Morna S...

REBELLION IN KILDARE, 1790–1803

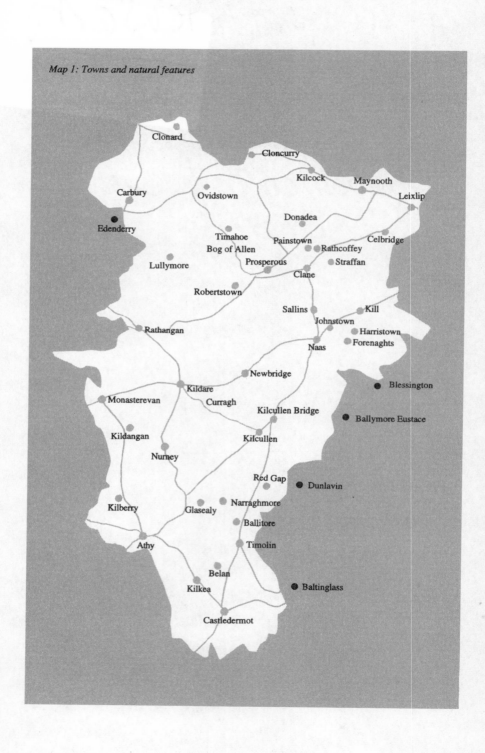

Map 1: Towns and natural features

LIAM CHAMBERS

Rebellion in Kildare 1790–1803

FOUR COURTS PRESS

Set in 10.5 on 13.5 point Caslon for
FOUR COURTS PRESS
Fumbally Lane, Dublin 8.
e-mail: info@four-courts-press.ie
and in North America
FOUR COURTS PRESS
c/o ISBS 5804 N.E. Hassalo Street, Portland, OR 97213.

© Liam Chambers 1998

A catalogue record for this title
is available from the British Library.

ISBN 1–85182–362–x cased
ISBN 1–85182–363–8 paper

All rights reserved. No part of this publication may be reproduced,
stored in or introduced into a retrieval system, or transmitted, in any
form or by any means (electronic, mechanical, photocopying,
recording or otherwise), without the prior permission of both the
copyright owner and the publisher of this book.

This book is printed on an acid-free and a wood-free paper.

Printed in Great Britain
by MPG Books Ltd, Bodmin, Cornwall.

To my mum and dad, Kathleen and Jimmy, and my brother Paul.

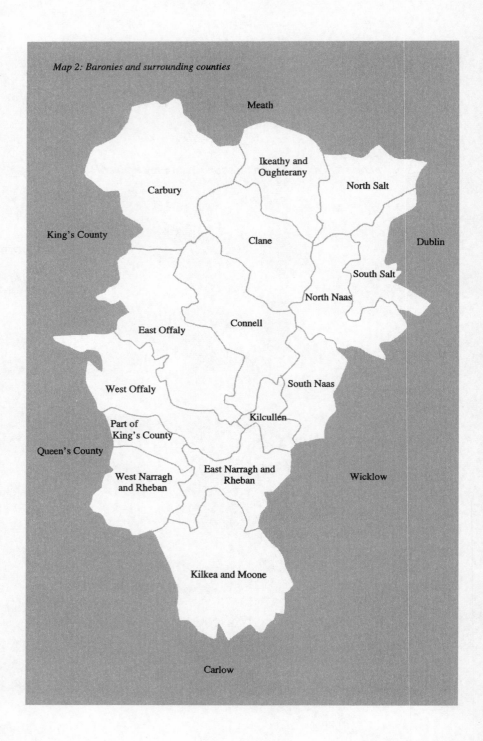

Map 2: Baronies and surrounding counties

Meath

Ikeathy and
Oughterany

North Salt

Carbury

King's County

Clane

Dublin

South Salt

North Naas

East Offaly

Connell

West Offaly

South Naas

Part of
King's County

Kilcullen

Queen's County

West Narragh
and Rheban

East Narragh and
Rheban

Wicklow

Kilkea and Moone

Carlow

Contents

List of abbreviations

BL	British Library
DEP	*Dublin Evening Post*
FJ	*Freeman's Journal*
H.M.C.	Historical Manuscripts Commission
I.H.S	*Irish Historical Studies*
Kildare Arch. Soc. Jn	*Journal of the Co. Kildare Archaeological Society*
NAI	National Archives, Ireland
NLI	National Library of Ireland
N.H.I.	*A new history of Ireland*
OP	Official Papers (second series)
PRO	Public Record Office (London)
PRONI	Public Record Office Northern Ireland
Reb. Papers	Rebellion Papers
R.I.A. Proc./Trans.	Royal Irish Academy Proceedings/Transactions
SOC	State of the country Papers (first and second series)
TCD	Trinity College, Dublin
UCD	University College, Dublin

Preface

This book is based on a thesis submitted for a master's degree at Maynooth College in 1996. While working on the original thesis and preparing the present publication I received the assistance of many people. Professor Vincent Comerford supervised the original work and continued to provide expert guidance and encouragement as I prepared the present text. I would also like to thank the other members of the Department of Modern History at N.U.I., Maynooth, for their interest and support. Dr Richard Alymer, Dr Dáire Keogh, Mr Seamus Cullen, Mr Des O'Leary and Mr Kevin Lynch shared my interest in the histories of late eighteenth-century Ireland and county Kildare and were generous in their assistance. The Department of Education (N.I.) awarded a scholarship which enabled me to carry out the original research. Kildare County Council 1798 Commemorative Committee kindly provided a grant-in-aid of publication for this book. Martin Healy, Martin Fanning, Michael Adams and Ronan Gallagher at Four Courts Press were efficient and courteous throughout. My greatest debt of gratitude is to my family and friends, to my mum and dad, Kathleen and Jimmy, my brother Paul and my girlfriend Niamh, for their love and support.

Introduction

This study provides a comprehensive examination of political developments and rebellion in county Kildare during the turbulent period from 1790 to 1803. Kildare is of interest not only because it produced a large-scale rebellion in 1798 but because of its dominant liberal establishment. The most powerful figure in the county, William Robert Fitzgerald, second duke of Leinster, was the most senior peer in Ireland. His presence encouraged a liberal-minded gentry. As political divisions became more polarised during the 1790s the liberal position became increasingly difficult to maintain. Maynooth College, founded in 1795, was viewed suspiciously by loyalists in 1798 and 1803 despite government patronage. In the years before the 1798 rebellion loyalist, liberal and radical divisions surfaced at a local level. They continued to a lesser extent in the post rebellion years. The disaffection created by and institutionalised in the Defenders and United Irishmen and its interplay with local politics provide the context to politicisation and the rebellions of 1798 and 1803.

The most significant manuscript source for a study of politics and radicalism in the late eighteenth- and early nineteenth-centuries are the Rebellion Papers and State of the Country Papers. Louis Cullen has recently made a convincing case for viewing these collections as 'an archive in their own right'.[1] The correspondence which comprises these collections came from military officers, government informers, local property owners and magistrates to Dublin Castle. In the case of Kildare they are particularly rich for the crisis period from 1795. The extant correspondence to Dublin Castle was considered by government as critical especially given the suspect nature of Kildare's liberal establishment. The papers of the Leinster family contain surprisingly little concerning political developments. The dearth of post 1794 material, particularly in the National Library collection, has led Stella Tillyard to comment that politically (and morally) compromising material was possibly removed.[2] Much of the private correspondence of John Wolfe of Forenaughts survives in an unsorted collection in the National Library. As a key loyalist figure, they provide an insight into his thinking during the period particularly on law and order issues.[3]

Thomas Moore's *The life and death of Lord Edward Fitzgerald*, Valentine Lawless' *Personal recollections* and Thomas Reynolds Junior's *Life* are all informative about the years before the rebellion. The former two portray their subjects as 'romantic' or innocent patriots not the revolutionaries they were. In many ways Thomas Reynolds Junior's biography of his father is the most revealing near contemporary publication concerning the pre-rebellion Kildare United Irishmen. Reynolds was appointed colonel in the rebel army in early 1798 but turned informer in February-March. Reynolds Junior's purpose was to clear his father's tarnished reputation. In this context he reveals the workings of the Kildare United Irishmen in the six months before the rebellion. The existence of the United Irish threat proved the necessity of Thomas Reynolds' betrayal. Therefore his son had no need to distance his subject from or downplay the level of radical politics.[4]

Unlike in Wexford, no post-rebellion debate occurred in Kildare.[5] The two most significant accounts of the origins and progress of the rebellion of 1798 in Kildare are those of Richard Musgrave and Patrick O'Kelly.[6] Musgrave's is the most detailed account of the rebellion. While he was bigotedly loyalist, his narrative is, in most respects, factually informative and correct. He was greatly influenced in his writing by the possibility that the act of union would be accompanied by Catholic emancipation. In this context he portrayed the rebellion as a popish revolt in the tradition of Sir John Temple.[7] Kildare afforded him no Scullabogue or Wexford Bridge but he gathered enough instances of individual sectarian assaults to construct a sectarian reading of the rebellion in Kildare. Rathangan, where nineteen Protestants were killed by the rebel army, provided concrete evidence of the religious nature of the rising. In a footnote to the incident he explained: 'The popish multitude are taught to believe, that the Protestants have no right to reside in Ireland, or to any property in it'.[8]

Patrick O'Kelly's *General history* is the only account of the 1798 rebellion published by a former rebel from Kildare. A native of Kilcoo near Athy, he participated in the rising in south Kildare. He spent the period 1803-32 teaching in America and France. In the early 1830s he published a translation of Abbé MacGeoghegan's eighteenth-century *History of Ireland*. He lived most of the rest of his life in Ireland where he died in 1858.[9] His reasons for writing a history of the rebellion are unclear. Perhaps as an academic he wished to record the events in his native county. His history is comparable to those of other former rebels. He acknowledges the existence of an extensive United

Irish network in Kildare by 1798. However, the rising itself is portrayed as a peasant uprising in reaction to the bloody disarming of April and May. His own role in negotiating a surrender at Knockallen is stressed. He is strongest when writing about events in south Kildare but cloudy on the north of the county. However, his comment that one of those to fight in the north '… was eminent for his classical effusions, [and] frequently quoted lines from a lyrical poet' is possibly a reference to himself.[10]

O'Kelly's rebellion was an ill-led, spontaneous and disorganised revolt, but nonetheless heroic. There are a number of reasons for the relative obscurity of the work. O'Kelly himself was a minor rebel figure from an area which produced an ineffectual mobilisation in 1798. Moreover it was published in the year when the first volumes of R.R. Madden's *The United Irishmen: their lives and times appeared.*[11] The essentially apologetic nature of O'Kelly's history is illustrated by Fr Patrick Kavanagh's use of verbatim extracts in his own work.[12] O'Kelly's interpretation suited Kavanagh's own argument which was coloured by the Catholic church's condemnation of organised fenian resistance in the later nineteenth century. Thus he sought to separate a justified (and spontaneous) rising from the militant secret society which inspired it.[13]

Three other descriptions of the rebellion in Kildare by native participants or witnesses were published in the nineteenth century. Thomas Rawson included a short account of the major engagements in Kildare in his *Statistical survey of the county of Kildare* in 1807.[14] The only lengthy account of the events of 1798 and 1803 written by a former Kildare rebel, other than O'Kelly, is that of Bernard Duggan of Prosperous. His narrative, composed in 1838, was published by R.R. Madden in 1846. The account is localised and makes little attempt to examine the underlying motivations for the events of 1798 or 1803. In fact Duggan had been a government informer since 1819. However the lack of an overbearing political subtext adds to the value of the source.[15] Mary Leadbeater's 'Annals of Ballitore' records the harrowing effect of the rebellion of 1798 on the rural tranquillity of the Quaker village of Ballitore in south Kildare. Despite the geographical confines of the work, its neutrality and honesty render this very human chronicle a valuable and informative source.[16]

The only modern attempt to place the 1798 rebellion in Kildare in the context of the preceding years was that written by An tAth Seosamh O'Murthuile in the 1940s. His account of the rebellion itself was translated from Irish and published as *Kildare 1798 Commemoration* to mark the 150th anniversary of the rising in 1948. While he made use of contemporary accounts and archive material Fr O'Murthuile's account belongs to the heroic genre.[17] Fr Peadar MacSuibhne's *Kildare in '98* concentrates on the rebellion itself. His study is composed of a disorganised series of accounts of the engagements in the county. He makes little effort to move beyond the interpretations of O'Kelly or Kavanagh.[18] The foremost recent attempt to analyse and narrate the events of 1798 in Kildare, and nation-wide, was Thomas Pakenham's *The year of liberty*. He recognises the existence of a militarily experienced leadership, some of 'exceptional ability' in Kildare. However he casts the rebellion as a largely peasant affair whose motivations were varied and confused. Thus the political import of the rebellion is lost.[19]

Whatever about the relative lack of attention received by county Kildare, study of the 1790s has witnessed a surge in interest particularly since the publication of Marianne Elliot's *Partners in revolution* in 1982. She illustrated the success of emissaries such as Theobald Wolfe Tone in attracting French support for an Irish republic.[20] Increasingly disaffection and rebellion in the 1790s have been placed in the context of politics and politicisation rather than purely agrarian or sectarian backgrounds. This is illustrated by the detailed research of Louis Cullen and Kevin Whelan, which has overturned the conventional view of Wexford in 1798 as a reactive sectarian uprising.[21]

As the revolutionary group with the most potential the United Irishmen who bridged conventional and out-of-doors politics, have received substantial study in recent years. The accepted view of a two phased movement forced from constitutional opposition to militant republicanism in 1795 has been broken down to reveal a more complex organisation. Internal divisions existed along organisational, strategic and class lines.[22] The success of the United Irishmen outside Ireland has prompted a reappraisal of their Irish success. Building on the work of J.S. Donnelly and others, Nancy Curtin has argued that the United Irishmen were highly successful in politicising and mobilising the population and '… possessed a genius for propaganda …'[23] The Defenders have been rescued from the obscurity of an anonymous group of Catholic peasants and emerged as a crucial revolutionary force of the period. Historians have begun to note the political dimensions of the group. The real problem with this group is the relative dearth of source material when compared in particular to the United Irishmen.[24]

The attention placed on radicalism in the 1790s has tended to obscure the nature of the forces of loyalism and reaction in the same period. However the strength of the radical threat poses the question, how did the Irish government survive? Some work has highlighted this conservative element during the decade. Studies of John Foster, and more recently John Fitzgibbon, reveal the workings of the Anglo-Irish elite.[25] Aspects of the Dublin administration's reaction to the growing crisis of the 1790s have been examined: their military response, their links with the Catholic church and their connections with the nascent Orange Order and sectarianism.[26] The period between the rebellions of 1798 and 1803 has received even less discussion in recent decades. Marianne Elliot illustrated the continued threat of Irish radicalism in these years. Essays by Thomas Bartlett and Daniel Gahan have examined the nature of post-rebellion society in Wicklow and Wexford.[27] While 1798 might be viewed as a culmination of the ferment of the preceding decade and thus a concluding point, it is revealing to expand the period under discussion to 1803. 'Emmet's rebellion' was a United Irish one. In Kildare at least, it was preceded by mobilisation against a background of inherent radicalism which continued to persist after 1798. The potential ramifications of this period has led Thomas Bartlett to suggest that: 'the events of these years may have had an even greater impact than the rebellion itself'.[28]

Outside the rebellion itself some aspects of Kildare history in the late eighteenth century have received attention from historians. Padraig O'Snodaigh has examined high politics in the period.[29] The populist figure of Lord Edward Fitzgerald has inspired a plethora of biographies.[30] These have largely been supplanted by Stella Tillyard's recent work: *Citizen Lord*. Tillyard stresses the ideological and radical nature of Fitzgerald's thought in producing a committed revolutionary. She traces the influences of his background and the philosophies of Rousseau and Paine. She seeks to eschew the 'romantic' version of Fitzgerald in favour of one which is 'logical, consistent and tragically inexorable'.[31] Other Kildare figures have been discussed by historians notably Lawrence O'Connor, a Defender leader executed in 1795, James Smyth a United Irish leader in Leixlip and William Aylmer a rebel commander in 1798.[32]

The other major centres of rebellion in Leinster outside Kildare – Wexford, Wicklow, Carlow and Meath – have all received attention from historians.[33] The present research fills a gap in the historiography of the 1790s in its examination of one of the most prominent centres of conflict in late eighteenth- and early-nineteenth cenury Ireland. An examination of Kildare during this period increases our knowledge of Ireland as a whole at this important juncture. This study traces the growth of popular politics, the creation of a revolutionary army, the United Irish rebellions of 1798 and 1803 and the conservative reaction against them.

CHAPTER 1

Kildare county

ဎ

1790

Kildare is an inland county in the province of Leinster. It is bounded by Meath to the north, Offaly and Laois (King's and Queen's Counties in 1790) to the west, Carlow to the extreme south and Dublin and the rising Wicklow mountains to the east. It is 36.8 miles in length by 26 miles wide. Two important natural features are particularly noteworthy. The vast Bog of Allen sprawls across the north east of Kildare. To the west of Kildare town lies the Curragh, described by Arthur Young as '… a sheep walk, of above 4,000 English acres, forming a more beautiful lawn than the hand of art ever made'.[1] The most important rivers in the county are the Barrow which winds along the western border via Athy into Carlow and the Liffey which enters Kildare from the Wicklow mountains and exits through Celbridge and Leixlip. This chapter provides an introduction to county Kildare at the beginning of the 1790s. It deals with the major family interests in the area, a description of towns and industry, population and finally political structures and recent political developments.

The Fitzgeralds of Carton dominated Kildare in the late eighteenth century. Edward Wakefield believed them to own almost one-third of the county.[2] The family's local and national prestige and their permanent residence in the county contributed to their popularity. Thomas Rawson who had been a political opponent of the second Duke (who died in 1804) wrote in 1807:

> The late much to be regretted duke of Leinster was a lover of his country; he almost constantly resided at his magnificent seat of Carton, where he set an example of honesty and benevolence and by every humane attention to the wants of the industrious people, to whom he gave constant employment and charitable assistance, he called aloud on the nobility and gentry of Ireland to imitate so great and good an example.[3]

The Kildare seat of the Fitzgerald's at Carton was a frequent resort for travellers. Marc de Bombelles, a French diplomat, visiting in the 1780s described the duke as 'Le premier seigneur de ce pays', and Carton itself as, 'grande et magnifique ou il a toute la representation d'un souverain, et la simplicite d'un honete gentilhomme'.⁴ William Robert Fitzgerald had succeeded his father James as duke of Leinster in 1773 at the age of twenty-five. He acquired family and political connections on both sides of the Irish Sea, through his mother Emily, daughter of Charles Lennox, second duke of Richmond.

His political significance derived from a number of sources: his connections, his nobility, his power in Kildare and his control of a phalanx of parliamentary seats. He played an important role in the volunteer agitation during the late 1770s and early 1780s. Nevertheless, writing in 1787 to his mother, he betrays a lack of political interest and acumen:

> ... if I could at once see them [his brothers] all settled in their professions I believe I should myself give up all politics as I am not calculated for it. Indeed I should give myself very little trouble about it was it not a duty I owe my family.⁵

By 1788 he was posturing to enter government and took up a position in that year.⁶

The regency crisis of 1788-9 completely altered his political fortunes. Siding with his Foxite relations he backed the decision to request the Prince of Wales to become Irish Regent. The King's sudden recovery in March 1789 spelt disaster for the family.⁷ Along with other Regency supporters he joined the newly formed Irish Whig Club and entered into a formalised parliamentary opposition. The Regency crisis served to highlight existing rifts within the Fitzgerald family along political lines. The duke's brothers Charles and Robert were avowedly Pittite, while Henry and Edward supported Fox, the faction which, for the moment, the duke allied himself.⁸ The coming decade would place much greater strains on William Robert, whose politics vacillated between populism and the need for stability.

The other national figure resident in north Kildare was Thomas Conolly (uncle-in-law of the second duke of Leinster) who lived at Castletown on lands adjacent to Carton estate. Castletown itself was widely acclaimed. Young noted that: 'Mr Conolly's at Castletown to which all travellers resort, is the finest house in Ireland, and not exceeded by many in England'.⁹ In politics Conolly prided himself on his independence, which frequently descended into fluctuation and indecision. Nevertheless, the nascent Whig club was happy to receive his membership following his high-profile embarrassment during the regency débâcle (after which he lost his seat on the board of trade). Conolly had neither the same property nor influence in Kildare as the Leinster family, the bulk of his land lay in Donegal and Derry.

The dominance of the Fitzgerald family in Kildare politics ensured that other families participated at a less influential and often more localised level. The Bourkes (Mayo), Stratfords (Aldborough) and Moores (Drogheda), all peers of considerable importance held property interests in the county. The earl of Mayo's influence centred on the town of Naas. Three earls died between 1790 and 1794, the family finally settled in that year with the succession of John Bourke, fourth earl (the first earl's grandson). The family did not play an important role in Kildare politics at large. The Moore family was in a similar position. The sixth earl of Drogheda, Charles had succeeded in 1758. His Kildare interest focused on his property at Monasterevan, however his influence lay outside.[10] The Stratfords played a somewhat more significant role in Kildare affairs, essentially because they spent more time in the county.[11] The head of the family was Edward, second earl of Aldborough whose major arena of political influence lay in west Wicklow, while his principal residence was at Belan in Kildare.[12]

Two recent arrivals represented very different interests in the county: the Lawless and La Touche families. Nicholas Lawless, a catholic, returned from France in the 1770s and conformed to the established church. By 1789 he had entered the house of lords as Lord Cloncurry, though his Catholic background did not completely disappear.[13] His son Valentine was to play an prominent role in the events of the next decade on both sides of the Irish Sea. The La Touches, Huguenots and bankers, with extensive connections, were more recent arrivals. They had purchased the Harristown estate from the Eustace family in 1783, John La Touche was the first occupant.[14] The Aylmers and Wolfes were long established and locally important. The Donadea Aylmer branch was headed in 1790 by Sir Fitzgerald Aylmer an extensive landowner in the north of the county though much of his property covered the Bog of Allen. He had been brought up a protestant and Hanoverian. He supported the duke of Leinster politically.[15] John Wolfe was head of the Wolfe family of Forenaughts in 1790. During the 1780s he sat as MP for county Kildare with the support of the duke of Leinster. Despite breaking his connection with the powerful Leinster interest at the 1790 election he continued to assume a powerful role locally.

Naas and Athy were the joint administrative centres of the county and the largest towns. Arnold Horner has estimated the population of Athy at 2,018 and that of Naas at 1,820 for the years 1798-1800.[16] Naas, owned by the Bourke family, was in a prominent geographical position, from its proximity to Dublin and its position on the road to both Limerick and the south. Athy, owned by the duke of Leinster, was the only Kildare town included in Richard Lucas' *General Directory* of 1788.[17] Leinster also owned the towns of Castledermot, Rathangan, Maynooth and Kildare. The latter was probably the third largest town in the county. J.H. Andrews has estimated the population in 1798 at *c*.1,600 based on Thomas Sherrard's map of the town produced in that year. Horner estimates it at 730.[18] In the north Maynooth, Leixlip and Celbridge, the latter two on lands belonging to Thomas Conolly, benefited from their proximity to Carton and Castletown.[19] Similarly Monasterevan on Kildare's western border with Queen's County gained from the attention of the earl of Drogheda.

The county in general was received quite favourably by visitors. Sile Ní Chinneide points out the absence of reference to poverty in Coquebert De Montbret's notes on the northern region, this is all the more striking when compared to his notes on the rest of the country.[20] De Bombelles and Thomas Campbell comment favourably on the county and on leaving the latter notes, 'on this side [i.e. south of] Castle-Dermot the country grows less pleasant'.[21] Indeed it is the towns which received most criticism from visitors, though poverty was evident in rural areas as well. Arthur Young noted on a journey from Dublin to Naas: '... I was again struck by the great population of the country, the cabbins [*sic*] being so much poorer in the vicinity of the capital than in the more distant parts of the kingdom'.[22] Agriculture was the principal occupation of the majority of the Kildare populace. Outside the Bog of Allen the land was excellent for tillage and suffered in consequence from overuse.[23] Thomas Rawson as agricultural inspector encouraged improvement in methods, but recognised short term leases and the resultant threat of 'Captain Bidbest' as a recurring hindrance to progress.[24] Certain landlords were attentive to the needs of their tenants. Young, for example praised Richard Nevill of Furness near Naas. However he goes on to comment, 'Their [i.e. labourers] circumstances are the same as 20 years ago'.[25]

Two large-scale projects dominated the proto-industrial landscape of Kildare in the period: Prosperous and canal construction. Prosperous was founded in 1780 by Robert Brooke on land west of Clane as a centre for the manufacture of cotton.[26] The project grew quickly and 5,000 people were in Prosperous by 1784. Despite government and local patronage, financial inefficiency led to the failure of the project.[27] It was closed down in 1792 thus

Year	No. of Houses	No. of People	Source
1788	11,272	[71, 570][32]	G.P. Bushe, 'An essay towards ascertaining the population of Ireland' *R.I.A. Trans.* vol iii, (1789), facing p. 143.
1790	11,205	56,000	D.A. Beaufort, *Memoir of a map of Ireland* (London, 1792) p. 57.
1791	10,605		Wray's hearth money returns in T. Newenham, *A view of the natural, political and commercial circumstances of Ireland* (London, 1809), app. xvii, p. 20.
1813	14,564	85,133	W. Shaw Mason, *A statistical account or parochial survey of Ireland* vol. iii (Dublin, 1819), p. xvii.
1821		99,065	Census of Ireland, 1821
1831		108,424	Census of Ireland, 1831

ending Kildare's earliest brush with large-scale industrialisation. The other major economic undertaking in Kildare in the period was the construction of two canals. Work on the Grand Canal began in 1756, the idea being to link Dublin to the river Shannon. It made steady progress through Kildare in the following decades, reaching Athy by 1791.[28] The construction of the Royal Canal was a financial disaster. Construction began in 1789 and by 1796 it had reached Kilcock via Broadstone and Maynooth. Its path through the Bog of Allen and its proximity to the Grand Canal seriously affected its prosperity.[29] Despite the financial difficulties of the ventures Kildare benefited greatly from the passing trade. Rawson was certain the increased navigability and ease of travel in the county was a great advantage to agriculture.[30]

Ascertaining the population of Kildare previous to the 1821 census is a necessary but difficult task. Pre-1821 population figures were largely calculated by multiplying the number of houses in a county (based on the hearth money collector's returns) by the average number of people in a house. Two obvious sources of error arise. Firstly, inaccuracy in the figure used for the number of houses on the side of deficiency due to a range of factors. The hearth collectors may have missed houses, ignored houses or simply failed to visit isolated houses, problems which were undoubtedly exacerbated by areas such as the Bog of Allen. The second difficulty was in deciding on an average number of people per house. Figures ranged from 5 to 6.5.[31]

The table on the previous page illustrates the various calculations of the number of houses and/or people in county Kildare in the late eighteenth and early nineteenth centuries.

Unfortunately Thomas Rawson makes no attempt, unlike many of the other statistical surveys undertaken by the Dublin Society, to establish the county's population.[33] Bishop Daniel Delany furnishes (average) population figures for Kildare in his statement made to government relative to the situation of his diocese in 1801. However the figure of 39,000 only covers the area under the jurisdiction of the Diocese of Kildare and Leighlin, whereas Archbishop Troy fails to provide figures for the Dublin Diocese sector of the county in his report.[34]

K.H. Connell settles on a figure of 5.65 for the average number of people in a house c.1790.[35] The figures for the number of houses in Kildare in the years 1788 to 1791 surprisingly drop by over 1,000. This is undoubtedly a reflection of inaccuracy rather than an indication of any decline in population. Taking the largest figure, 11,272 and Connell's average people per house figure of 5.65 we arrive at a population total of 63,687. While this figure seems realistic, the number of houses at 11,272 almost certainly errs on the deficient side. While an exact population is impossible to arrive at Bushe's figure of 71,570 may not be excessive.

An attempt to enumerate the religious affiliation of the populace is to add a further layer of complexity. Only Edward Wakefield furnishes complete data based on Beaufort's population of 56,000. He states there were 54,134 Catholics and 1,866 Protestants.[36] Mason includes figures based on the incomplete returns of members of the established clergy in 1814 (only five parish returns are included). He calculates 6,573 Protestants and 19,028 Catholics in a total of 25,601.[37] The respective ratios are 29:1 and 3:1. These are so strongly divergent it is difficult to draw conclusions, though Kildare was recognised as a largely Catholic county.

The political structure of Kildare in 1790 may be analysed at two levels; parliamentary representation and local government. Both levels were dominated by the second duke of Leinster, William Robert Fitzgerald. This is reflected in his control of parliamentary seats in the county, which returned ten members to the Irish house of commons. Two were returned for the county itself and two others for each of the boroughs of Athy, Naas, Kildare and Harristown.

One contemporary commentator believed Kildare to be 'a close Leinster county'.[38] In fact the duke was one of the few patrons able to carry a county election singe-handedly. This is clearly demonstrated by the events of the 1790 election, particularly the inability of the sitting MPs to stand for re-election. Both men deserted the Leinster interest in 1790 and joined the administration. Lord Charles Fitzgerald, the duke's brother opposed William Robert's stance on the regency question and publicly announced his incapacity to stand.[39] John Wolfe had been expected to stand again for the county as late as 1790. However he purchased a seat in the borough of Killybegs and joined the administration under the influence of his uncle, Arthur Wolfe the Attorney General.[40] A further impetus to the independent nature of the MPs returned for Kildare was the county's proximity to Dublin and its resultant acquaintance with the events of the Irish Parliament.[41] In 1790 the duke's brother Edward was elected with Maurice Keatinge of Narraghmore. The latter was nominally an independent but the support of the Leinster interest was crucial to his position. Both men were liberal in their political sympathies.

William Fitzgerald directly controlled three of the boroughs in county Kildare responsible for electing MPs – Athy, Kildare and Harristown – through his control of membership of the corporations. The former two were freeman boroughs in which the franchise extended to the freemen of the borough and members of the corporation.[42] Harristown was a corporation borough in which the right of franchise extended only to members of the corporation. It was a classic rotten borough. Only one house stood in 1790.[43] Whereas the boroughs of Athy and Kildare exercised some minor functions, that of Harristown existed merely to perpetuate itself and elect MPs.[44] No officers were elected after its disenfranchisement in 1800.

Lord Henry Fitzgerald and Lt.-Col. Arthur Ormsby were elected as members for Athy in July 1790. Lord Henry however chose to represent Dublin for which he was elected with Henry Grattan on the Whig platform. Ormsby seems to have been a friend of the Leinster family. He was joined by

Fredrick John Faulkner, a relation of the same family through Emily, the duke's mother.[45] Simon Digby of Landenstown and Robert Graydon of Kilashee were elected to represent Kildare. Digby was MP for Kildare for thirty-five years from 1761 to 1796. Both were strongly attached to the Leinster interest. Harristown was represented in 1790 by Sir Fitzgerald Aylmer head of the Donadea Aylmer family and Arthur Burdett, both brought in by the duke of Leinster. By 1790 the corporation borough of Naas was owned by the Bourke family. The head of the family had been created earl of Mayo in 1785, for his strong attachment to government.[46] The head of the family in 1790 was the first earl, John Bourke. That year his son John Bourke Jnr (Lord Naas 1785-90) and another John Bourke (son of Joseph Deane Bourke, archbishop of Tuam, the earl's second son) were elected. According to one commentator the latter opposed government.[47] However the first earl died and was succeeded by his son John Bourke who was in turn replaced in parliament by Sir James Bond. Bond supported government and seems to have purchased the seat from Mr Burgh of Oldtown who was granted possession of the seat 'during Lord Mayo's [i.e. the second earl of Mayo] lifetime'.[48]

For the purposes of local administration Kildare was divided into four-teen baronies and half baronies and 113 civil parishes. It was by barony for example that the Grand Jury allotted money for road building and other works. At the head of the local political machinery, nominally at least, was the county governor. Not surprisingly the post was held by the duke of Leinster. The other key positions were the high sheriff and the grand jury. Theoretically the Lord Lieutenant appointed the high sheriff who in turn chose the grand jury. To complete the circle, the grand jury submitted three names annually to government from which a high sheriff was chosen. However the reality was less rigid. The post of high sheriff was held by Maurice Keatinge in 1790. He was replaced (probably due to his impending election) by John Taylor on 6 March. The two previous incumbents had also been noted liberals: Richard Griffith (1788) and Thomas Wogan Browne (1789).[49] The duty of the grand jury was to raise and spend money on the county; on roads, gaols, various officers etc.[50] The grand jury presentment lists for a number of assizes survive from 1791 through to the early nineteenth century (only 1794, 1798 and 1803 have not been traced in the years 1791-1803). Not only do they list the money to be raised and spent per barony but the majority list the grand jury for that particular meeting, which enables us to ascertain the state of local politics in a given year.[51]

Responsibility for law and order rested basically with the men of property in the country. The task was unpaid, but was a method of demonstrating one's attachment to government and thereby soliciting promotions and favours. It is unclear exactly how many magistrates or justices of the peace were in Kildare in 1790. *The Gentleman's and Citizen's Almanack* lists seventy one justices of the peace for the county in 1795. A further twenty one had been added by 1798, though certainly not all of them were active.[52]

Thomas Packenham characterised Kildare as 'the county of great wooden demesnes' and 'liberal landlords'.[53] Many of the politically active inhabitants of the county were of liberal views, something aided by the politics of the dominant interest – a source of patronage at a local level. A number of wealthy and influential Catholics were quite powerful locally for example, James Archibald, Dominic O'Reilly, Daniel Caulfield, John Cassidy, John Esmonde and Thomas Fitzgerald. Thomas Wogan Browne, of an influential Catholic family, converted in 1785, but Wakefield noted as late as 1812, 'Wogan Browne although a convert, is still considered a catholic'.[54]

Kildare quite openly demonstrated its liberal character by its stance on the regency question. The following resolutions were passed at a meeting held on 12 March 1789 (two days after George III's recovery) and reveal a mixture of defiance and a repetition of the principles of 1782;

> That there is no parliament competent to appoint a regent for Ireland for any purpose whatsoever save the parliament of this realm.

> That the royal assent given to Irish acts of parliament is the assent of the King of Ireland.

> That our thanks be returned to the Lords and Commons of Ireland for asserting the rights of parliament and the independence of this country against the unconstitutional attacks lately made thereon by the ministers of the crown.[55]

The county's political establishment was to be severely tested during the 1790s as the basis of political participation expanded considerably. The liberal political stance became increasingly difficult to adhere to as radicalism and reaction polarised society in the second half of the decade.

CHAPTER 2

Politics and politicisation
&
1791-5

The period between the start of the 1790s and the end of Fitzwilliam's viceroyalty was one of unprecedented political activity throughout Ireland.[1] The campaigns for Catholic relief 1791-3, and parliamentary reform radicalised public opinion and encouraged widespread participation. Kildare was relatively peaceful during these years. Political issues did not prove to be highly divisive on a public level among the county establishment, a circumstance aided by the absence of Defender violence which spread from Ulster to north Leinster in 1792-3.

Kildare Catholics had received a measure of political acceptance during the 1770s, including limited membership of the Naas Volunteers and the Anna Liffey Club.[2] A number of prominent Kildare Catholics were involved in the Catholic Committee in the 1780s. Thomas Wogan Browne attended frequently until his conformity to the established church in 1785.[3] James Archibald, Dominic W. O'Reilly, Michael Aylmer and Christopher Nangle also attended.[4] The return of elected delegates from Kildare to the committee from 1784 added a new dimension to Catholic politics in the county. In that year the Catholics of Naas returned Pat Dease, Thomas Braughall (both were also elected for Drogheda, Dundalk and Dublin) and Francis Dermot.[5] In 1791 delegates were returned from Athy, Thomas Fitzgerald, Garrett Fitzgerald and Jos. Pat Cahill. Dan McGuire was elected to represent Castledermot.[6] Some of these names remain completely elusive, appearing in neither local nor national agitation. Thomas Fitzgerald of Geraldine was the most prominent Kildare activist and was to play an important role in both arenas. The 1791 election produced a broader based and more liberal committee with more frequent meetings.[7] By March of that year Fitzgerald had demonstrated his liberal allegiance within Catholic politics by replacing one of the sub-committee members forced to stand down due to non-compliance with the forceful wishes of the general committee. He continued to perform an important role at a national level and chaired a meeting in 1792.[8]

The Kenmareite secession of December 1791 extended Catholic politics even more broadly. Sixty-eight members of the Catholic committee headed by Kenmare, Fingall, Gormanstown and Troy left the body on its refusal to pass a declaration of unconditional loyalty and presented a separate address on 27 December 1791. Dominic Wm. O'Reilly was the only Kildare signatory.[9] The radical leadership had the backing of the county. A meeting of Kildare Catholics was held in Athy on 14 January, chaired by Thomas Fitzgerald. It resolved that the Catholic committee were 'the only body competent to declare the sentiments of the great body ... that we earnestly exhort our prelates and pastors from any interference in politics ... theirs the spiritual, theirs [sic] the temporal'. It is noted at the end of their resolutions that: 'The above resolves supported by the voices of some hundreds of reputable landowners'.[10] The reference to 'hundreds' of landowners may indicate general support among Catholics for this stance rather than the attendance of a large number of landowners. They may have been prominent tenants. Nonetheless their actions provoked an angry response from local Protestants.

The meeting produced a reaction from the corporation of Athy. At a meeting held on the 26 January it passed resolutions addressed to its MPs. They stated, 'We know well the firm basis on which our constitution is raised, and are too well assured of its value, to wish, or to approve any change, in which the Protestant Ascendancy may be endangered'. It requested its members to vote against any further 'measure that may tend to alter our present happy constitution under which we have all so long prospered'.[11] Ormsby and Faulkner, the sitting MPs promised to pay the 'greatest attention to the address'.[12] The borough was directly controlled by the duke of Leinster, which has led Padraigh O'Snodaigh to assert the Athy resolutions were a 'rather pathetic device used ... to get off the hook of Catholic emancipation' and proves he was 'not a political radical'.[13]

While it is true that the duke was never a political radical, conflicting reports of his position at this point may provide an insight into his reasoning. William Drennan noted in December 1791 that the duke had 'declared warmly for the Catholics'.[14] In the same month the *Freeman's Journal* reported that the duke had made overtures to government about the possibility of entering the administration. His offer had been turned down on the grounds of expense.[15] Uncertainty concerning the duke's position on Catholic politics and his own need to placate both sides of the debate might have produced his acceptance of the Athy resolutions. A simpler consideration may have resulted in them i.e., the radical tone of the Catholic address and large-scale support it mustered in the duke's backyard.

The rift with Leinster was a serious and unexpected one for the Catholics of the county. It damaged prospects of support for their cause and detached them from the prime source of local patronage. The breach was speedily repaired by an address presented following a meeting at Naas on 23 March. The deputation presenting it was headed by James Archibald and Thomas Fitzgerald, chairman and secretary of the meeting respectively, and Dominic Wm. O'Reilly, Charles Aylmer, John Fitzgerald, Richard Dease, John Esmonde and Daniel Caulfield. It expressed thanks for the duke's 'protection and brotherly kindness' and hoped that his influence would 'dispel the mist of intolerance which unhappily perverts the minds of some of our country-men'.[16] He returned his gratitude for the address and stated '… whenever the legislature has thought it proper to take up the cause of Catholics, it has always met with my support …'[17] Thomas Conolly was also attached to the Catholic cause in September 1792 following a meeting at Castletown with Edward Byrne, John Keogh, Thomas Fitzgerald and Theobald Wolfe Tone.[18]

Sir Hercules Langrishe's Catholic relief act was passed grudgingly in April 1792. Pro-Catholic petitions were overwhelmingly rejected and the attacks on Catholics which accompanied the legislation resulted in the introduction of fresh strategies to the relief campaign. Tone was formally appointed secretary to the committee in July 1792 signalling a shift in policy. Reconciliation with the Kenmareite faction was also achieved during the summer. The plan for a convention was a truly radical departure. Protestant opinion immediately made its opposition felt through grand jury resolutions, as many as twenty-three were presented in mid-1792. The Kildare grand jury remained silent.[19]

Nancy Curtin has contended that: 'The election of delegates encouraged the extension of the Catholic question deep into the Irish countryside, further politicising and polarising inhabitants'.[20] Kildare chose: Thomas Fitzgerald, Charles Aylmer, John Esmonde, Christopher Nangle, James Archibald and Randall McDonnell. Three other Kildare men William Dunn (Queen's Co.), Walter Fitzgerald (Carlow Co. and Town) and Richard Doyle (Wicklow Co.) were returned. The 1791 delegates from Athy and Castledermot also attended.[21] The process of calling a convention significantly heightened public mobilisation. In its choice of delegates the electorate clearly placed itself on the liberal-radical wing of Catholic politics. Fitzgerald, Aylmer and Esmonde were all to have radical links later in the decade. Archibald was one of the county's most prominent activists. The absence of the equally prominent O'Reilly may indicate a reluctance to choose one of the older guard.

The commotion of Catholic politics in December and January 1792-3 was accompanied by a development in the Whig political camp under the leadership of the duke of Leinster. At a meeting on the 5 December 1792 the Whig club had split over whether to introduce the Catholic question for discussion.[22] The Kildare liberal Richard Griffith urged the duke of Leinster to form a new political association to combat the republicanism of the Volunteers, United Irishmen and the duke's brother Lord Edward, as well as the timidity of the Whig club.[23] Leinster replied favourably and the Association of the Friends of the Constitution, Liberty and Peace was formed in Dublin on 21 December.[24] The duke chaired the meeting with Griffith as secretary. Central to their political credo was the belief: 'That the permanent peace and welfare of Ireland can only be established by the abolition of all civil and political distinctions arising from difference in religious opinion, and by a radical and effectual reform in the commons house of parliament'.[25] The duke even make approaches to the liberal wing of the United Irishmen through Thomas Addis Emmet.[26] The association was initially quite successful and a number of branches were formed in early 1793.[27] However, the Dublin organisation split over its plan of parliamentary reform (which was never produced) in early March.[28] The war with France which was declared in February was instrumental in the groups demise. Even with its element of respectability it failed to attract the support of many Whigs who viewed it as too radical or many radicals for whom is was not radical enough.

The granting of Catholic relief in April 1793 and the accompanying dose of restrictive legislation (gunpowder, militia and convention acts) ended Kildare's Catholic agitation until Fitzwilliam's arrival. The summer assizes of 1793 held in Athy marked the official entry of Catholics into local politics. At the quarter sessions held in July the duke of Leinster himself attended. He was met by 'an immense crowd the horses instantly taken from the carriages and drawn through the town with shouts and acclamations of "success to the House of Leinster", a general illumination at night, bonfires, etc.'. He was entertained by Catholic inhabitants, attended also by the MPs and bench, while 'ale was given to the populace'.[29] Thomas Fitzgerald was granted a commission of the peace by the government to add to the deputy governorship he had received in May.[30]

The grand jury panel included six Catholics called by the high sheriff, Maurice Keatinge.[31] The *Dublin Evening Post* urged the counties of Ireland to 'look with a steady eye to Kildare and imitate her glorious example'.[32] Ominous signs were already evident. A bonfire held by O'Reilly of Kildangan was not so successful. According to James Alexander his provision of porter to 'drink his majesties [*sic*] health' directly resulted in a small turnout. For Alexander this was one of a number of signs of growing disaffection.[33]

The involvement of the 'populace' at Athy reveals how broad the political base had become. In 1793 a pamphlet was recovered by government circulating from Rathcoffey. The author condemned the war with France in the name of poor manufacturers, on the basis that war would result in economic ruin for that group. It concluded: 'We do not want charity. We do want work. We are starving. For what. A war?'[34] Thomas Collins, a government informant, initially reacted with surprise but later portrayed Archibald Hamilton Rowan's house at Rathcoffey, complete with a press and the source of numerous 'squibs', as a centre of radical activity.[35] While many were undoubtedly destined for the Dublin population, a number must have found their way around the Kildare countryside.

The hinterland of Rathcoffey was a nexus for a group of active liberal and radical politicians. Five miles lay between Hamilton Rowan and Richard Griffith at Millicent, with Wogan Browne at Castle Browne and Theobald Wolfe Tone at Bodenstown between. (Tone was named after a local landowner, Theobald Wolfe, an active magistrate and conservative throughout the 1790s.) His diary reveals substantial contacts with Wogan Browne and Rowan during 1792. At dinner in September they drank 'The spirit of the French mob to the people of Ireland'.[36] In December 1793 Thomas Russell dined at Millicent with Tone, Griffith, 'a sensible man' and Wogan Browne, 'who reads an essay on universal representation'.[37] These glimpses provide an insight into the links between Kildare liberals and United Irishmen which was further augmented by ties between both groups and Catholic politicians such as John Esmonde of Osberstown or Charles Aylmer at Painstown.

The most compelling evidence for the politicisation of county Kildare in the early 1790s is that of James Alexander.[38] A resident of Ross in Wexford, he was a native of Harristown, near Monasterevan and visited there for a period from January 1793. He contended that: 'The late rebellion has been much longer setting on foot in this kingdom than very many people are aware of. I perceived strong symptoms of it, when I was last in Harristown'.[39] Having heard 'expressions of disaffection' among the peasantry, he attended their social gatherings, 'in order to feel their political pulses'. Loyal toasts he quickly discovered were either overruled or 'passed over in silence'.[40]

Political radicals were becoming more vocal. George Cummins, a Kildare apothecary, is reported by Alexander as observing that: 'The people of this kingdom are beginning to open their eyes to perceive their natural rights'.[41]

Mary Leadbeater noticed the same trait in Malachi Delany of Ballitore whom she described; 'Though a great talker and qualified to handle various subjects he confined himself to two – religion and politics. His mode of treating the first consisted in ra[n]ting at the clergy, and the last in abusing the government'.[42] Both Cummins and Delany were deeply involved in United Irish activities later in the decade. Alexander was unable to uncover the origin of political fomentation in west Kildare and concluded, 'I believe some newspapers went a good way into the business; for I never knew the people in your [his brother's] neighbourhood anything like so attached to these vehicles of information and political sentiment'.[43]

Opposition to the embodiment of the Militia was viewed by Alexander as a symptom of widespread political radicalism. The Militia act was passed in April 1793. By March of the following year only two county units remained unembodied: Cavan and Kildare.[44] Maurice Keatinge was initially appointed colonel of the Kildare body in April 1793. Henry McAnally states he simply did not take up the post.[45] During the summer of 1793 anti Militia riots occurred throughout Ireland. Despite disturbances in Carlow and Queen's County, Kildare remained tranquil.[46] James Alexander's account of Militia opposition in the Monasterevan region refers to 1793. Harristown itself was not in Kildare but was situated in a part of King's County to the south of West Offaly barony. This area was largely comprised of bogland and bounded to the west by Queen's County and to the north, east and south by Kildare. The disturbances which affected this district obviously spilled over into its natural hinterland in Kildare. He states that: 'When the parochial lists of persons qualified to serve in the Militia appeared, there was no bounds to their expressions of indignation'.[47] He observed 'remarkably strong and healthy looking beggars about the county at this point'. These he learned were emissaries of some sort spreading disaffection about the Militia. They were working in Harristown, Walterstown, Nurney and Kildoon (the latter three in West Offaly). A local man informed him, 'as for Kildare [town] it is too full of them already!' Cummins was prepared to use the opportunity to spread sedition.[48] Priests became objects of suspicion as it was they who had to provide lists of fit persons for military service from which names would be selected. In Monasterevan and Kildangan chapels were shut up.[49] Alexander, however, reports no major gathering in opposition to the Militia.

Why was the Kildare unit not embodied in 1793? McAnally offers two reasons. Firstly the duke of Leinster was only offered the colonelcy after it was 'hawked about' due to his opposition to government. Secondly, 'the fact that Kildare was a rather unruly county'.[50] The former is certainly more plausible than the latter given Kildare's relative tranquillity in a period when other counties witnessed severe outbreaks of violence. (McAnally tended to minimise Militia resistance in any case). This concurs with the view of Charles W. Fitzgerald, who stated that the duke of Leinster's opposition meant he did not attend the levees of the Lord Lieutenant 'and it was only after consulting some of his friends that he waited upon him to receive it'.[51]

Leinster seems to have been in favour of the Militia Bill early in 1793 and was finally offered the command in May 1794.[52] The duke appears to have been confident of his ability to raise a unit (only 280 men were needed under the terms of the act). The press reported he intended to raise it voluntarily; difficulties however arose.[53] Lord Edward who had recently moved to Kildare town, in a letter to his mother on 19 July wrote, 'We have been busy here about the Militia the people do not like it much – that is the common people and farmers – even though Leinster has it, they do not thoroughly come into it, which I am glad of as it shows they begin not to be entirely led by names'.[54]

Militia disturbances appeared in Kildare in the same month. A hundred men entered the village of Ballitore 'tendering an oath to all of their own class whom they met, that they should not join either military or army, but be true to their own cause'.[55] Near Kilcullen a 'riotous assembly' gathered at Redgap where 'they swore several of the inhabitants, not to pay rent or taxes'. The crowd was dispersed by a Militia unit stationed there.[56] The *Dublin Evening Post* reported further 'petty disturbances' in August, but failed to specify the location. A 'mob' attempted to swear gentlemen against accepting commissions or aiding in the Militia. On the institution being 'humanely explained ... they dispersed without committing the smallest violence or depredation'.[57]

Bartlett has argued that: 'the anti-Militia riots of 1793 helped to create that atmosphere of fear and repression that made the '98 possible and some sort of '98 inevitable'.[58] In Kildare the limited disturbances which occurred marked a new departure. The loose association of the lower orders against the Militia (and its tentative promotion of agrarian issues) prefigured more organised Defenderism. Lord Edward had noted, without regret, the loosening of paternalistic ties between his brother the duke and the lower orders i.e. the breakdown of the moral economy which is the topic of Bartlett's study. The duke's policy of voluntary enlistment probably helped limit resistance by rendering it unnecessary. The fact that Kildare's disorder took place in 1794 (with the exception of west Kildare), not 1793, points to the importance of purely local and immediate factors. The Kildare Militia was embodied in July

1794, the last in the country to do so. The commissions were signed in that month and from August the Militia were stationed in Athy.[59] At the end of September a full embodiment had still not taken place, the total membership of the unit was only 101.[60] The small number of protests which had occurred did not lead to any organised disturbance. No fresh violence was reported during the rest of the year.

Recent research has suggested that the 'lull' which entered radical politics in 1794 was more apparent than real.[61] In Kildare political agitation had ceased in the aftermath of the 1793 relief act. The news in late 1794 that Earl Fitzwilliam, one of the Portland Whigs who had joined Pitt's government, was to be appointed Lord Lieutenant triggered a jolt in activity among liberal and radical activists. In spite of his opposition to the war with France (an issue on which he sided with the Foxite Whigs) the duke of Leinster was appointed Clerk of the Hanaper at the start of the year.[62]

Kildare Catholics speedily convened a meeting in Kildare town in January following Dublin meetings in December. They agreed 'a humble application be made to parliament in the ensuing sessions praying for a total repeal of the penal and restrictive laws still affecting the Catholics of Ireland'. A petition was drawn up by Ambrose O'Ferrall, Charles Aylmer, John Esmonde and Christopher Nangle. It was requested that the county's MP's lay the address before the house of commons.[63] The address was presented directly to the Lord Lieutenant by a deputation on 16 February. This included the duke of Leinster, Col. Keatinge and Dr Daniel Delany, Catholic Bishop of Kildare and Leighlin as well as fourteen prominent Catholics.[64] It marks the apogee of unity among the pro-Catholic group in the county, particularly given the presence of Delany and Leinster. The suddenness of the opportunity offered by Fitzwilliam's appointment facilitated this alliance which included all elements of the Catholic political spectrum.[65] Fitzwilliam was recalled exactly one week later, shattering hopes.

A meeting held at Kildare town under Daniel Bergin (chairman) and Thomas Braughall (secretary) quickly condemned the removal and predicted dire consequences.[66] A full meeting of the 'Gentlemen, freeholders and inhabitants of the county of Kildare' was held at Naas on 4 March, chaired by the high sheriff, Sir Fenton Aylmer. Fourteen resolutions were drawn up concluding that dismay and the continuation of abuses would be the result of Fitzwilliam's departure. Two petitions were to be drawn up. The first, to the viceroy himself, expressed 'deep despondency' at his removal and was to be delivered by Aylmer.[67] The second addressed to the King was presented by Michael Aylmer and John Taylor on 18 March. It lamented Fitzwilliam's recall and sought the King's intervention.[68] The county meeting reassembled on 26 March (Fitzwilliam departed the previous day). It passed fresh resolutions, repeating its regret and stating the best method of judging the new administration was 'the success or failure of the serious question of Catholic emancipation'.[69] County Kildare's reaction to the 'Fitzwilliam episode' served to outline its own liberal stance on the renewed issues of Catholics relief and parliamentary reform. Its resolutions and addresses were full of bitter disappointment. While the county establishment's vocal response indicates a united front, the role of government linked elements, such as John Wolfe remains unclear.

Recent research has illustrated that radicalism in the 1790s cannot be divided simplistically by the 'Fitzwilliam Episode' into constitutional and militant phases.[70] However, Kildare fits the division in one major sense, that is, organised violence became common from 1795. The limited Militia riots did not lead to an atmosphere of 'fear and repression' but were put down quietly and effectively.[71] It is tempting to view the Defender incursion as a direct result of the popular expectations and frustrations of early 1795. National political events, however, would only partially explain their introduction and would not account for their continued activity and spread further into Kildare. Nonetheless the apparent lack of open disagreement among the Kildare elite did not stunt the politicisation of the lower classes, indeed it encouraged radical activity. The large liberal section of the county attempted to continue their stance after 1795. As Defenderism and the United Irishmen were introduced into an already quite politicised county divisions naturally appeared and were compounded by the growing weakness of the Leinster faction in the county.[72]

CHAPTER 3

'To be true to the French': Defenders and United Irishmen in Kildare

ও

JULY 1795—APRIL 1797

Agrarian disturbances were a continuous feature of eighteenth-century Ireland since the initial Whiteboy outbreaks in Munster in 1761.[1] Kildare was affected by the second wave of Whiteboy violence in the late 1770s.[2] The Defenders emerged from the Armagh troubles of the late 1780s. David Miller has placed the origins of the troubles in the socio-economic sphere.[3] However, Louis Cullen and more recently Jim Smyth have argued the Defenders must be viewed in a political context. Cullen writes that: 'Political circumstances are the only unifying factor in accounting for what took place across a progressively wider area. If a political theme is taken as the main issue in Armagh, it links the county with a much wider region'.[4] The political mobilisation of the early 1790s and the embodiment of the Irish Militia and the 'Armagh Outrages' of 1795-6 encouraged Defender expansion.[5]

The Defenders moved steadily south during the early 1790s. By December 1792 they had appeared in north county Meath. J.G.O. Kerrane points out the importance of the sectarian element in this region where a colony of 'Scots' (i.e. Presbyterians) came under attack. He sees both political developments and economic grievances behind their appearance.[6] This dissemination continued through 1793 as Defender violence was emulated by the establishment, particularly in the form of the Meath Association.

The eruption of Defender violence in Kildare in July 1795 must be viewed in the context of the resurgence which occurred in county Meath in the early summer of 1795. Kerrane has commented on the nature of the fresh disturbances which most strongly affected the south of the county. He argues the motivating factors behind the attacks were economic rather than religious in the less sectarian atmosphere of south Meath. This is articulated in the 'Market Town Document' of June 1795. The notice was posted up in all the market towns of the county and sought to regulate rent, wages, food prices and tithes. Kerrane contends the pamphlet was written by Lawrence

O'Connor, 'one of the few men of education to be a Defender'. However if O'Connor was not a unique example of 'middling' class Defender member-ship there is no real evidence to substantiate this view.[7] The outbreak in Kildare may also be connected with national politics. In the same way that Jim Smyth links political mobilisation and the disturbances of 1792-93, the sudden departure of Fitzwilliam and swift negative reaction in Kildare may have created a climate in which popular hostility to the new government (whose coercive intentions were revealed in Carhampton) was channelled into the Defenderism, already encroaching on the Kildare border.[8]

Defenderism was first publicly revealed in Kildare on the arrest of Lawrence O'Connor and Michael Griffin at Kilcock, for attempting to swear Bartholomew Horan of the South Mayo Militia, on 12 July. The court's description of the oath O'Connor had tendered was as follows: '... to be loyal to all brother defenders, and the French, and that they would soon land, and they would have the Kingdom of Ireland to themselves'.[9] O'Connor received much contemporary and later attention being one of the few Defender leaders tried during the period. He was steward and manager to the Rowley family of Summerhill in county Meath, parish clerk and a successful school-master.[10]

The events of the period between O'Connor and Griffin's arrest and their trial in late August are crucial in understanding the spread of Defenderism into the county. The day after their arrest both men were conducted from Kilcock to Naas jail, along with several other prisoners, under the supervision of Sir Fenton Aylmer (as high sheriff), Wogan Browne, Michael Aylmer and Thomas Ryan when a rescue attempt was made.[11] According to Richard Nevill a crowd of 'about 600' had gathered in Kilcock and news of the intended rescue had reached the Sheriff. The party arrived at Clane safely. However a number of gentlemen were waylaid and Ryan was shot at twice, the second attempt wounding him.[12] A proclamation issued later stated the 'armed mob' administered 'unlawful oaths' and plundered houses.[13] Nevill importantly stated 'they [i.e. the mob] mostly came from cy [sic] Meath'[14] a claim augmented by the need to administer oaths locally. This seems to indi-cate the initial burst of violence was not perpetrated by sworn but previous-ly inactive Defender cells in the area, but by fresh recruits backed by south Meath Defenders, possibly from O'Connor's own area around Summerhill. Camden reported to Portland that O'Connor '... declared himself to be at the head of the combinations in Meath and that no person of wealth or sit-uation was concerned with Defenderism in that county'. While he was prob-ably not a county leader (if indeed such a post existed) he was obviously important in the south Meath-north Kildare area.[15] He was held at Naas, but transferred to New Prison, Dublin at some point in August.[16]

O'Connor's reputation was secured not only by his stature locally. The scale of the violence in a previously tranquil county ensured maximum publicity. Defender threats were serious. The house of George and Sarah Napier was attacked on 20 July, causing panic at nearby Castletown.[17] The violence posed a serious problem for the county establishment. Camden recognised the problem and recounted the events in a letter to Portland.

> I should not have thought it necessary to have troubled your grace with this representation of a transaction which does not appear to deserve particular notice, was not the country where it happened so near the capital, had it not taken place in a country which has usually been quiet and had not the ingenuity of detailers of intelligence here magnified this ... into a regular engagement between the military and the people of this country.[18]

A meeting of local magistrates held at Sallins on 18 July, chaired by the duke of Leinster, offered a £300 reward for the capture of those involved in the ambush of Ryan.[19]

A full county meeting was held at Naas on 24 July. It issued a lengthy proclamation offering various rewards in a serious attempt to arrest the spread of Defenderism.[20] The meeting resolved in the strongest terms to unite against Defenderism. A subscription was collected to aid this process; the amount donated increased steadily during August.[21] Local initiatives were also undertaken in an attempt to prevent the spread of Defenders. In Kilcock an anti-Defender oath was taken by forty three 'principal inhabitants' before the local justice of the peace, John Walsh.[22] The tenants of Richard Nevill of Rathmore, east of Naas, swore a similar oath on 22 July.[23] Defenderism continued however to spread throughout the north of the county during August and September, at least fifty arrests were made during this period.[24] A number of Defenders were found guilty at the Athy assizes of various offences, including three executed for the shooting of Ryan.[25] They reputedly repented at their execution stating, 'the sole object of their pursuit was to get about two acres of cheap land and to raise the price of workman's labour'.[26]

The Revd John Walsh, vicar at Kilcock, the epicentre of Defenderism in Kildare, emerges from the Rebellion Papers as the most spirited resister of Defenderism in the north of the county. In August he reported to government, 'to recount all the occurrences which have engaged the attention of the active justices of the peace of Kildare since I had the honour of an interview with you would at present be more than I could wish to perform'.[27] Walsh, as landlord and vicar, was of course a particularly potent object of wrath for Defenders. In a letter addressed to Sackville Hamilton in October he indicates the problems he faced. He had determined to level a commons in his neighbourhood, 'inhabited by a people who have been closely leagued together by combination oaths'. He claims it was from here the life of Ryan had been sought. However he did not receive the full support of unnamed local landowners. The killing of a bullock provided the opportunity to urge the handing up of arms and the threat of levelling. At this point the area became peaceful, and several gentlemen offered to provide compensation if the dwellings were destroyed. Walsh felt this intervention undermined his proposed actions.[28] The determined unity of the Kildare establishment of July 1795, was much more difficult to maintain at ground level, particularly given the inevitable clash between those of heavy handed tendencies such as Walsh, and the numerous liberal landowners of north Kildare.

The trial of Lawrence O'Connor and Michael Griffin held at Naas on 31 August, following an adjournment from Athy, provides the historian with information on the Defenderism O'Connor and others were disseminating in north Kildare. Two oaths were found which revealed a strong connection with hopes of French assistance, as well as an indication of an organised system of Defender committees. Defenders had been sworn in Kilcock before the arrests.[29] After guilty verdicts were returned O'Connor proceeded (in a frequently quoted passage) to explain the symbolical meaning of the words 'Love, Liberty and Loyalty' written on one of the oaths:

> By *love* was to be understood that affection which the rich ought to shew [*sic*] the poor in their distress and need but which they withheld from them … *Liberty* meant that liberty which every poor man had a right to use when oppressed by the rich in laying before them and expostulating with them on their sufferings – but the poor man in this country had no such liberty … *Loyalty* he defined as meaning that union which subsisted at present among the poor – he would die in that loyalty – it meant that the poor who formed the fraternity to which he belonged would stand by each other.[30]

O'Connor then congratulated the judge for letting his lands directly to his tenants.[31]

O'Connor's comments have not failed to draw observation from historians. Lecky noted that: 'There appears to have been nothing in it either of politics or religion'.[32] Dr Michael Beames concluded that: '... its underlying concept of a just social relationship between the classes ... may be taken as indicative of how little real impact nationalist and republican sentiments had on the Irish peasantry outside Ulster in this period.[33] O'Connor's evidence reveals the importance of socio-economic grievances in the spread of Defenderism out of its sectarian heartlands into areas such as south Meath and north Kildare. His aim was not social revolution, but a form of social justice, within which social and economic relationships would be regulated.[34] The political subtext is important however. Molyneaux, writing in the *Dublin Evening Post* noted '... they [the Defenders] are now sworn, and in the hitherto peaceable county of Kildare, TO BE TRUE TO THE FRENCH'.[35] Marianne Elliot has traced tentative Defender-French links to as early as 1792.[36] O'Connor's complete silence on the conspiratorial import of Defenderism is revealing in itself. The oath produced in court also had a revolutionary cap of liberty.[37]

Lawrence O'Connor was executed outside Naas jail on 7 September. He was given no opportunity to address the crowd. His head was 'fixed on the top of the jail upon an iron spike seven feet high,' a measure Camden claimed '... had a great effect on the people'.[38] Griffin as a old man was recommended for clemency. He was still in jail in early 1796 awaiting execution scheduled for April of that year.[39] O'Connor's reputation in the martyrology of the 1790s was further established by the appearance of a poem in 1798 entitled *The martyr of liberty*.[40] The arrest, attempted rescue and trial of Lawrence O'Connor, all of which occurred with maximum publicity, fuelled the encroachment of Defenderism into the county.[41] Once introduced it took firm root in the north of the county.

The key local response to escalating violence was a military one. Dublin Castle used execution and transportation against convicted Defenders in an attempt to quell the situation. The Fermanagh and Sligo Militias were dispatched from Dublin.[42] The north of the county was saturated with military stations, at Kilcock, Hortland, Carbery, Clane, Prosperous, Naas, Celbridge, Maynooth and Leixlip, to add to the existing military presence.[43] In late September Camden continued to report Defender disturbances in north east Kildare.[44] However by October 1795 the initial outbreak of Defenderism, which was confined to the north of the county, died down. The Defender movement in Kildare appears to have simply remained inactive or dormant rather than dissolving.

In late 1796 convicts on a prison ship at Cobh offered to give information on Defenderism in Kildare. In October they contacted a Cork doctor through John Kenny a fellow convict. He wrote:

> They are two Defenders and their names is [*sic*] Patrick Connor and Edward Byrne. They say that they can make information against thirty men in the county of Kildare for high treason and Defenderism and will from that the leading men come into the informant's houses and gave them powder balls and guns for the purpose of entering gentlemen's houses and say that when they refused to be concerned that they threatened their lives in case of their refusal and informed them that the high sheriff of the county of Kildare (Mr Aylmer) and a Mr Brown[e] were Defenders and if they were not that they should not live in that country.[45]

John Wolfe informed government in December that 'Aylmer' had also received 'repeated application' from the same prisoners. He also named Lawrence Drennan and Michael Gavacan. He was sceptical but nonetheless advised the information should be pursued.[46] Mr Franson, a neighbouring curate of John Walsh, had received two letters from Byrne and Connor.[47] Walsh seems to have arrested them sometime between late 1795 and early 1796, and states they were committed on 'Hanlon's evidence'. Hanlon was a solider in the Royal Irish Artillery. An attempt was made on his life on 31 January 1796 in Thomas Street, Dublin, to prevent him giving evidence at Naas assizes.[48] Edward Byrne stated in his letter 'I mean to inform your honours of a conspiracy which still is in existence against you …' He goes on to list names and reveals a plot to murder Franson. Connor in a separate letter reveals a conspiracy 'to take away the lives of Squire Aylmer, Squire Brown[e][49] and Squire Ryan and Sir Fenton Aylmer,' (i.e. all those involved in escorting Lawrence O'Connor from Kilcock to Naas). The Defenders in the area seem to have been quite well organised and spreading.

> Thomas Hopkins and James Miny were two committee men and swore in a great number of Defenders … and also told us that as soon as the French were landed and should conquer the kingdom that we should have the principal gentlemen's places and that we should be raised out of slavery and misery …[50]

It is unclear what happened to the convicts and their information must be treated carefully given their desperate situation. Their letters do reveal a well organised though locally motivated Defender organisation. The conspiracy targeted local magistrates though no major attacks are reported during the winter of 1795 or early 1796. John Wolfe reported in December 1795 that: 'The country around here and at Kilcock and its vicinity appears perfectly at rest, so far as Defenderism is concerned, but there have been a great number of highway robberies, and some burglaries lately committed'.[51] The beginning of a United Irish/Defender amalgamation can be traced to early 1796 in the south Meath, county Dublin and north Kildare areas. In Kildare one figure was particularly influential in the emergence of the United Irish movement, Lord Edward Fitzgerald.

The enigmatic figure of Lord Edward played a pivotal role in the growth of the Kildare United Irishmen. His francophile leanings were well established and enshrined in his romantic marriage to Pamela de Genelis, the reputed daughter of duc d'Orleans. His radical reputation was established by outbursts such as that in the house of commons on its anti-volunteer stance in 1793 when he stated: 'I do think that the Lord Lieutenant and the majority of this house are the worst subjects the king has'.[52] In June 1794, the Edward and Pamela moved into a house in Kildare town.[53] Thomas Moore states Fitzgerald joined the United Irishmen in early 1796.[54] Fitzgerald and Arthur O'Connor had undertaken a mission to France via Hamburgh in May 1796. It is more plausible that the pair joined the Leinster movement in the Autumn of 1796, after internal wrangles over the form and control of the group had ceased.[55]

Fitzgerald's interaction with local communities in Kildare is crucial. In 1796 James Alexander's sister informed him '… that about the year 1796 his lordship resided in Kildare, danced among the rustics at bonfires and in short conducted himself with such condescension, freedom and affability that, like Absalom of old, he stole away the hearts of the people'.[56] His activities were undoubtedly part of the creation of a revolutionary United Irish movement in Kildare. The earlier phase of the United Irish movement had no Kildare branches and few Kildare members. This is largely explained by the presence of a large and powerful liberal group in the county. Three early members with Kildare connections are noteworthy: Archibald Hamilton Rowan, John Esmonde and John Lube (a brother of George Lube a rebel leader in 1798).[57]

The initial United Irish focus of its organisation building in Kildare was the established Defender movement of the north. The reappearance of Defender disturbances may have taken place at the instigation of United Irish activists, working in Kildare. Serious disorder emerged during the late summer and early autumn of 1796. As early as June John Walsh was shot at while searching for stolen sheep. He reported a riot involving the Carlow and South Mayo militia. 'This unfortunate business,' he wrote, 'has brought to light a deep laid scheme to alienate the mind of the soldiers from their duty.'[58] In August Fenton Aylmer reported Defender activity in the Meath/Kildare/King's County area.[59] Lord Aldborough was seriously worried by the presence of three notorious 'Defenders' or 'Regulators' near Belan.

> They ... frequent each fair market and ale house threatening to knock the brains of every Protestant and to regulate the price of labour ... of land and value of provisions ... if left here they will poison the minds of the ignorant there about this neighbourhood.[60]

This was an isolated incident though it does demonstrate the ability of Defenderism to spread quickly, if somewhat erratically. Camden reported the reactivation of Defenderism 'within these two months' to Portland in August.[61]

In Kildare the impetus towards United Irish/Defender alliance had both northern and Dublin roots. James Hope, the Templepatrick radical, visited Kildare on a number of occasions during 1796 and 1797. In his memoir he writes,

> A secret delegation was resolved on [from Ulster in 1796] and I was one of two persons who were appointed to proceed there to disseminate our views among the working classes. We succeeded in our wishes and likewise formed connections with Meath and Kildare which soon extended to the other counties.[62]

His lengthy treks around the country must be viewed in this context. He made one trip from Dublin specifically to Prosperous in 1796.[63] Lord Edward Fitzgerald also had extensive northern links and stayed in Belfast with O'Connor in November 1796. A paper seized by a Lieutenant Ellison confirms the northern involvement. A United Irish provincial committee had been formed in Leinster and Dublin itself was organising well. Kildare had petitioned to Ulster for support. It also stated, '[Dublin] will pay as soon as possible for the forwarding of the business in the upper part of the county of Meath and Kildare; Dr C. Q. takes from Newry fifteen constitutions to the county Kildare, and promised to distribute them there with much attention'.[64] The Newry connection is further illustrated by eleven Kildare subscribers to John Corry's *Odes and elegies* published in the town in 1797, including Lord Edward.[65] A paper seized in early November stated that Meath, Westmeath, Kildare and Dublin had 16,000 United Irishmen.[66]

The arrest of a number of prominent Ulster radicals including Thomas Russell and Samuel Neilson, in September 1796 caused some panic in Leinster. Boyle reported in October that: 'The Defenders in Co. Dublin, Meath, Kildare and Westmeath are very quiet since the taking up [of] the Belfast men – the magistrates and associations in the above counties are very attentive'.[67] A further event militated to some extent against the continuing United Irish/Defender co-operation in Leinster; the formation of the Irish Yeomanry. Col. Keatinge had argued for such a force in his *On the defence of Ireland* published anonymously in 1795.[68]

While Keatinge's ideas proved too radical for government, they sanctioned the formation of a Yeomanry in the early winter of 1796. The government's initiative was quickly taken up in Kildare by men like Fenton Aylmer, Keatinge and Alborough.[69] The Kildare corps were not the Protestant/loyalist rallying point of other counties. A meeting held to elect officers to an Athy force under the command of the duke of Leinster resulted in conflict between liberal figures, particularly Thomas Fitzgerald and conservatives.[70] An early 1797 list contains fifteen units in the county. Eight units had officers who had been involved in Catholic and/or liberal politics earlier in the decade.[71] The loyalist-liberal wrangle for control at a local level is further illustrated by the quarrel between Richard Griffith and Henry Stamer of Prosperous, ostensibly concerning the raising of corps.

In October the Clane cavalry had been granted commission with Griffith as Captain and John Esmonde his First Lieutenant. The disagreement with Stamer can be traced to the same month. Griffith had written to John Wolfe recommending the duke of Leinster as Commander of the yeoman cavalry in county Kildare, he added:

> What have you done with Mr Stamers? His real object is to be a man of consequence and to raise an independent corps of 'unwashed artificers' in Prosperous. He could muster about ten or twelve to serve on foot. There are but five horsemen in the town and they swear they will not go out of the barony.[72]

Griffith's argument was based on social prestige and practicality, but Wolfe did not fail to side with the loyalist Stamer against Griffith, a prominent liberal. Writing to Cooke in January 1797 he stated that:

Great exertions have been made (as Mr Stamer tells me) by Griffith and Esmonde (who's Griffith's Lieutenant) to get the people of Prosperous, who are all Stamer's tenants, to quit their landlord and to join them – the people are disposed to stand by Stamer – but it is a matter of struggle and nothing would so completely run Stamer down as government countenancing the efforts against him.[73]

In a further letter dated the same day (perhaps mistakenly), Wolfe informed government of his own decision not to raise a corps in the area. Stamer had decided to reside in Prosperous and raise an infantry corps in the town.[74] The incident not only illustrates the increasing local divisions, particularly at the beginning of an election year, but the importance of John Wolfe as a local power broker.

The *Memoire of the state prisoners* asserts the military organisation of the United Irishmen was not formed until November or December 1796.[75] Recent research suggests the military aspect of the United Irishmen was in existence, to some degree, as early as 1792. The links forged with Defenderism during the latter half of 1796 undoubtedly involved the formation of armed societies. The failed Bantry Bay expedition seems to have inspired the nascent United Irish groups in north Kildare and provoked interest elsewhere. Mary Leadbeater noted, 'We were relieved from the present apprehension of invasion, but it caused a ferment in the minds of the people'.[76]

From December 1796 to January 1797 reports of radical political activity in Kildare increased as the United Irishmen spread, initially in the north Kildare region which had been the Defender heartland. Gradually reports arrived in Dublin from further south. In December Wolfe asked Cooke to send him a description of Keenan '… whom you mentioned as recruiting for the rebels at Sallins'.[77] On 3 January he noted the appearance of Defenderism 'in this neighbourhood', (i.e. outside Naas), and stated his intention of 'going on a patroll [*sic*] to prevent any nocturnal meetings'.[78] Two days later he reported 'Defender activity' at Kilcock, and a failed attempt six to eight weeks previously to 'administer oaths' in Kilcullen. Perhaps on the strength of this fact, he concluded, 'I have every reason at present to believe the people in general of this country – quiet, loyal and contented'.[79] Later in the same month John Walsh wrote a despairing letter to Thomas Pelham, requesting a transfer, '… beyond the horizon of those places where my exertions have rendered me odious to a vile democracy …' and hinted strongly at the inactivity of the neighbouring magistrates.[80]

The repeated reports of attempts to administer oaths as far south as Kilcullen are a reflection of the United Irish extension in Kildare. In late February the Meath loyalist Revd Thomas Knipe reported disturbances in the Clonard area involving the 'French Militia'. They made 'one dreadful distinction,' according to Knipe, 'while they robbed papists, they robbed and endeavoured to murder Protestants'.[81] The recruitment drive was carried on both by local zealots and wandering emissaries. In late May a warrant was issued for the arrest of James Murphy for administering illegal oaths. A witness stated he had been active in Maynooth, Lucan, Leixlip, Kilcock, Dunboyne and Westmeath.[82]

At what point the Defender groups of north Kildare became part of the United Irish system is unclear. Information received from the informant Nicholas Maguan, put the Kildare United Irishmen at 850 on 4 April 1797. He noted however 'The number in the business is immense, though unacquainted with the system or organisation'.[83] This is probably a reference to undigested Defender cells. A return dated 25 April, puts the Kildare total at a credible 3,452.[84] This would suggest the Defenders of north Kildare were affiliated to the united system by April 1797 though the spread south had yet to start in earnest. Thomas Boyle reported in the same month that: 'All the people of the counties of Dublin, Meath and Kildare are now raised again and become as wicked as ever'.[85]

As noted even by late April few signs of radical activity are evident further south than Naas or Kilcullen. The growth of a United Irish organisation in north Kildare gave the county group a momentum of its own, particularly given the weakening position of the Ulster movement in 1797, aided by key radical figures further south. Lord Edward Fitzgerald remained crucial. Lady Lucy Fitzgerald, Edward's radical younger sister noted the frequent presence of the Kildare apothecary George Cummins at Kildare Lodge in late 1796. Cummins close association with Lord Edward suggests the creation of a countywide organisation dates to this period.[86]

The Defenders in Kildare are important because they provided the United Irishmen with a pool of organised radicals when the movement began to organise nationally. Its primary targets were the landlords of the north of the county, in a sense a physical articulation of the socio-economic code expressed by O'Connor. Defenderism provided a serious challenge to the liberal county establishment. However by winter 1795-6, as the immediacy of the events of July-August 1795 waned, so did Defender activity. It was the possibility of United Irish links that reactivated the movement in the second half of 1796. In early 1797 a solid United Irish structure was established in north Kildare. By late April 1797 the deteriorating situation in Carbery Barony had led to a move to proclaim it under the terms of the 1796 Insurrection Act. The ensuing public debate on how to pacify the county was to split Kildare's establishment and further radicalise the populace.

CHAPTER 4

Liberal failure: Kildare United Irishmen and the conservative response

֍

MAY 1797—MAY 1798

May 1797 was a crucial month for all sections of Kildare's political spectrum. The proclamation of Carbery barony and failure of a county meeting encouraged loyalists and simultaneously rendered the liberal position obsolete. The events revealed, publicly, deep establishment divisions. These divisions were manifested to a lesser degree over smaller scale issues during the preceding years but they were now linked to countywide problems. Liberals were concerned at the spectre of military disarming in Ulster, while conservatives viewed the mounting level of violence as part of a political conspiracy. Public debate and disaffection were fuelled. The United Irishmen subsequently spread rapidly into southern Kildare.

Carbery was one of the most disturbed baronies in the county. Two organised attacks close to the Meath border were particularly serious. On 30 April 300 armed men attacked the house of the prominent loyalist Revd George Knipe at Castle Rickard. Knipe was shot dead.[1] At the trial of the group's leader Captain Fearnought, alias John Tuite, it was claimed Knipe was shot because he was an Orange leader.[2] A similarly large party of 250 attacked the house of Stephen Sparks at Castlecarbery on 7 May.[3] Sparks himself noted 'great appearance of regularity' among the assailants. The attack lasted over an hour and the beleaguered loyalists were saved by the intervention of the Wicklow Militia under Captain Hempenstall, from Edenderry.[4] Both attacks underlined the vulnerability of loyalists and the organisation of the United Irishmen in these localities. Later in the month a rebel was hung where '… he had been heard to say he would plant the tree of liberty'.[5] The attacks were characterised by both preparation and cohesion.

The 1796 Insurrection Act empowered two or more justices of the peace to summon a meeting of justices of the peace at which those assembled could petition the Lord Lieutenant to have all or part of a county 'proclaimed'. The proclaimed area would effectively be under martial law, anything construed as disorder was to be dealt with severely.[6] John Tyrrell notified government of his intention to convene a meeting to discuss the situation in Carbery barony in late April.[7] This was held on 8 May at Naas. Those in favour of proclamation outnumbered the liberals by almost two to one. This marked a serious decline in the duke of Leinster's control in Kildare. The following list of those present evidences the political divisions at the meeting:

In favour of proclamation	*Against*
earl of Mayo	duke of Leinster, chairman
Viscount Allen	Thomas Wogan Browne, teller
Fenton Aylmer	W.B. Ponsonby
John Wolfe	M.B.StL. Keatinge
John La Touche	Revd Dean Cadogen Keatinge
Richard Nevill	John Taylor
Richard Griffith	Thomas Fitzgerald
Theobald Wolfe	James Archibald
John Tyrrell	Richard Dease
Charles Palmer	Thomas Ryan
John Montgomery	Dom. Wm. O'Reilly
Thomas Tyrrell	William Donnellan
James Carlisle	
John Greene	
John Johnson Darragh	
Thomas Fredrick Knipe	
Thomas Kelly	
Michael Aylmer	
Edward Hendrick	
William Patrickson	
Garret Tyrrell[8]	

The division is slightly deceptive, particularly in the case of Sir Fenton Aylmer. A letter to the castle written on the day of the meeting clearly demonstrates his opposition to the measure. He recounted the rising number of rebel attacks in search of arms: 'Instances of this sort are becoming every day more and more serious ... there are few nights the villains are not out and few nights we [presumably his Yeomanry unit] are not out ... notwithstanding they avoid all our vigilance ...' He recognised the need for action but declared his opposition to proclamation despite signing the memorial: 'I preferred it to suffering a continuation of the system of murder and assassination and robbery both of arms and money that pervaded confident am I that there are other means that would be more likely to keep down the flames'.[9] Wogan Browne expressed similar sentiments in a letter dated the next day. Indeed L.M. Cullen has argued the letters of Aylmer and Wogan Browne present a 'concerted protest'.[10] He was firmly opposed to proclamation which he feared would incite further violence.

> ... it appears to me that the wound lies very deep and that means of conciliation as well as repression are necessary to heal it and that I fear, such a measure in such a place will by the publick [sic] be considered less a social regulation extended for the purpose of quieting this county than a political expedient used to prepare Leinster as Ulster has been for proscription and execution.[11]

Plans for the convening of a county meeting seem to have materialised towards the end of April 1797 around the same time plans to proclaim Carbery were first floated. For liberals the answer to the desperate situation in Ulster and the worsening condition of Leinster was conciliation – based on the major plank of their programme: parliamentary reform. The duke of Leinster informed Camden he would support renewed liberal activity in Kildare in April.[12] The *Dublin Evening Post* reported on 2 May this action had cost the duke his position as clerk of the Hanaper and his command of the Kildare militia.[13] The proposed meeting mimicked similar Whig efforts in other counties, however the Kildare meeting was to be convened on the widest base possible – i.e. inhabitants. This possibly reflects the democratic leanings of organisers such as Wogan Browne.[14] A requisition was presented to Robert La Touche the high sheriff, signed by, among others, the duke of Leinster and Lord Cloncurry. The meeting intended to discuss the propriety of petitioning the king for the dismissal of his Irish ministers.[15]

La Touche refused to convene the proposed gathering on the strength of a counter requisition signed by sixty-four prominent conservatives including: Drogheda, Aldborough, Carhampton and Mayo. They argued 'a meeting at this time would be highly injurious to the peace and tranquillity of the county'.[16] Richard Griffith recognised the importance of this move. He had changed allegiance from the Leinster camp in late 1796 (he resigned his Whig club membership in November of that year). However he also realised the weakness of the loyalist position: 'You tell me of the great lords etc. etc. who have signed it,' he wrote to John Wolfe, 'I should rather see the names of a score of good substantial farmers, and some Roman Catholics'.[17]

An attempt to circumvent the rebuff was made by the liberals by convening the meeting through the county governor – the duke of Leinster. Following a meeting in Dublin on 15 May the Kildare liberals released a statement dated 26 May. A county meeting was arranged for 29 May at Naas. This notification was followed by a long list of names occupying almost a whole page in the *Dublin Evening Post*.[18] Lawless and Wogan Browne were personally informed by Pelham that the danger of such a meeting was apparent to government and suitable military force would be used to prevent it.[19] A proclamation dated 17 May banned unusually large gatherings of people primarily in a clamp down on the United Irishmen. This machinery was applied against the Kildare liberals. A military force, under the command of Arthur O'Connor's brother was despatched to Naas by an apprehensive Dublin Castle.[20] From 26 May handbills were distributed by Wogan Browne and others encouraging the Kildare populace not to meet at Naas but to sign a petition which would be circulated.[21] Wogan Browne also enclosed the handbill in a letter to Pelham the following day, explaining his actions. He concluded:

> ... that this county was prevented from meeting lest we should petition his majesty for the dismissal of ministers ... But steady to our purpose we will not thus be deterred sir, from an attempt to convey our opinion to his majesty.[22]

In place of a meeting a petition was circulated throughout the county from late May. It was a firm declaration of the Whig position in the country. A number of copies printed on broadsheets survive in the Rebellion Papers. Charles Hamilton Teeling reprinted the document in 1832.[23] The petition was a populist strategy and was circulated and posted up around the county. Stephen Sparks found one posted to Carbery church door. 'I am sure it is not what it proposes,' he wrote, '*the petition of the magistrates and freeholders of this county* and I think put up merely to encourage that feeling of disaffection carried on in the lower order of people in this county'.[24] The author, claimed Leonard McNally, was Wogan Browne. One thousand copies were to be printed and distributed by John Chambers of Abbey Street.[25] Valentine Lawless claimed the petition was prepared by Wogan Browne, Patrick Latten and himself. He noted it was signed by 'several hundreds of the first men of that county,' while Teeling claimed it eventually bore 6,000 signatures.[26] It was finally presented to the King at St James by Lord Henry Fitzgerald in October.[27] The liberal attempt to harness the weight of public opinion behind their cause was seriously damaged by the lack of a meeting. They would find it increasingly difficult to hold the middle ground in Kildare, which was viewed as suspicious by worried conservatives.

The duke of Leinster's support for the liberal campaign cost him not only his minor administration place, but also his seat on the privy council and, by mid-May, his command of the Kildare militia. All three were the subjects of an extensive correspondence between the duke and Camden during April and May 1797. Camden realised the importance of the duke to Irish politics and stability and ensured the duke of Portland was continually informed of the situation. The protracted correspondence signifies the difficulty in dealing with a major liberal figure in Ireland. While the duke's public anti-government stance could not be tolerated, his treatment was a delicate matter.[28]

On 10 May Lady Lucy Fitzgerald recorded, colourfully, in her diary

> May 10 – We had an alarm in the evening that brother Leinster and Edward were both to be taken up. Brother Leinster had yesterday a most curious scene with Lord Carhampton who is a wicked madman. He scolded and stormed, said brother Leinster was at the head of that gang of assassins the United Irish. He did him too much honour for he is not one.[29]

A brief exchange of letters followed, copies of which exist in the Wolfe Papers and are reprinted in full in *The earls of Kildare and their ancestors*. Leinster angrily defended the action of his regiment and demanded an apology.[30] However Carhampton replied, underlining the serious disaffection among the Kildare Militia.[31] Two United Irishmen of the Kildare regiment, Daniel Mahon and Thomas Carty, were found guilty of sedition and mutiny on 30 May 1797. One witness stated Carty had declared to Captain Walker: 'That there were more of them than him ... that the duke of Leinster had given up his commission, and that they need not be afraid, for that the head men of the kingdom were to take charge of them'.[32] Carhampton had similarly accused Michael Aylmer – not of disaffection but of inactivity.[33] Carhampton's attitude is indicative of the conservative response to the liberal challenge. Carhampton viewed the political situation as a conflict between loyal subject and insurgent in which the position of Leinster and others particularly in Kildare was at least suspect and at worst traitorous.

The appointment of John Wolfe as commander of the Kildare militia on 20 May 1797 illustrates the government's need to support the loyalist minority in Kildare.[34] The appointment also explains Wolfe's possession of the Carhampton-Leinster letters. An undated letter from John Carlisle, a captain (and later major) in the Kildare militia congratulated Wolfe on his appointment and noted, 'You will be agreeably surprised by finding it not in so desperate a state as is universally believed'. He implicitly noted the existence of United Irishmen in the unit but asserted many were now prepared to 'repent' possibly given the situation of their comrades.[35] A number of officers resigned their position following the duke of Leinster's departure. These included: Major Dominick William O'Reilly, Capt. Richard Rice, Lt. William Aylmer and Ensign William Donnellan.[36]

The liberal-conservative wrangle over the proclamation of Carbery barony and county meeting was rendered further significance by the forthcoming elections. The decision of Henry Grattan and his fellow Whigs to withdraw from the house of commons on 15 May placed liberal interests in a difficult position.[37] In Kildare the Leinster party abstained from the election. However the abstention was neither rigid nor certain, even as late as July. On 10 July Robert La Touche, the high sheriff requested the duke's support in the event of Lord Edward's not standing. The duke's reply evidences the uncertainty.

> I am not yet certain whether Lord Edward declines standing for the county *between you and I* I am inclined to think he will … I certainly cannot give my interest to anyone that does not declare for Catholic emancipation. At any rate I shall not give my interest to Mr Wolfe.[38]

Lord Edward's decision, a week later, not to stand allowed the La Touche interest to assert itself.[39] An address to the county's electors appeared in the press the following day. Valentine Lawless claimed the work came from his pen. 'What is to be expected from a parliament returned under martial law?' he wrote.[40]

The ambiguous position of the Leinster family created uncertainty during the election. A further difficulty was caused by the apparent drop in the number of electors from 1,500 (in 1790) to 300.[41] Maurice Keatinge stood again as an independent candidate. Three others offered themselves as candidates in late July. John La Touche (Robert's father) on 18 July, Joseph Henry of Straffan on 22 July and John Wolfe on 24 July.[42] Henry offered himself as a liberal in the vacuum that had emerged. An address to the freeholders of the county signed 'A Freeholder' urged him to stand down: 'What can you hope for at the present juncture in returning an independent member?'[43] Henry subsequently withdrew his short lived candidature after one week. He had not received the support of his potential power base – the liberals of north Kildare.[44]

The pro-government vote hung in the balance between La Touche and Wolfe. However traditional Leinster voters such as William Grattan or Robert Graydon declined to support Wolfe and he withdrew his candidacy on 28 July.[45] A letter to the castle dated the same day indicated Wolfe's frustration. John La Touche had obviously canvassed Leinster's support and Wolfe complained he did not expect an election until after the next session and therefore had deferred registering his friends; '... had any other person but Mr La Touche stood on the duke of Leinster's interest I should have succeeded, but he went to the duke without holding any communication to me'.[46] Louis Cullen comments that Leinster's policy 'appears to have been guided by the prospect of ditching a more determined loyalist in favour of a less declared one'.[47] John Wolfe's more proclaimed conservative stance in local matters, his government ties and his defection from the Leinster camp seven years earlier swayed the Leinster strength to La Touche. Maurice Keatinge and La Touche were duly elected without a contest. Mary Leadbeater recorded the popular celebration at Keatinge's victory in Ballitore.[48]

Leinster's fading dominance in local politics was illustrated by the results of the borough elections in county Kildare in 1797-8. The boroughs of Athy (William and Richard Hare) and Kildare (James Fitzgerald, the prime sergeant and Bridges Henniker) were sold to pro-government supporters. Harristown had been sold to the La Touche interest in 1793. The deaths of the sitting MPs, Sir Fitzgerald Aylmer in 1794 and Arthur Burdett in 1796, enabled Robert La Touche and his brother John to take possession of the seats. Both men were returned in 1797. By 1797 both seats for the earl of Mayo's borough of Naas had been sold, to George Damer (Viscount Milton) and Walter Yelverton. Thomas Pelham and Francis Hely Hutchinson were elected in 1797. Pelham chose to sit for Armagh Borough and was replaced by Sir John McCartney.[49]

The duke of Leinster effectively abandoned his important local position in the autumn of 1797. He travelled to Bristol Hot Wells with his wife who was seriously ill. He remained there until the following May when he went to London.[50] Valentine Lawless returned to England ostensibly to continue his studies at the same time. Fitzpatrick claimed he was elected to the executive committee of the United Irishmen in autumn 1797.[51] The very public liberal-conservative wrangle which had commenced in late April further radicalised public opinion by underlining the impotency of the moderate approach. Moderate politicians were increasingly pulled towards radical or loyalist camps. The liberal campaign had been specifically designed to mobilise the weight of public opinion. Their failure to field a candidate at the election implicitly recognised the worthlessness of parliamentary tactics and for some indicated the expediency of 'out of doors' mobilisation. From May 1797 reports of United Irish activities in south Kildare rapidly increased.

Letters arriving at Dublin Castle in May 1797 illustrate the disturbed nature of county Kildare. A number of attacks and arrests were reported from Celbridge.[52] The duke of Leinster's town of Maynooth further exhibited the extent of disturbance in the area. Richard Cane a yeoman Sergeant explained to Pelham, '… perhaps there is not in the kingdom a town more seditious and disloyal'.[53] A list of disturbances compiled by Richard Nevill in the same month depicted the level of terror. 'The banditti,' he wrote, 'carry about fire in tea kettles to set fire to cabins.' He listed eleven attacks on respectable citizens in six days largely in search of arms and ammunition for the expanding society.[54]

While Nevill believed the area around Naas itself was tranquil John Wolfe did not. He noted large assemblies of people and requested troops of the Romney Fencibiles be sent to the area.[55] Indeed Wolfe's opinion seems to have hardened during this period. Information received from his uncle Theobald Wolfe suggested the unreliability of Yeoman corps commanded by his political opponents.

> He tells me that the duke's Yeomanry, Browne's and Sir Fenton Aylmer's exercised together at Kilcock last Sunday, that Browne took the command or at least the lead and Sir Fenton Aylmer remained quiescent; he does not say the duke was there: I have thought this worth communicating to you because I think it leads or may lead to something very mischievous.[56]

In a letter to John Wolfe, Theobald stated bluntly that the Leinster corps were 'noted for associating with croppies'.[57] A neighbour at Naas, John Ravell Walsh favoured a conciliatory attitude. He suggested the use of an oath 'comfortable to the oath of allegiance' to be used to gauge the loyalty of the populace. He also criticised the heavy-handed actions of some magistrates whose behaviour 'contrasts with the conduct of proper magistrates' and put them in danger.[58]

Reports began to reach Dublin Castle of radical activity on Kildare's southern borders. A radical newspaper was read to the inhabitants of Baltinglass each Sunday and oaths administered.[59] Robert Cornwall reported Carlow people travelling to Kildare for meetings in August.[60] Benjamin

O'Neale Stratford reported from north Wicklow in June, 'I hear that the contagion of the county Kildare is likely to erupt into this part to which I fear it is too near'.[61] His brother Lord Aldborough, writing in September outlined a desperate situation in his locality:

> ... bandittis burn houses and pillage them and steal lead in whatever shape they can find it ... and rob the Yeomanry at night in their lonely houses of arms under the pain of murdering them or burning their houses.[62]

He argued only a military solution was suitable but his suggestions were not moved upon at this point. Despite the almost hysterical tone of Aldborough's letter, it was rather solitary. Very few reports arrived from Kildare from July to October. The stationing of a military camp on the Curragh in August seems to have curtailed the ability of United Irishmen in the area, though Pollock a crown councillor believed its effects were limited.[63]

The summer assizes held at Athy at the end of August served to publicly manifest again the radical-conservative divisions in the county. The grand jury panel included both Lord Edward Fitzgerald and Valentine Lawless.[64] A number of 'Defenders' were sentenced to execution including William Kennedy tried on 24 August for his part on the attack on Carbery charter school.[65] Kennedy's case allegedly involved serious abuses. The evidence of Stephen Hyland was extracted by Lt. Hempenstall of the Wicklow Militia through violence. Hempenstall acquired the epithet the 'walking gallows' for his barbarity. One of the jurors on refusing to convict the defendant was promptly informed he would be thrown out a window if he did not. A number of gentlemen, including grand jurors presented the solicitor general with a petition on Kennedy's behalf, but he was executed before it reached the Lord Lieutenant.[66]

Pollock one of the crown councillors who attended the Athy assizes wrote a worried letter to Dublin Castle: 'I think there is in that county a most decided and unequivocal determination to subvert the King's government'. Prisoners were 'supported' by Lord Edward Fitzgerald, Valentine Lawless, Thomas Ryan and George Cummins and all the Catholic jurors. The duke of Leinster's behaviour during a short visit was also viewed suspiciously. Cummins he believed was particularly dangerous and organised the United Irish prisoner's fund. Thomas Fitzgerald he described as 'a tanner, distiller and republican' and urged the disbandment of his yeoman corps. The obvious reluctance to prosecute United Irishmen was a reflection of the strength of local organisation. 'The county is to be saved yet,' Pollock concluded, 'but no time is to be lost.'[67]

In Kildare the show of the radical party at the assizes convinced Pollock of their underlying tendencies. The events must have had a powerful impact on the local community. Two cases aroused particular attention. Captain Simon Fraser and John Ross of the Inverness Fencibles were found not guilty of murdering an elderly carpenter Christopher Dixon in May. *The Press* published notes on the trials of Fraser/Ross and William Kennedy in the same issue in a blatant attack on the prejudice of the judiciary.[68] In a further case John O'Brien and another United Irishman were acquitted of administering oaths. Following the verdict, reported Pollock, 'Lord Edward and Lawless ... walked back with the refractory jury men and publicly that evening drank the health of the 5 virtuous *citizens* who would not find their friends guilty'.[69]

If Pollock, a government official, was so abhorred by the power of the radicals in Kildare at the summer assizes, what must the effect on the local population have been? They demonstrated to the Kildare United Irishmen that they were a powerful body. If Pollock alone is relied on, the judicial process was, at least, seriously undermined. Patrick O'Kelly's reference to the episode is surely significant. Loyalists were placed on the defensive. A visiting judge Robert Day, informed the Attorney General in August:

> Gentlemen here [i.e. Philipstown] and in the county of Kildare have converted their houses into garrisons their windows and doors barricaded with bullet proof plank, pierced in various places for spike holes – and notwithstanding the present calm they have no idea of abandoning that defensive system or relaxing their precautions till after the winter.[70]

Day's 'present calm' did not last long. The months of November and December witnessed a resurgence of violence, particularly in the southern baronies. Indeed gauging the strength of the United Irishmen on this evidence is difficult. Disturbance may be a sign of radical penetration or poor leadership (or both) in a particular locality. A tranquil area could reflect either a disciplined underground movement or ineffective mobilisation.

Reports of disturbances which arrived at Dublin Castle during late 1797 and early 1798 emanated largely from mid and south Kildare. Based on this evidence north Kildare remained relatively tranquil. Most of the attacks were on isolated houses in an attempt to gain arms and ammunition. The long winter nights were an ideal cover for such raids.[71] Murders occurred with increasing frequency. In November John Wolfe reported the savage killing of Patrick Nicolson and his sister. They had been taken from their house by 'a number of savages with their faces blackened and shirts over their coats' (the description is more akin to Whiteboy raids). The reason for the murder was a mystery. Wolfe suggested the 'deceased man sometime last summer gave offence to our modern reformers for which they burned his house'.[72] The episode demonstrates the link between violence and political considerations.

For Wolfe the only solution was a military one. He favoured proclamation. 'Speedy trial and proclamation,' he wrote, '... nothing can strike greater terror into the common mind.'[73] Even when those responsible were arrested their prosecution was threatened by the safety of witnesses. In December Captain Swayne reported a prosecuting Dragoon Guard feared he would be poisoned.[74] Richard Nevill reported at least six robberies occurred in his neighbourhood during a week in December, 'some of them attended with great barbarism'. Gatherings, for example for boxing matches, were utilised by United Irishmen to meet and organise. He also found the *Union Star* was posted up in a canal store at Sallins. The braodsheet's inflammatory rhetoric composed (anonymously) by Watty Cox, urged the execution of informers and magistrates, Kildare figures were occasionally included.[75]

Possibly the most daring and certainly the most profitable raid was an attack on the Athy packet boat carried out in early December. Two cachets of arms were seized from a boat destined for Leighlin Bridge from Philipstown. Lord Downshire at Edenderry commented the event 'has made a deep impression on the minds of the disaffected here'.[76] A. Weldon, an established church minister and prominent south Kildare loyalist, was of the opinion that the attack was launched from or at least planned from Dublin not Athy. He felt the conductor and boatman were themselves involved.[77] An extensive enquiry failed to uncover the roots of the enquiry or the arms. Patrick O'Kelly claimed the arms were hidden in surrounding bogland. 'Captain Fitzgerald's corps being generally of the United Party, no great display for searching the arms was manifested.'[78] The canal's advantages were effectively exploited by the United Irishmen. Canal workers were involved in both the Defenders and United Irishmen in Carbery Barony. In April 1798 it was reported 'improper persons' used it to travel to and from Dublin. It was suggested a magistrates pass should be introduced to prevent this.[79]

What was the state of the Kildare United Irishmen as they faced into 1798? How many had been sworn in and who were the leaders? Two sources are particularly instructive on the Kildare United Irishmen emanating from one person: Thomas Reynolds. They are his son's history of his life published in 1839 and Reynolds' testimony on oath before the Privy Council taken in May 1798.[80] The son's biography was an apologia designed to clear his father's tarnished reputation. He attempted to illustrate his father's innocent involvement in a politically (not militarily) motivated United Irish society. Reynolds himself was a silk manufacturer and had been involved in Catholic agitation during the early 1790s. He was sworn into the United Irishmen by Oliver Bond in Dublin in February 1797. His son argues he joined merely from his support for a society whose avowed objectives were Catholic emancipation and parliamentary reform, but heard little of its revolutionary plans. Reynolds attitude was non-committal. While he was not an infiltrator, he viewed the United Irish cause in terms of personal benefit not political ideology or revolutionary zeal. He attended society meetings at the Brazen Head and later a Baronial meeting where he learned the conspiracy aimed at: 'overturning the present government, of establishing a republican form of government instead ... and of assisting the French in any invasion they may make upon this kingdom to forward their views'.[81]

Towards the end of 1797 Reynolds received possession of Kilkea Castle and estate, owned by the duke of Leinster, and seems to have retired there to make preparations for residence.[82] In November Lord Edward approached him and requested he replace him as Colonel of the Kilkea and Moone Barony temporarily. He was informed the military organisation of Kildare had been completed but Fitzgerald himself wished to lie low for a period. Reynolds seems to have given a 'very reluctant assent' for a number of reasons. Foremost was his connection with the Leinster interest which he perceived had been damaged politically by recent events in Kildare. In effect Reynolds viewed the approach as an invitation (albeit a dangerous one) to social prestige in his new home and given the request's origins one he could hardly refuse.[83] He was not sworn to the post until the following January when he met the key local activist Matthew Kenna of Birstown. Kenna informed him the baronial committee contained twelve members who commanded 2,300 men.[84]

What was the strength of the United Irishmen in the county? The reports emanating from the county's beleaguered loyalists suggest the organisation was overwhelming the county and had percolated into southern Kildare effectively from May 1797. A return of numbers captured from a county Down meeting in early June 1797 puts the Kildare organisation at 12,703.[85] This is the highest figure for the county's association, higher even than the generous returns of 1798. United Irish figures served not only the purpose of assessing the movement's strength but possessed an implicit inspirational factor. The revamped United Irish constitution produced in August 1797 created a hierarchical structure based on simple societies (twelve members); lower baronial committees (representatives of ten simple societies); upper baronial committees (representatives of at least four lower baronials); county committees (representatives of at least four upper baronials) and provincial committees with two representatives from each county.[86]

An undated report produced below details the strength of Kildare by men and arms. The original is held in the Public Record Office HO 100 papers. Its location with papers marked received between January and March 1798 suggest it may have been compiled as early as late 1797. Thomas Reynolds mentions a return of arms was presented at a county committee meeting held on 10 February 1798 at which he was elected treasurer.[87] His new position would have give him access to such documents and he possibly passed this one to William Cope.

This is the only surviving document which breaks Kildare United Irish figures into baronies. Despite its deficiencies it is significant for this reason alone. The total number of United Irishmen in the county was put at 10,855. The figures illustrate the organisational structure of the county. It was divided by barony rather than half barony therefore the divisions in the baronies of Salt, Narragh and Rheban and Offaly were ignored. The rather large figure for the 'town of Naas' must apply to the baronies of North and South Naas as a whole. At over 10, 000 the paper strength of the organisation was healthy and credible assuming it refers to a late 1797 or early 1798 date. Kilkea and Moone's figure was actually 1,000 below Kenna's figure. One important regional variation emerges. The two northern baronies of Carbery and Salt seem rather under organised. Carbery's large tracts of bog only partly explain the inconsiderable figure of 384. The force of proclamation conceivably damaged the area's organisation. The figure for Salt suggests four lower baronial committees existed, hence the nominal figure 480.

Where figures for arms are included they indicate baronies were at least arming. Many did not have an ample quantity of heavier weaponry; guns, pistols and bayonets. Ikeathy for example, was in a very poor state. Pikes however, were an easily manufactured source of armament. The figure of 3,060 bayonets for Narragh and Rheban obviously indicates the arms seized from the canal in December remained in the area. It also supports the view that the return post-dates that attack. When Thomas Reynolds was requested to become Colonel of the Kilkea and Moone Barony he was informed the military organisation of the county had been completed. O'Kelly stated mil-

County of Kildare Returns

Town of	Men	Guns	Pistols	Swords	Pikes	Ballcartridges	Balls	Bayonets	Blunderbusses
Naas	1360	117	108	70	588	1030	3291	45	7
Baronies of									
Offaly	2032	No returns–censured							
Kilkea & Moone	1339	215	44	89	1029	10000	—	123	7
Narragh & Rheban	1646	240	86	57	1050	1000	—	3060	6
Clane	1114	70	100	40	—	—	—	20	7
Connell	1020	No returns–censured							
Ikeathy	880	40	40	50	—	—	—	50	—
Carbery	384	No returns–censured							
Kilcullen	600	50	34	42	600	—	—	50	—
Salt	480	30	10	15	50	—	3000	—	2

[*Source:* PRO HO 100/75/209 (5) County of Kildare Returns, n.d.]

itary organising and weapons manufacturing commenced in the winter of 1797 (which the above return may reflect).[88]

Lord Edward retained a crucial position on the county movement and a functioning and effective leadership had been fashioned by him. Many of the leaders were closely connected to him. George Cummins acted as his agent.[89] Malachi Delany of Ballitore was reported to be 'very great with Lord Edward'.[90] Other key players – Thomas Reynolds, Matthew Kenna or Michael Reynolds were all similarly positioned. James Smyth, a calico print-er at Leixlip, who according to one source had been involved in radical pol-itics in Belfast, forged links with Lord Edward following his election as delegate for Salt in February.[91] R.R Madden asserted that c.1798 William Putman McCabe, a northern radical who had become a confidant of Lord Edward, was assigned the task of 'organising Kildare'. However there is no mention of his presence in the county in the Rebellion Papers and the evi-dence is much stronger for his involvement in Wicklow and Wexford.[92] Lord Edward's resignation of the Colonelcy of the Kilkea and Moone Barony to Thomas Reynolds signalled his partial vacation of control in Kildare, although he retained some involvement at a county level.[93] He continued to actively participate in United Irish affairs in west Kildare and attended two 'sub baronial' meetings in January and March 1798 in the houses of George Cummins and himself, in Kildare town. At the meeting in March his posi-tion as treasurer appears to have been taken by Roger McGarry.[94]

Reynolds named those who attended his first county committee meeting held at Nineteen Mile House near Kilcullen on 10 February: Thomas Reynolds [Kilkea and Moone], Matthew Kenna [Kilkea and Moone], Michael Reynolds [Naas], Mr Flood [Kilcullen], Mr Daly [Kilcullen], George Cummins [Offaly], Two persons from Athy [Narragh and Rheban], One person from Mr La Touche's Yeomanry [Naas?].[95] The lack of any del-egates from the northern baronies of Salt, Ikeathy, Carbery, Clane or Connell is surprising. Perhaps the geographical distance from Kilcullen was a factor or Lord Edward had been relied on to represent these baronies. Coupled with the evidence in the return above, however, it could reflect an organisa-tional backwardness in the area. Most of the local leaders were young and quite affluent, many were farmers. Others such as Smyth, a calico printer, or Cummins, an apothecary, were skilled artisans. According to Reynolds, Lord Edward had regularly attended county meetings previous to his resignation. On 10 February Reynolds was elected treasurer in his place. George Cummins was elected secretary in the place of Michael Reynolds. Daly was also elected as a delegate to the Leinster provincial.

The 'treachery' of Thomas Reynolds presented the government with an opportunity not only to uncover the national leaders of the United Irishmen, but also the conspirators in the heavily politicised county of Kildare. Reynolds' son stated his father decided to pass information to government when he learned the full details of the proposed rebellion and its use of assassination.[96] He initially passed information to government via William Cope with whom he was transacting business, possibly as if received from a third party.[97] In hindsight Lord Edward's approach to Reynolds was an understandable, but critical, mistake. It was made from the viewpoint of expediency. Reynolds had neither proved his loyalties as a radical politician nor abilities as the commander of a large underground army. Information he supplied led to the raid on Oliver Bond's house on 12 March and the capture of most of the Leinster provincial. Reynolds spent the previous week collecting the county returns in order to learn the location and date of the meeting. George Cummins was arrested, but overall the arrests were not a serious setback to the Kildare organisation though the possibility of infiltration certainly unnerved some members.[98] Cummins revealed nothing and 'being obstinate in denying evidence he was committed'.[99]

Were the leaders of radical politics from the previous years involved in the Kildare United Irishmen? A numbers of such figures were connected to the movement by Thomas Reynolds: John Esmonde, Thomas Fitzgerald, Wogan Browne, Maurice Keatinge, Daniel Caulfield and Col. Lumm.[100] John Esmonde of Osberstown was certainly a United Irishman. At a meeting held on 18 March he replaced Thomas Reynolds as treasurer.[101] In January 1798 his yard was even searched for arms.[102] Another member of the medical profession Dr Johnson of Ballitore was apparently a local United Irish leader.[103]

A relatively large body of evidence suggests Thomas Fitzgerald of Geraldine was connected with the United Irishmen. Two confessions stated he was a commander. One asserted he was 'over', another that he and Lord Edward 'were to take their part and to command them'.[104] Colonel Campbell, officer commanding at Athy, claimed he obtained similar information.[105] Campbell discovered a number of 'suspicious papers' at his home, which was placed under free quarters in April.[106] The twenty-one documents contained in the latter collection reveal the involvement of Fitzgerald in Catholic, radical and Kildare politics throughout the decade. Two of the documents are particularly incriminating; a United Irish address, dated February 1798, which included the August 1797 constitution of the society and an 'Orange Oath' of the type circulated among Catholics to incite fear and anger.[107] Following his arrest in May he denied any connection with the United Irishmen.

Interestingly he admitted advising his nephew, Thomas Reynolds against continuing his dealings with Mr Cope – but on financial grounds.[108] The evidence in favour of Fitzgerald's involvement in the United Irishmen is not conclusive. In March 1798 he reported disturbances in his area (perhaps as a cover). He declared his innocence again in July 1798, claiming again that he was never involved in any committees.[109] Nonetheless the Yeomen under his captaincy were publicly disarmed in Athy in April.[110]

Thomas Reynolds information before the Privy Council implicated a number of prominent Kildare liberals. At a county committee meeting held in March it was agreed to accept some persons if they came forward:

> ... as it was irksome to the gentlemen of the county to come forward to societies where they might meet persons of low descriptions Col. Lumm, Col. Keatinge, Mr Esmonde and Mr Wogan Browne should be informed that if they would accept the commissions of colonel they should be admitted at once into the county meeting without passing thro' the inferior societies.

Thomas Reynolds was informed Col. Lumm had attended a later county meeting. Col. Keatinge agreed to join the Ballitore committee, while Daniel Caulfield of Levetstown had requested to be named joint colonel of Kilkea and Moone barony which, according to Reynolds, duly occurred.[111]

Camden had informed Portland on 11 March that the following were the names of the Kildare Colonels: Wogan Browne, Col. Lumm, Col. Keatinge, Valentine Lawless, Mr Pender, Michael Reynolds, George Cummins and two close relations of the unnamed informant.[112] The list possibly reflects the castle's desire to view the Kildare insurgents as a liberal-radical plot led by a dangerously articulate and affluent group. However the informant's omission of two delegates (probably Thomas Fitzgerald and Lord Edward), on the grounds of his (or her) relationship to them suggest Thomas Reynolds as the informant. An undated and anonymous account in the Rebellion Papers purports to state a number of Kildare gentlemen were contemplating 'to act with the people' and seems to confirm Reynold's information. The account is rather vague but again Col. Lumm is stated to have come forward.[113] Lumm is one of the most shadowy United Irish figures in Kildare, though he seems to have been connected with Lord Edward Fitzgerald.[114]

Wogan Browne was not directly implicated by information other than that cited above. He was, however, deeply suspected. At the beginning of 1797 he was severely reprimanded by Lord Clare for kicking off a football match.[115]

Football matches and other large gatherings were used by United Irishmen as covers for their gatherings. For example, Richard Nevill reported in May 1797 that: 'instead of funerals the meetings [of United Irishmen] on the Curragh are for weddings'.[116] One of Wogan Browne's tenants, William Aylmer of Painstown had joined the United Irishmen by late 1797. Valentine Lawless asserted Aylmer was sworn by William Sampson who often accompanied Lawless to Laughlinstown camp where the Kildare Militia were stationed. Aylmer seems to have been sworn between late 1796 and early 1797. He resigned his Lieutenancy in the Kildare regiment on 12 June 1797.[117] Perhaps he resigned in sympathy with Leinster or in apprehension of John Wolfe's appointment.[118] His activities between this date and the outbreak of rebellion remain unclear. He possibly wished to restrain his United Irish links to a minimum.

The Kildare return to the United Irish national committee meeting held on 26 February 1798 was 10,863, a slight increase on the previous return.[119] Coupled with Reynolds' information, the existence of an organised and determined Kildare United Irish movement is confirmed. Despite the proto-democratic ideology and structures of the movement it instinctively sought connection with middling (and upper) classes at its leadership level. This is most striking in the Dublin movement. The involvement of liberal-radical politicians in rural Kildare was designed to encourage the participation of the sections of 'lower orders' who remained hesitant. The cult of Lord Edward is the most obvious indication of this attitude. However as Thomas Reynolds recognised many affluent figures had too much to lose in coming forward – the free quarters of April and May 1798 made this patently obvious.

During the winter of 1797-8 prominent loyalists in south Kildare were attacked; John Greene, Captain Beaver, Thomas Rawson and Major Allen all suffered.[120] Rawson reported to Wolfe in January that: 'The trade of timber cutting for pike handles has been carried on with great success – not a plantation escaping'. At Grangemellon thirty-seven pikes were found, however enough timber for 2,300 more was discovered.[121] In January a sergeant of the Romney Fencibiles was apparently murdered at Newbridge and reprisals were taken against a local shopkeeper. A letter to *The Press* suggested the man had seized an opportune moment to desert.[122] The most publicised attack was the attempted murder of John Johnson Darrah, a magistrate from Eagle Hill, on 1 March. Darrah was so seriously wounded General Dundas initially reported he had died. He was shot in broad daylight by a man delivering post to his door. A man was arrested for the attack a few weeks later and confessed to the crime.[123]

Conservatives were increasingly drawn towards the use of the Insurrection Act. Nevill had floated the idea briefly in early December.[124] During December and January John Wolfe began to accumulate accounts of disturbances in the Athy area with a view to petitioning for proclamation, particularly through Thomas Rawson. He began one letter, 'I fear I tire you but you know its your own desire'.[125] In another he noted: '[I]… agree with you that if the whole county had been proclaimed last September it would have stopped the contagion spreading as it has into Queen's County and Carlow'.[126] In the first week of January no fewer than seventeen houses were attacked in the Athy-Stradbally area.[127] In mid-January a requisition requesting a meeting of justices of the peace was signed by four southern magistrates. Thomas Fitzgerald and James Archibald refused to sign the document.[128] A meeting was arranged to be held in Athy but proclamation remained an uncertainty. As in the case of Carbery the previous year the use of draconian military legislation was opposed by liberal politicians such as Fitzgerald, Archibald and Wogan Browne. Rawson advised Wolfe that if the measure was to be secured magistrates from the north needed to travel to Athy.[129] Wolfe informed Pelham on 21 January the meeting would take place on the following Thursday [25 January]. He utilised the information of Rawson and Weldon to state the case in favour of proclamation. He added that the mere threat of the action had produced 'a complete change' and stated the baronies of Kilkea and Moone, West and East Narragh and Rheban and 'perhaps East Offaly' were to be considered.[130]

Nonetheless Sir Fenton Aylmer was sufficiently worried about the extent of possible proclamation to write to Wolfe on the matter, warning:

> … *that no advantage* [should] *be taken* of the absence of me and others to proclaim Connell. Should it be the wish of any, privately to set on foot by whom it may to proclaim the whole county I alone cry out against it but I hope and trust that no such measure may be attempted.[131]

Wolfe's reply rejected the existence of any 'secret intention or private management' with respect to the meeting, or any intention to proclaim the whole county. Indeed Wolfe himself had considered Athy an unwise venue.[132] The meeting produced a memorial requesting the proclamation of five baronies (with only one objection): Kilkea and Moone, East and West Narragh and Rheban and East and West Offaly. In all some two to three hundred houses were represented to have been plundered for arms. It emerged that those opposed to the measure including Keatinge and Thomas Fitzgerald had decided not to attend.[133] The baronies were proclaimed on 2 February 1798 and joined a growing territory in Leinster including all of Queen's County (Jan. 1797) and Carlow (Nov. 1798).[134]

Proclamation was the most obvious conservative reaction to the United Irish problem. Mary Duggan has argued the Orange Order played an important role in unnerving the movement in Carlow.[135] Given the beleaguered situation of many loyalists in Kildare the weakness of the Orange movement is initially surprising. There was one lodge formed at Monasterevin in 1798 though its composition is unclear.[136] A letter in the Rebellion Papers attests the existence of a lodge in Naas in 1798 as well. The group met twice a week in the town and included 'a great many militia men'. One Atkinson, a shopkeeper is named in the letter, but the four signatories gave only their initials.[137] A number of Kildare men joined the Dublin Lodge No. 176 at an early date in 1798. John Montgomery, who acted as Kildare Grand Master and his neighbour Revd John Keating both lived near Naas. Two other conservative families provided members for the nascent lodge – the Knipes and Stratfords.[138] The Orange Order in Kildare remained isolated and never presented the United Irishmen with a serious threat. However the latter movement was not unaware of the propaganda affects of fear of the Orange Order in the county.

Thomas Rawson's Loyal Athy Infantry, formed in late April, were suspected to be an Orange corps.[139] The idea was implicitly recognised but rejected by Rawson himself. In November he wrote to Wolfe:

> I had much objection to any party which could give a handle to the disaffected and as such prevented any Orange society in my corps. I knew them to be steady loyal Protestants and did not imagine anything could increase their zeal. I have done everything in my power to reconcile but all to no purpose with the Roman Catholics every protestant is an Orange man – and every Orange man looked on as an enemy.[140]

In January 1798 Rawson published a denial of the very existence of orangeism.[141] The Montgomerys, Stratfords and Knipes were all well known ultra-conservatives, but none exerted a powerful local influence. The Kildare order's lack of support is not surprising given the county's largely Catholic demographic composition and liberal stance of many Protestants. Neither did Kildare possess a possible basis in the form of a concentrated population of lower class Protestants except perhaps in Naas.

On 30 March 1798 a Privy Council proclamation declared Ireland to be in a state of rebellion and imposed martial law. The county was to be forcibly pacified while stolen or concealed weapons or ammunition were to be recovered. Castlereagh directed the commander in chief of the army, Sir Ralph Abercromby to employ his troops on the disturbed counties of the country, including Kildare.[142] Some arms, including 626 muskets were surrendered to General Wilford during the last week of March. However the great bulk of rebel armoury remained in their hands.[143] Abercromby's preferred method of pacification was the use of free quarters. Accordingly 4,000 copies of a proclamation were released in Kildare requesting the return of stolen arms within ten days.[144] Free quarters commenced by late April. In neighbouring Queen's County a disciplined force under Sir Charles Asgill quickly produced positive results.[145]

In Kildare the measure was most forcibly applied to wealthy liberal landowners. William Drennan was aware that free quarters had commenced in Kildare by 24 April, at the home of Wogan Browne.[146] The policy was applied particularly vigorously under the direction of Col. Colin Cambpell from Athy.[147] Thomas Reynolds paradoxically became a victim of the military rampages because of his suspicious degree of influence with the local populace.[148] His residence was billeted with 200 soldiers and 80 horses, initially under Captain Erskine, later Col. Campbell. Kilkea Castle was thoroughly searched and plundered. Reynolds was arrested in early May and quickly revealed himself as the person who had supplied the information which led to the Bond's arrests in March. He subsequently provided government with a full statement before the privy council. Reynolds later calculated his total losses at £12,760.[149]

Thomas Fitzgerald of Geraldine suffered similarly. He was forced to quarter 10 officers, 110 troops and fifty horses for 29 days beginning on 20 April. He was initially placed under house arrest but later taken to Dublin.[150] After his arrest a number of rebel captains in the Athy area including James Walsh, Patrick Dowling, Terence Toole and Pat Bearns drew up a rescue plan. However Fitzgerald himself dissuaded them from this course of action.[151] Those associated with Lord Edward were particularly suspect. Patrick Dunne, Thomas Dunne and Daniel Caulfield were all visited by Campbell's Dragoons.[152] Caulfield was arrested in mid-May and charged with high treason.[153] Drennan reported in early May that Col. Keatinge and Col. Lumm Sampson had been arrested.[154] Whatever possibility existed of prominent liberal-radical politicians leading a rebellion it now vanished.

Anticipated leaders such as Reynolds, Thomas Fitzgerald, Caulfield, Keatinge, Lumm and possibly Wogan Browne had been detached from the projected rebellion. In that sense the period of free quarters was crucial.

General Lake's succession to the command of the Irish army on 25 April following Abercromby's resignation signalled a shift in military policy – free quarters were dropped in favour of more direct military pressure. Draconian measures were now directly applied to the lower orders. Campbell at Athy again appeared at the forefront of the assault. Flogging was to be used to extract confessions from suspected persons. William Farrell a Carlow United Irishmen asserted the flogging produced immediate results in Athy: '… one single informer in a town was sufficient to destroy all the United Irishmen in it …'[155] Among those specifically targeted were blacksmiths and carpenters suspected of manufacturing pikes.[156] In many cases the innocent naturally suffered with those involved in United Irish activities.[157] Campbell writing in mid-May acclaimed the success of the measures which had produced arms, ammunitions and confessions. On 15 May he reported the names of captains had been received and added '… a great number of pikes some hundreds … within these two days' had been handed up. Leaders however, for example Matthew Kenna, remained in hiding.[158] By mid-May the draconian measures produced positive results in terms of detection and recovery of weapons throughout south Kildare. A source from Baltinglass reported that: '… the sight of the pikes were shocking, from 18 inches to 2 feet long, with two wings about 10 inches long, reversed in a bow for cutting bridle reins …'[159]

In Ballitore Col. Keatinge's appeals for leniency were ignored and 'great waste was committed and unchecked robbery' by the professed Orange men of the Tyrone Militia. Mary Leadbeater's account reveals the misery this policy wreaked on areas of Kildare. The policy may have produced pacification but it also hardened attitudes further among those who suffered.[160] The rigorous disarming was applied less forcefully further north. In Monasterevan suspected rebels were arrested among them a publican, a smith and a schoolmaster. Fifty stands of arms were taken from the canal but 'sent back'. At Kilcullen the Dragoons recovered forty to fifty pikes and received information on suspected rebels.[161] In late April Dundas received detailed information on the United Irishmen in the Kildare-Kilcullen area from a 'man of family and fortune', perhaps someone who feared the prospect of free quarters which had commenced. The information included a detailed report on twenty-three 'suspected persons'. The informant was perfectly correct in his statement of United Irish structures. He also stated, 'every man upon the Curragh has a pike; they are hid underground'.[162]

On 11 May Camden reported to Portland that the severe measures adopted at Athy produced beneficial results. Information supplied to General Wilford led to the capture of persons under Reynolds' command in Kilkea and Moone. Great numbers of pikes had been delivered up and were still arriving. 'The organisation of the military committee [in Kildare]' he concluded, 'is broken and pursued'.[163] Four days later General Dundas, the midlands commander, wrote complacently to Dublin Castle:

> The last few days have furnished me with very affecting scenes – my house filled with the poor deluded people giving up their arms, receiving protections and declaring that moment to be the happiest in their lives. Be assured that the head of the hydra is off – and the county of Kildare will for a long while enjoy profound peace and quiet.[164]

The measures reached the north later in May. Louisa Conolly wrote to William Ogilvie on 21 May describing a familiar scene of burning houses and surrendered pikes. Regiments of a Scottish force had worked their way through the towns of Kilcock, Maynooth, Celbridge and Leixlip obtaining mediocre results in terms of arms. The Conollys themselves busily urged the local populace to co-operate.[165] At Prosperous the level of violence used by Captain Richard Swayne became notorious. However, the narrative of Bernard Duggan, a participant, conflicts with that of Musgrave on certain points of detail.[166] For example, Musgrave states Captain Swayne and a detachment of City of Cork Militia and Ancient Britons arrived in the town on 20 May. He also argues exhortations to produce arms, including one by Dr John Esmonde, failed miserably.[167] Duggan states Swayne arrived on 22 May and immediately implemented free quarters, arrested twelve men, burned property and tortured suspects, though he admitted pitch capping was not used.[168]

What effect did proclamation, free quarters and military excesses have on the United Irishmen in Kildare in the weeks before the rebellion? Martial law was applied to the most disturbed areas of county Kildare itself, particularly those baronies which had recently been proclaimed. By mid-May the leadership of the Kilkea and Moone barony was decimated. The Corporal had turned informer and was later arrested. At the same time a number of prominent Captains were taken up – Luke Brannick, a Yeoman, John Pendred, Philip Germaine, Patrick Germaine and David Fardy. Their county associates were aware of Reynolds' treachery at this point and urged their colleagues to implicate him which they did. In turn these prisoners provided information concerning the lower composition of the barony. Two long lists of names are included with Brannick's testimony. Most of those named were from Castledermot.[169] The measures applied by Campbell at Athy also yielded results in the form of information on United Irish activists.[170]

While Camden was correct to assert the military committee in Kildare was 'pursued' he was mistaken in concluding it was 'broken'. His conclusions were based on the complacent reports of Dundas. A county meeting was convened on 18 March at which Thomas Reynolds read letters he had received from Lord Edward Fitzgerald three days earlier. An address urged the members to fill vacancies and remain calm. The Kildare organisation was deeply worried by the Bond arrests. A member was apparently killed before the meeting, held at Reilly's on the Curragh, and buried nearby.[171] At the meeting new officers were elected as a precaution. Michael Reynolds replaced George Cummins as secretary, John Esmonde replaced Reynolds as treasurer. Tom Daly being absent remained an officer. The following day Reynolds met a number of his captains at Athy. He terminated his involvement with the United Irishmen at this point. His son stated Daniel Caulfield was appointed Joint-Colonel with him but his information on the April-May period is either fleeting or non-existent.[172]

Reynolds' Kildare associates quickly learned of his treachery. At a meeting of the Leinster Provincial in the Brazen Head, Dublin, (held at some point after the Bond arrests) Michael Reynolds proposed he be killed. In early April one of the Sheares brothers met the Kildare committee at Dr John Esmonde's house at Osberstown and informed them that Reynolds was definitely the informer. He was then requested to attend a meeting to be held on the Curragh at Bells on 19 April, but refused. The meeting in his absence decided to assassinate him. Matthew Kenna and Michael Murphy, a butcher from Naas, were deputised to carry out the attack but failed.[173]

The evidence from Kildare during April and May suggests the draconian military measures initiated by government were not applied forcibly to those areas which were tranquil. There are no accounts of the Athy atrocities repeated further north, though important discoveries were undoubtedly made. Some of the county delegates were known to the government but had escaped, particularly Michael Reynolds. According to Patrick O'Kelly a meeting of Kildare Colonels was held in Dublin in early April to fill vacancies, possibly under the guidance of Lord Edward Fitzgerald. He certainly met a number of Athy Captains around the same time, indicating the continuing perception of his importance.[174] In mid-April the Leinster Provincial issued a fourteen-point set of instructions, these were effectively intended to prepare the country's United Irishmen for war. They concerned practical measures to be taken both individually and collectively.[175] A paper found on Lord Edward on his arrest further evidences the ongoing military preparations in the county. It listed the military strength of government in each Kildare barony, estimating a total force of 3,819. The forces were most heavily concentrated in the disturbed areas proclaimed in February and the key strategic towns of Kilcullen and Naas.[176]

The April instructions also included a return of men in eight Leinster counties and the city of Dublin. The Kildare organisation was put at 11,910, an increase of over 1,000 since the return of February. A return emanating from Sirr the Dublin police chief at the same time seems to have been based on this return.[177] The figure was produced before the violent disarming had commenced in earnest and is quite credible. The United Irishmen in Kildare had recruited members through a plethora of propaganda techniques in early 1798, however, the threat of Orange men seems to have made an appearance. Thomas Fitzgerald's possession of an Orange oath is one indication.[178] As early as January Thomas Rawson had issued a statement denying their very existence and implying the use of 'Orange fear' as a radical tactic, '… to agitate the public mind …'.[179] The extent of the use of this mechanism is unclear but it may have resulted in an increase in United Irish numbers. Meanwhile those who had previously attempted to remain neutral were now driven towards the United Irishmen by repressive measures which seemed to indicate impending destruction.

The strength of the Kildare movement is also reflected in its six colonels, noted on the April instructions. Only two other Leinster counties had chosen colonels – Dublin and Meath with three each. An almost identical return of men marked 'a smith at Celbridge' but undated, stated Kildare had twelve Colonels and possibly reflects the situation by late April.[180] The events of April and May undoubtedly disabled some areas but communication was maintained until the outbreak of rebellion. Michael Reynolds, George Lube and Hugh Ware held 'frequent communications with the executive'.[181] Madden states Thomas Andoe and George Lube disseminated Dublin's instructions for a rising to Kildare on 20 May.[182] Given the capricious nature of the Dublin executive in the weeks before the outbreak of rebellion, Lord Edward held a crucial position as the only experienced militarist. Infighting in the executive produced uncertainty and anxiety, particularly given the worsening situation in a strong county like Kildare. T.A. Emmet later cited disarming in the county as an immediate cause of the rising.[183] However the arrest of Lord Edward on 19 May in Dublin affected not only the national hopes of co-ordinated rising but Kildare's aspirations of a Fitzgerald-led rebellion.[184]

It is difficult to gauge how many arms were surrendered by the rebels before the rebellion started. Gosford at Naas stated in July that previous to the rebellion he recovered 150 pikes and eight to ten firelocks. On the day of the rising he recovered 800 pikes and twenty to thirty firelocks from the defeated rebels.[185] The paper army of 12,000 Kildare United Irishmen were neither completely disorganised nor disheartened. A rising was daily expected by local leaders. When Thomas Reynolds was arrested in early May he betrayed one of the yeomen who was escorting him to Dublin. The man, who served on the county committee, informed Reynolds that his namesake Michael had received information from Dublin, a rising was to take place in ten days.[186] The violent disarming, combined with Thomas Reynolds' information on the Kildare organisation left rebellion as the only practical course for many United men in the county.

CHAPTER 5

The 1798 rebellion in county Kildare

cs

24–30 MAY

While the events in Kildare often figured prominently in history, they paled in significance in comparison to those in the Wexford theatre. Furthermore, at the moment when the Kildare rebellion began to lose momentum that of Wexford exploded – a fact reflected in the written histories.[1] This has tended to obscure the events which occurred in Kildare between late May and the arrival of Wexford and Wicklow forces in the county in July. For the purposes of analysis the rebellion may be divided into two phases. This chapter will deal with the first phase from 24 May to 30 May. The Kildare insurgents achieved their territorial zenith between 24 and 26 May. By the latter date they controlled a large swathe of territory in southern Kildare. This fact temporarily masked their rapid loss of momentum. The United Irish army suffered defeats at Naas, Carlow, Tara and a failed to attack Athy. This resulted in the loss of urban centres captured, a process completed by 1 June. For almost two months the Kildare insurgents posed a serious threat to government within a few miles of Dublin itself. The rebellion engulfed the entire county and involved thousands of men and women.

Lord Edward's arrest seriously undermined prospects of a united county effort. This fact, however, conceals the reality that different parts of the county were to fulfil various functions within the strategy of the United Irish army. Thomas Graham has argued the United Irishmen formulated a basic three-part plan which was gradually passed to government from March 1798. The first phase involved the capture of key sites within Dublin. Forces in the surrounding areas; north county Dublin, Meath, Kildare and Wicklow were to bolster this attack by forming a ring around Dublin. Outer counties were to capture the important centres in their own counties.[2]

It remains unclear exactly what areas of Kildare were involved in the second phase of the plan. Undoubtedly the north Kildare rebels were expected to take part in a march on Dublin. Prospective jottings found on Lord Edward's possession on his arrest indicate this was considered:

> Suppose R. force divided into three columns. The left *of the Kildare*

[71]

line to ... [assemble at] Cloncurry, or between it and Clonard Bridge; a detachment to be sent to Clonard Bridge, as soon as possible; that *body* [column] to advance by Kilcock, Maynooth, Leixlip and Chapelizod towards Dublin.[3]

Information on the Kildare element of any plan is scant. A more unsatisfactory method of determining the nature of United Irish strategies is to examine what did occur. It is difficult to determine if attacks on Naas, Clane or Kilcullen were part of any semi-circular assault on Dublin. More significantly the dearth of large-scale rebel activity in north Kildare during the first week of rebellion may be indicate the important role designated to the United Irish forces in that area. The immediate reason for the apparent disorganisation was the failure of the Dublin city element. It is tempting therefore to conclude the north Kildare rebels – in close contact with the city – held back for this specific reason.

By 23 May Dublin Castle was aware of impending insurrection in Dublin and surrounding areas.[4] Government forces dealt effectively with the United Irish threat in the capital. The failure of the internal Dublin plan meant phase two of the rebel strategy was rendered ineffective. However this in turn provided the attack on Naas with increased importance within the context of a Kildare rebellion. Michael Reynolds of Johnstown suddenly became very important. He was still secretary of the Kildare county committee, and as such technically the leader of the Kildare United Irishmen. More immediately he was the commander of the rebel forces in the vicinity of Naas.[5] The arrival of the Munster mail coaches in county Kildare indicated something had gone wrong in Dublin. However the fact that they were attacked in Naas also indicates some previous level of mobilisation near the town.

The garrison at Naas was heavily fortified and adequately soldiered under Lord Gosford. At 2:30 on the morning of 24 May an attack commenced under Michael Reynolds and about 1,000 men.[6] They quickly penetrated the town streets particularly from the Johnstown road. Their efforts were concentrated on government troops stationed near the gaol. The rebels possibly intended to liberate prisoners. Troops were engaged for three-quarters of an hour, but three surges failed to produce results and the rebels finally dropped their weapons and fled. This was followed by a cavalry charge. At least thirty-two men were found dead in the streets and up to one hundred outside. Three men with green cockades were taken and hanged in the town. Government troops suffered only six fatalities. While Gosford expressed satisfaction at the actions of the infantry and cavalry generally, 'as to the

Yeomanry,' he wrote, 'I wish we could make a good report of them'.[7] Contrary to Patrick O'Kelly's assertion of indiscipline among the rebels which made defeat inevitable, Reynolds' force was remarkably disciplined in making such a determined strike against a strong force. Reynolds himself escaped drawing some of his force to Blackmore Hill near Blessington.[8]

While the loyalists at Naas were informed of an intended rising the more isolated garrisons were not. The risings in the vicinity of Naas illustrates that Reynolds did not act 'solely from himself' as O'Kelly intimates.[9] The attack on the small town at Prosperous provided the Kildare rebels with their first victory. Despite the level of violence used by Capt. Swayne immediately before the rebellion Bernard Duggan makes no assertion that the rebellion when it arrived was purely reactive, although twelve men arrested on 23 May were scheduled for execution the next day. The order to rise came from 'the United men's committee'.[10] Esmonde and other local leaders persuaded Swayne to order his sentinels not to challenge those approaching the town to facilitate the surrender of rebel weapons, probably in anticipation of the intended rising.[11]

Duggan clearly states Dr John Esmonde was 'commanding general over the people'.[12] He was accompanied by Phil Mite, a yeoman, and local farmers and artisans, most prominently: Andrew Farrell, John Mahon, Thomas Wylde, Bryan Rourke, Bernard Duggan, Bryan McDermott, Edward Hanlon, Patrick Tobin and Denis Hanlon. Their forces gathered at the canal to the south of the town. Swayne's troops were concentrated in the barracks vacated by the Armagh Militia, a former cotton factory and a number of houses throughout the town. The rebel attack, which possibly commenced before the assault on Naas (Musgrave stated it began at two o'clock) quickly turned into a rout. The rebels rushed the barrack where Captain Swayne slept, killing him and trapping most of the soldiers inside.[13] The rebels quickly realised the ground floor of the barracks was full of straw which was used to burn the building. Some soldiers were consumed by the flames, others leapt to their death or were received on pike ends attempting to flee. One witness Thomas Davis reported he ' … heard the soldiers exclaim "The house is on fire, we shall be burned or suffocated: we can fight no longer!" … and the said rebels exclaimed that the day was their own, and they would then plant the tree of liberty'.[14] Richard Griffith claimed fifty Militia and twenty Ancient Britons perished – practically the entire garrison based on Musgrave's calculations.[15]

With the battle won, Esmonde, on the fringes of the town, perceived a small military party (the nature of this group is unclear, perhaps a Yeomanry patrol) as a larger army from Dublin, and, being ill-informed of the battle, he ordered a general retreat. Many of those in the town soon realised their mistake but Esmonde and his aide-de-camp Phil Mite galloped away.[16] Victory gained, the rebels began to search for arms (and enemies) in the town and the surrounding countryside. Two men were immediately targeted; Mr Brewer, an English cotton manufacturer and Henry Stamer, the local justice of the peace and a large property owner. Both were killed.[17] A number of families in the neighbourhood were terrorised, mainly Protestants. These activities produced some dissension among the rebels but a plea for assistance from their Clane comrades withdrew most of their attention.[18]

While Prosperous rebels were completing a sweeping victory rebels unsuccessfully mounted an attack on neighbouring Clane. An initial attack by 300 men was repulsed, despite the fact that a body of the rebels secreted themselves in the town before the assault was launched. The second offensive was more audacious. It was led by six men in Ancient British uniforms (which suggests some Prosperous rebels were involved) but was foiled by the vigilance of the local commander Captain Jepson of the Armagh Militia.[19] At three o'clock Richard Griffith was awoken and informed of the engagement. The intervention of his Yeomen succeeded in dispersing the insurgent force threatening the town. Soon after five in the morning an assault was launched by the Prosperous rebels, but the garrison at Clane quickly rallied and pursued the assailants to near Prosperous.[20]

As Duggan noted the failure to take Clane was 'but to little effect,' as both the Armagh Militia and Yeomen were ordered to retreat to Naas.[21] As he left Clane, Griffith was joined by his first lieutenant, Esmonde. Phil Mite had already informed Griffith of Esmonde's actions. The latter was arrested when the party arrived in Naas. He was sent to Dublin on 8 June, court martialed and hanged from Carlisle Bridge on 14 June 1798 where he met his fate 'with the greatest fortitude and composure'.[22] Esmonde was a serious loss to the rebels of the Prosperous area as an influential and recognised leader among the local United Irishmen. His behaviour after the battle of Prosperous are confusing. Perhaps he joined his yeomen believing the rebels were defeated or wanted to gather intelligence at Naas without realising he had been identified. The opposition of Esmonde and Griffith on the battlefield of 1798 evidences the simplicity of equating the liberal cause of the mid-1790s with the radical cause of 1798.

General Dundas at Castlemartin received information on the eve of the rising that the Kilcullen rebels were preparing for assault.[23] Kilcullen Bridge remained tranquil in the morning. However a body of rebels, possibly 300 were installed in the church yard of Old Kilcullen, on high ground. On marshalling his forces Dundas impetuously ordered his cavalry, consisting of Ninth Dragoons and Romney Fencibles to charge up the stony hill on the rebel position, led by Captains Cooke and Erskine. On the third charge most of the soldiers were swallowed up by the mass of pikes at the summit. Both Cooke and Erskine died, up to two-thirds of the privates also perished.[24]

Dundas retreated north to Kilcullen Bridge with a unit of Suffolk Fencibles under Captain Beale. The rebels meanwhile were considerably buoyed by their success and wished to press home their advantage. The growing United Irish force moved north, passing Kilcullen Bridge to the west and took up position to the north, on the Naas road beside a small hill. Dundas marched out to meet them with the small force at his disposal. After an initial exchange of fire the rebels broke and the cavalry completed a victory attended with heavy rebel loss. Both Musgrave and Thomas Rawson stated the rebels lost 300 men. The rebels regathered on Knockallen to the south but Dundas retreated to Naas shortly afterwards effectively leaving the area in rebel hands.[25] Dundas' underestimation of the rebel forces, the advantage of the pike on high ground and the ultimate superiority of disciplined government forces were to be recurrent themes of the rebellion.

From its geographical situation, the rebellion in west Wicklow was crucial to the effort of the United Irishmen in east Kildare.[26] A significant assault was mounted on the garrison at Ballymore Eustace on the morning of 24 May. The nature of the attack initially gave the rebels an advantage but while the assailants began to burn parts of the town the troops rallied under Beevor's command and they succeeded in defeating the rebel force.[27] By nine o'clock the rebellion on the border had 'gathered momentum'. Hundreds of rebels appeared in the Baltinglass area. An attack was mounted on Stratford-on-Slaney on 24 May was repulsed with heavy losses.[28]

Meanwhile at Dunlavin one of the most ruthless actions of the early rebellion occurred. A decision to execute more than thirty-five suspected rebels was taken following the arrival of a party of Ancient Britons. Ruan O'Donnell argues the reason for the excess was reprisal (for losses inflicted at Ballymore Eustace) and intimidation rather than panic or fear of attack.[29] Those killed included fourteen members of Col. Keatinge's Narraghmore Yeomen.[30] Later in the day an intended attack was rebuffed before it reached the village.[31] The overall failure of the United Irish effort in west Wicklow to establish a base in any one of the border towns did not help the cause of their comrades across the border. However the Wicklow Mountains provided a particularly sheltered camp in case of defeat.

According to Patrick O'Kelly, Patrick Walsh, a respectable landowner from the Narraghmore area, brought instructions for insurrection to the United Irishmen of the region on 22 May. Anonymous information received by government described the situation in the district on the morning of 24 May: ' ... men, women and children joined in procuring arms of all descriptions, they sung horrible songs ... never before heard by loyalists, to excite the rebellion'.[32] During the morning Thomas Rawson, at Glasealy, learned of a large gathering outside Narraghmore. However attempts to enable the Protestants of the area to retreat failed. Malachi Delany, a prominent local United Irishmen was briefly taken by Yeomen in the morning but the rebel force which Rawson estimated at 2,000 men and women forced his release. Narraghmore loyalists later swore an attack on Narraghmore took place at 10 o'clock by an estimated 200-500 rebels. Their testimony placed Malachi and Peter Delany at the head of long lists of participants.[33] After two hours, nine Protestants defending the courthouse were defeated. Four were butchered fleeing blazing building while five others were hanged afterwards.[34] Keatinge's Yeomen provided the rebels with willing activists. James Byrne, James Murphy, Hugh Cullen and John Lawlor all were or became captains. Over forty of the sixty-eight members joined the rebels.[35]

Meanwhile Lieutenant Eadie and a unit of Tyrone Militia and Suffolk Fencibles who were stationed at Ballitore were ordered north during the morning. Eadie and his force encountered the rebel force in the woods outside Narraghmore, where five loyalists had been hung. A general discharge forced the rebels to flee.[36] Some of the Suffolk Fencibles remained at Shackleton's Mill to defend their barrack and baggage. Mary Leadbeater's diary recorded the uncertain atmosphere in the town: 'A report that Naas Gaol was broken open – that Dublin was in arms and so forth. All was uncertainty except that something serious had happened, as the mail coach had been stopped'.[37] Following their engagement with Eadie, a large number of the rebel force moved south towards the village (Leadbeater estimated up to 300 headed by Malachi Delany, now mounted). The small number of soldiers at the mill attempted to flee, at least two were killed. At Ballitore Delany attempted to retain a semblance of order, however, a captured loyalist and officer in Lord Aldborough's Yeomen, Lieutenant Richard Yeates, was killed. Aldborough was further horrified to learn his coachmen, footman and groom were all sworn United Irishmen.[38]

At Ballitore the numbers of the insurgents began to swell once more, to around 3,000 according to one estimate. The rebels, having provided for the defence of Ballitore, marched north towards Red Gap Hill on the road between Ballitore and Kilcullen.[39] Meanwhile Rawson had despatched a message to Campbell at Athy for assistance. In consequence two columns were marched out, one commanded by Campbell himself, the other by Major Montresor. The latter column dispersed a small rebel force north west of Narraghmore at Fonstown, before linking with Eadie's group. Eadie's force encountered a rebel army of up to 3,000 at the end of the 'bog road' which linked with the Kilcullen turnpike near Red Gap Hill. Eadie's unit managed to hold position before Montresor arrived. His appearance seems to have unnerved the rebels whose ranks were broken. In the ensuing panic 'some hundreds' were killed. Government lost only a handful of men. The clash became known as the 'battle of the bog road'.[40]

The soldiers retreated, O'Kelly stated, to the courthouse at Narraghmore but Mary Leadbeater believed they retreated to Athy following their victory. The rebels returned to their *ad hoc* base at Ballitore 'worsted'.[41] Their initial advantage and victories at Ballitore and Narraghmore had proved to be neither decisive nor strategically advantageous. For now the government troops were prepared to concede ground. Later during the day the rebel numbers began to increase again. It was decided to attack Castledermot to the south in an attempt to link with the Carlow United Irishmen. Perhaps at this point Delany, Cullen and the other leaders realised Athy had not fallen and possibly realised the exaggerated reports circulating in the morning were false.

The same morning Revd Christopher Robinson, Chaplain to Lord Aldborough's Yeomen witnessed the effect of the mere news of impending rebellion at Castledermot.

> ... all was quiet here till about 9 o'clock when ... the whole fair dispersed and ran in all directions with their cattle towards their respective homes, news then arrived that the mob had risen in Dublin, Naas, Ballimore [i.e. Ballymore Eustace] etc. and had beaten the King's troops, had possession of cannon, had let out prisoners and were rising everywhere over the kingdom.

Robinson's house was attacked. However no general assault was made on the town. He escaped first to Dunlavin and later Baltinglass.[42]

The rebels moved south on the town on the evening of 24 May. The small garrison, commanded by Captain Mince, had all day to prepare for attack. As the rebels attacked they were initially shot at from the windows of houses. When their ranks broke Mince's force pursued and captured some men. Exhaustion after the earlier battles must have seriously weakened the United

Irish army. Leadbeater recorded that following the defeat large crowds stopped gathering in Ballitore, but camped on the higher ground to the east of the town.[43] Musgrave believed the 'main object' of the south Kildare rebels was to link with their comrades in Carlow and Queen's County, to attack Carlow town. It is unclear if the rebels in East Narragh and Rheban considered this as part of their plan or simply considered it strategically advantageous to link with a larger force. Perhaps they intended to rouse the United Irishmen of Kilkea and Moone whose leadership had been decimated before the rebellion.

In west Kildare signs of disaffection and impending assault appeared during 24 May, particularly at Rathangan and Monasterevan.[44] At some point on 24 May General Dundas made a crucial decision which accelerated the progress of rebellion in Kildare. He decided to order a general retreat of troops to Naas. Hence Clane, Ballitore and Kilcullen had all been evacuated. The decision held most far reaching implications for those larger towns which had still not suffered a major attack – particularly the trio in most immediate danger – Monasterevan, Rathangan and Kildare town.

On the afternoon of the 24 May General Wilford, at Kildare, ordered his troops to Naas to reinforce General Dundas. Captain Winter at Monasterevan was in consequence also ordered to headquarters. On passing through Kildare he was persuaded, by Dominic William O'Reilly of Kildangan, not to burn the baggage of Wilford's troops which was lodged in the guard house.[45] Following the retreat of government troops, 2,000 rebels according to one estimate, headed by Roger McGarry entered the town. The abandoned baggage was now seized providing the rebels with better weaponry. The town was plundered, loyalists forced to flee, while those who remained, such as George Crawford, were attacked.[46] The same night the Limerick mail coach was stopped in the town. One of the guards Lieutenant William Giffard was killed.[47] The capture of Kildare town albeit by default, placed an important area near the Curragh in rebel control. It also blocked one important communication route to Dublin. The communication problem in the county was compounded by the rebel occupation of the Kilcullen area. Monasterevan was now effectively cut off from east Kildare and Naas. The arrest of the leading United Irishmen form the baronies of West and East Offaly, George Cummins and Lord Edward Fitzgerald, possibly explains the hesitancy of the insurgents of the area to attack the important urban centres. McGarry, who assumed control in Kildare town was probably a captain and had been a baronial committee member. James Molloy's evidence suggests he was baronial treasurer in March.[48]

Monasterevan's evacuation made an attack imminent. The town was now protected by eighty-five yeomen (recently embodied) commanded by Lieutenant Bagot and Captain Hoystead and a company of South Cork Militia.[49] The United Irish army attacked on the morning of 25 May. Patrick O'Kelly, who stated his account was based on an eye-witness report, asserted the principal assailants were from the area south west of the town under the command of Padraig Berne, a miller from Nurney. The force apparently numbered around 1,500 men.[50] Musgrave, however stated the assailants left Kildare town in the early hours of the morning under McGarry. It is likely a combined force attacked the town, at 4 o'clock in the morning.[51] The rebel force was marshalled into at least two columns and attacked via the canal and the church. The action in the town was for some time 'very serious', but the patience of the infantry finally broke the rebels and the cavalry completed a rout. O'Kelly saw the root of the failure in the inability of the two rebel groups to link.[52] Campbell estimated sixty-five rebels killed, while Musgrave named five dead yeomen.[53] The defeated rebels fell back to Kildare town.

By 25 May most of the swathe of Kildare territory between Athy and Naas was under control of or threatened by United Irish forces. Athy was second only to Naas (given the latter's proximity to Dublin) in strategic terms. Rebels at Castledermot were already repulsed but Athy held the real key to the south of the county. No serious threat emerged from Kilkea and Moone. Patrick O'Kelly clearly demonstrates that an attack on Athy was contemplated. On 23 May the rebel commanders 'received regular orders' to assemble in three distinct bodies for an assault:

1 from Geraldine to the west
2 from Cloney and Kilberry to the north
3 from Queen's County to the south

The failure to launch the attack was placed squarely on the shoulders of the colliers of Queen's County by O'Kelly. Having learned of the massive rebel defeat in Carlow (on 25 May) they failed to take part in the projected plan.[54] A number of rebels from East Narragh, under Patrick Dowling, also travelled to participate in the attack. They lay concealed three-quarters of a mile from Athy all night. The signal for advance never sounded – it was to be the bell of the packet boat to be captured by Queen's County rebels.[55] An estimated 400 assailants died during the battle for Carlow. It virtually ended any possibility of connections between south Kildare and north Carlow rebels in the near future.[56] Campbell's troops did not withdraw from Athy and the town quickly became a loyalist refuge. Mary Leadbeater recorded, 'the garrison town of Athy was thronged with those who were afraid to remain in the country yet where was safety?'[57]

On 25 May Rathangan was in a similar position to Athy. The prominent local, James Spencer, land agent to the duke of Leinster and Yeoman commander, persuaded Captain Langton and his company of South Cork Militia to remain. This was despite an order from Wilford to evacuate the garrison to Sallins. Langton finally departed on the afternoon of the 25 May but Spencer chose to remain behind.[58] A rebel attack was not actually mounted until the following morning, possibly due to the setback received at Monasterevan. Rathangan, however, was a much softer target. The same morning Major Latham at Mountmellick despatched a small party with a message, via Rathangan. This body encountered 'five thousand Defenders'.[59] It was this force which attacked Rathangan. They were commanded by John Doorly, described as a 'respectable young farmer' from Lullymore in the Bog of Allen.[60] The victory was achieved quite easily. Spencer and some Yeomen simply barricaded themselves in a house. On being forced out Spencer was murdered. Musgrave asserted Doorly was directly responsible. However O'Kelly claimed: 'Doorly, as it has been acknowledged by some of his bitterest enemies, was not at all present at the murder of Mr Spencer'.[61] The victory at Rathangan sparked a spree of plunder and murder. An account written by anxious Edenderry officers stated twenty-six Yeoman privates were killed.[62]

Victory at Rathangan left the rebels in control of a vast sweep of territory south of Naas. However the government's hold on Athy, Monasterevan and Castledermot provided a valuable buffer against a push south, for the moment. There was little to be gained by a push south east into the Wicklow Mountains. United Irish advantage was the direct result of Dundas' extremely defensive policy, not the result of direct rebel activities. Meanwhile the large force at Kildare had failed to overcome a much smaller one at Monasterevan. The 26 May marked the apogee of rebel control in the south of the county. Their basic problem was what to do next, given the partial nature of their success. Athy and Naas were still in government hands and troops were surely on the way from Dublin. Concentrated rebel action in north Kildare was necessary if the capital was seriously to be threatened.

Patrick O'Kelly was obviously confused about events in north Kildare during the first week of the rebellion. He was aware a United Irish force was camped in the Bog of Allen by late May but did not know why William Aylmer was inactive during the period. He concluded that Aylmer and his associates, Hugh Ware and George Lube, initially held back from Mick Reynolds' 'impetuosity' and later initiated a 'second rising' in the area. This is to some extent correct but rather vague.[63] William Aylmer later claimed he did not join the rebellion until 'about a week after it broke out'.[64] Aylmer and Ware informed Revd Charles Eustace, a son of General Eustace who was held at Timahoe in early June that, they attempted to leave the country on the outbreak of rebellion, ' ... with the intention of going to America but from the ports being shut would not escape'.[65] The fact that Aylmer's name is not strongly connected with any rebel activities until early June supports his testimony. This does not mean there was no United Irish activity in north Kildare.

Across the border in south Meath the tiny garrisons of Ratoath, Dunshaughlin and Dunboyne were all attacked on 24 May. Events in north Kildare were closely linked to those of south Meath.[66] A letter written by W. Wilson, from Maynooth, illustrates the panic of the area. The Lucan mail coach had been robbed and 'dreadful reports' arrived from Naas and elsewhere. Though no attack occurred, he concluded, 'It is hard not to say what may be the case in this and the adjoining countery [sic]'.[67] Col. Gordon reported on 26 May three attacks were made the previous day, on Kilcock, Leixlip and Lucan.[68] Michael Lynam, a gardener from Celbridge was, he claimed, 'seized' by a group of rebels and 'compelled' to take part in the attack on Leixlip. He believed the rebels wished to connect with the group at Tara.[69] Lousia Conolly was certain a group of 200 rebels who quietly passed through Castletown on the morning of 26 May took part in a planned attack on Leixlip later that day. They possibly intended linking with the United Irishmen in south Meath. Seamus Cummins notes that the United Irishmen in the Leixlip area actually continued to surrender weapons on 25 May.[70]

The battle of Tara which took place on the evening of 26 May involved a limited number of north Kildare United Irishmen. The battle, like that at Carlow to the south, was crucial to the Kildare rebels generally. No significant rising materialised to the west of the county, the roads to the south were blocked and Dublin was relatively peaceful. If connections via south Meath were also broken the Kildare rebels were effectively stranded. However the 4,000 insurgents on Tara Hill were defeated, with about 300 fatalities, largely by the power of the government troops' field pieces.[71] Charles Teeling stated: 'Many returned to their homes, the most determined remained in arms and proceeded to join the ranks of the brave and persevering Aylmer in Kildare'.[72] While some United men may have encamped in the vast bogs of north Kildare in the aftermath of the Tara defeat, probably linking with

Prosperous rebels, Aylmer was not there. The defeat at Tara effectively crushed large scale, open rebellion in South Meath

The 26 May certainly marked the zenith of United Irish fortunes within Kildare itself, but the rebellion which had achieved short-term objectives was now at a standstill.[73] The rebellion was in fact stalled without a Dublin offensive. By 26 May the various rebel forces in Kildare had gathered into strategically placed camps, usually on hills, in inaccessible areas, or both. Richard Musgrave believed six camps were formed during the first week of rebellion: at Knockallen, a hill outside Kilcullen; Barnhill, outside Kildare town; Hodgestown, south of Timahoe; Hortland, north east of Timahoe; Red Gap Hill, in the vicinity of Ballitore and Timahoe in the Bog of Allen.[74] The rebel camp at Blackmore Hill, inside county Wicklow was populated by Kildare rebels, including those defeated at Naas. Musgrave later asserted that camps at Timahoe, Mucklin and Drihid in the Bog of Allen were established by the 30 May but ascertaining their exact origins is difficult.[75] Pat Delemar of Prosperous was taken from the town in late May, forced to take the United Irish oath and held at the rebel camp at Timahoe for ten days. Those he named as commanders were leaders of the rising at Prosperous, including Andrew Farrell. At the time of his escape on 6 June, an estimated 1,000 people were encamped at Timahoe.[76]

On 27 May the Kilcullen rebels encamped at Knockallen made overtures to General Dundas suing for peace through Joseph Perkins, a rebel leader.[77] The following morning Patrick O'Kelly (author of *General history*) arrived at Knockallen from Athy. He informed the camp of the poor situation of the rebels in the Athy area. O'Kelly, according to himself was appointed colonel so as to take part in negotiations for surrender.[78] O'Kelly's mission may have been connected with the march north of troops under Col. Campbell.[79] On 28 May O'Kelly and two United Irish officers, Patrick and John Finerty of Kilrush met Dundas. By the time General Lake arrived from Dublin Dundas had concluded a peace with the rebels. A large quantity of arms was apparently handed in: 'The pikes and arms of every description being given up, the heap could be compared in size to the Royal Exchange'.[80]

Neither Musgrave nor Gordon mention O'Kelly's role in the proceedings.[81] It is impossible to authenticate the veracity of O'Kelly's account but it would have been a curious story to fabricate. His claim to have been 'in his 17th year' certainly appears to have been bogus and was possibly an attempt to excuse his United Irish activities through immaturity. The combined evidence of cemetery records and an obituary notice in the *Freeman's Journal* suggests he was between twenty-two and twenty-five in 1798.[82] Accepting the surrender of thousands of rebels without punishment was an unpopular move among loyalists. Dundas reputation was seriously questioned in parliament.[83] Camden believed it had been 'indiscreetly carried on'.[84] In Kildare loyalists were worried by Dundas' actions. Richard Griffith believed it was 'a foolish capitulation … my decided opinion is now the sword is drawn nothing but extreme severity will cure the evil'.[85]

The dispersal of rebels at Kilcullen relieved the blockade on communication between Naas and the south of the county. However the rebel encampment around Kildare town left the south of the county cut off. General Lake urged the route should be reopened by force.[86] At the same time the Knockallen surrender was concluded rebels at Kildare attempted to sue for peace with Dundas. On the morning of 29 May it appears a surrender was agreed. Dundas deputed Wilford to receive it.[87] On the same morning Major General Sir James Duff arrived in Kildare from Limerick with almost 500 troops, worried by the breakdown of communication with Dublin. At seven o'clock, that morning, he sat down to write to Lake from Monasterevan. He planned to surround Kildare town and 'make a dreadful example of the rebels'. He was probably not aware of the impending surrender.

As Duff's troops approached Kildare town the rebels retreated, assembling on Gibbet Rath on the Curragh, apparently abandoned by Roger McGarry. According to O'Kelly, Duff subsequently disarmed the group and ordered them to kneel and beg pardon. This being complied with, Duff ordered his troops to 'charge and spare no rebel'. This resulted in the death of 325 people.[88] At two o'clock Duff added to his letter to Lake, describing what happened:

> My Dear General, (I have witnessed a melancholy scene). We found the rebels retiring from this town on our arrival armed. We followed them with the dragoons. I sent some of the yeomen to tell them on laying down their arms they should not be hurt. Unfortunately some of them fired on the troops, from that moment they were attacked on all sides, nothing could stop the rage of the troops. I believe from two to three hundred of the rebels were killed. [They intended we were told, to lay down their arms to General Dundas]. We have three men killed and several wounded. I am too fatigued to enlarge.[89]

Gordon believed the soldiers acted on the defiant discharge of a muzzle (upwards) by one of the rebels.[90] The massacre at Gibbet Rath swiftly ended Dundas' policy of large scale pardon. Duff's actions are difficult to explain.

One possible contributing factor was revenge. During the rebel occupation of Kildare town the mails from Limerick were plundered and Duff's nephew piked to death.[91] The massacre did serve to quell open rebellion in the area and reopen lines communication with Munster.

While the Kildare rebellion was to a large extent stalled by 26 May, one rebel achievement provided a serious threat – that at Rathangan. On 27 May officers at Edenderry, a few miles north west of Rathangan, wrote a worried letter to Castlereagh expressing their need for reinforcements. Refugees from Rathangan and the intervening village of Clonbulloge had all fled to Edenderry. The officers concluded ominously: '… without [reinforcements] … this country and a number of his majesties loyal subjects will inevitably be destroyed'.[92] The threat of incursion into Queen's or King's Counties produced a response from government forces on 28 May. Lt.-Col. Mahon was despatched from Tullamore to prevent any attack occurring. He initially pursued rebels into the town of Rathangan killing 'sixteen to twenty'. However he was forced to retreat outside to wait for reinforcements. He was subsequently joined by a regiment from Edenderry and a Yeomanry force. The second attack was equally unsuccessful coming under assault from the windows of the town.[93] Not only did the government troops lose twenty men but dead horses were subsequently used as barricades. 'You need not mention this disaster,' R. Marshall concluded in a letter to Brigadier General Knox, 'We did not make any bulletin of it.'[94]

Later in the morning Lt.-Col. Longfield and a force of North Cork Militia and Dragoons arrived at Rathangan. He found the streets barricaded but unlike Mahon possessed two battalion guns. The second discharge of these weapons and subsequent cavalry charge dispersed the rebels. His comments on the rebel dead are interesting: '… I saw 14 or 15, and what I consider of particular consequence is that all of those I saw dead are of the better kind of people …' He later discovered up to sixty rebels were killed.[95] Many must have ventured north into the Bog of Allen. Doorly's house at Lullymore was burned and he now joined the United Irishmen encamped at Timahoe.[96] The recapture of Rathangan firmly ended any hopes of extending rebellion west.

The rebel force in West Narragh and Rheban, which was modestly successful, moved in the same direction as their Kilcullen counterparts on 26 May. They attempted to sue for peace with Col. Campbell, but delayed when he demanded six hostages.[97] On the morning of 29 May Campbell with almost all his force left Athy with the express aim of forcibly pacifying the West Narragh area. Keatinge's house at Narraghmore, which may have been used by rebels, was destroyed by a discharge of cannon. At 3 o'clock in the morning Ninth Dragoons entered the village of Ballitore with orders to fire on anyone with 'coloured clothes'. However the rebel force had evacuated the area on the approach of the troops.[98] During the next few hours the village was at the mercy of the troops. Houses were burned, smashed and plundered. Dr Johnson, possibly a United Irish leader in the area, who played a rather vacillating role during the early fighting, was accused of leading a rebel force and was shot. Timolin, Narraghmore and Crookstown all suffered similarly.[99] Hugh Cullen, father of the future Cardinal, Paul Cullen, was arrested in late May or early June and narrowly escaped execution. His brother Paul was executed as a rebel in 1798. Works dealing primarily with Hugh's famous son downplay the active role of Hugh Cullen in 1798. It appears likely he was a leading United Irishman in his locality.[100]

On 30 May a large rebel force assembled at Blackmore Hill was dispersed by troops under the command of Major General Duff. Once again cannon was put to particularly effective use by government forces and proved decisive.[101] A further rebel surrender took place on the Moat of Ardscull and seems to be that referred to by Col. Campbell in a letter dated 2 June, which indicates 300 rebels participated. Others came forward individually in Athy.[102] On the morning of 2 June an attempt appears to have been launched by United Irishmen to attack Athy. According to Campbell two columns approached the town from the bog road. Campbell in turn split his troops in pursuit of the rebels. His left column encountered one group near Bert where he estimated 100 were killed; a number lowered only by the impenetrability of the bog.[103] When Campbell's troops were finally moved to Kilcullen around 10 June to counter the growing threat in north Kildare, no actual attacks were mounted on the garrison under the defence of Rawson's Yeomen.[104]

By 30 May the strategic victories of the Kildare United Irishmen were all retaken with the exception of Prosperous. The county south of an invisible line drawn between Rathangan and Naas was now in government hands. Many of the defeated rebels did not return home, some travelled north to the Bog of Allen, others to the Wicklow Mountains. As the collapse in Kildare occurred from the 26-27 May, the Wexford rebellion suddenly exploded into action. This later became important to the rebels who remained in arms in Kildare and Wicklow. The focus noticeably shifted around the 30 May. The early phase of the struggle focused on the capture of urban areas, in line with the original United Irish strategy. As those centres were recaptured it became clear their occupation could not be maintained for long periods without the support of a successful rebellion outside Kildare. While the rebels of north Kildare intermittently attacked and plundered towns they did not attempt to occupy them. The rebels now made increased use of the most obvious natural advantage in the county: the Bog of Allen.

CHAPTER 6

The 1798 rebellion in county Kildare
❦
1 JUNE—21 JULY

The second phase of the Kildare rebellion may be delineated between early
June and 21 July and centred on northern camps, particularly at Timahoe. It
was characterised by what Teeling labelled, 'a species of fugitive warfare'.[1]
William Aylmer and his comrades entered the conflict at this juncture. The
key turning point occurred at the rebel defeat at Ovidstown on 19 June. From
early July the remaining rebels in Kildare attempted to negotiate terms with
Dublin Castle following Cornwallis' efforts to encourage surrender.
Channels of communication opened around 4 July. During the month the
introduction, briefly, of rather less cautious Wexford and Wicklow rebels into
the county temporarily derailed the process. But their defeat and departure
enabled the Kildare forces to conclude a surrender by 21 July.

On 30 May United Irishmen in the barony of Carbery finally rose. A
large force, as many as 2,000, attacked and burned the charter school at
Castlecarbery which was abandoned by Stephen Sparks and his students.[2]
Patrick O'Kelly described what he believed occurred at this juncture:

> The men of Kilcock, Maynooth and the north eastern boundaries of
> the county of Kildare, being now called upon by young Aylmer of
> Painstown, George Luby of Ovidstown and Hugh Ware of Maynooth
> [Ware was from Rathcoffey] to rise, a second rising in the county was
> brought about by the people.[3]

What occurred was not a second rising. Many of those now drawn to camps
in the Bog of Allen, principally Timahoe, had fought during the previous
week. However a recognised leadership now emerged in the north which
encouraged large-scale participation in the rebellion. William Aylmer had
not only been an officer in the Kildare Militia but hailed from a respectable
Catholic family of the area which accorded him 'an extensive influence
among the United corps of that part of the county ...'[4] According to the family biographer he was born in 1772. However Aylmer himself gave his date of

birth as 1778 when he enlisted in the Austrian army in 1899. His military ability is evidenced by a successful career in the Austrian army in the early nineteenth century.[5] George Lube had been particularly active, based on evidence available, in the Kildare United Irishmen before 24 May. Hugh Ware, born in 1772, was a professional land surveyor, a knowledge especially useful to the rebels when combined with their detailed knowledge of local geography. He later had a highly successful career in the French army. Miles Byrne, the Wicklow rebel, who fought under his command described him as 'the bravest of the brave'.[6] All three were young men of respectable backgrounds.

Timahoe was particularly suited to maintaining a rebel base. It was situated in the Bog of Allen on an area of dry ground. In July 1803 Fenton Aylmer commented on the strategic importance of Timahoe if a rising occurred in its locality: '… it is most advantageously situated and they always have as in the last rebellion a safe retreat across the bog and from the hill the most commanding view of everything stirring in the country'.[7] By early June Aylmer and Lube were both based at Timahoe and began roaming the hinterland. On 1 June Aylmer 'was positively seen' leading a rebel force into the town of Kilcock. Sir Fenton Aylmer, who informed the Castle of this development also implicated William's brother Robert, who was also seen at the Timahoe camp. Up to ten Kilcock residents were forced to the camp but subsequently escaped. Fenton Aylmer expressed reservations about their usefulness in obtaining prosecutions due to fear of reprisals. Another Aylmer connection, 'Barnwall', a brother-in-law was arrested at Trim around the same time. It was hoped this 'may break the whole business'.[8] Richard Musgrave indicated rebels at Timahoe were prepared to surrender around 29 May and attempted to treat with Fenton Aylmer.[9] By early June, however, a campaign of 'fugitive warfare' began in earnest. On 4 June the Timahoe insurgents launched an attack on the small garrison at Kilcock defeating a force under Sir Fenton Aylmer. Following the occupation of the village, Courtown, the seat of Michael Aylmer was burned to the ground. Fenton Aylmer's seat at Donadea narrowly escaped destruction. The rebels were diverted by information that their own friends had lodged valuables in it, according to Aylmer. Perhaps even at this point William Aylmer and the other leaders were careful not to alienate potentially useful connections.[10]

Even before the attack on Kilcock was launched a plan of operations against the north Kildare rebels appears to have existed. On the morning of 4 June General Champagne sent a reconnoitre party to Timahoe which discovered the area 'posted strong' despite rumours it was deserted. In his letter dated 4 June Fenton Aylmer noted: 'The plan of operations commences tomorrow at 8 o'clock'.[11] The date of Champagne's attack is unclear. Oliver Barker at Clonard who participated in the move on Drihid to the west of Timahoe dates his account 6 June. Musgrave however states the assault occurred on 8 June. Champagne secured extra troops at Edenderry. The bog was surrounded and the camp attacked and dispersed. Barker believed a simultaneous attack took place on Timahoe from Kilcock.[12] This was nothing more than a temporary victory. Numerous attacks on the rebel strongholds occurred throughout June and July ultimately to no real effect.

The direct action on Timahoe failed to prevent the continuance of assaults in north Kildare. On the afternoon of 19 June, the town of Maynooth, which was garrisoned by a small contingent of the duke of Leinster's Yeomen under Thomas Long and Richard Cane was taken by 500 rebels under William Aylmer. Some of the Yeomen taken prisoner remained at the rebel camp as volunteers. On 13 June the town was attacked and plundered again. Lt. Cane subsequently retreated to Leixlip having insufficient troops to garrison Maynooth.[13] The rebel base or bases in the Bog of Allen developed as launching pads not only for attacks on lightly garrisoned towns but also on the surrounding countryside. Richard Griffith described the situation in late June:

> We have been shut up in Naas ever since I wrote to you [4 June], standing on the defensive and allowing the insurgents to possess the whole county of Kildare, except a few towns. The consequence has been terrible the rebels have plundered and defaced the whole country.[14]

The activities of the United Irish army encamped at Timahoe seemingly remained static and localised and compared unfavourably to the action of the Wexford rebellion. The only source of information on what occurred at the camp during the first weeks of June must be extracted from statements of escaped prisoners. None of the leaders at Timahoe (except Bernard Duggan[15]) later published autobiographical material. Nevertheless the significance of the north Kildare rebellion has been understated. The insurgents were not confined to the small area of dry land at Timahoe. The Bog of Allen provided a natural buffer zone which allowed rebels to launch attacks over a wide area. Oliver Barker expressed incredulity at '… the way they lived. Horses, cows, sheep etc. were found after them …'[16] Furthermore the insurgents threatened a crucial route into Dublin from the west. Indeed the camps very existence threatened the capital itself given the disturbed nature of north Wicklow and of course Wexford.

On 4 July Sir Fenton Aylmer provided Dublin Castle with the earliest extant list of leaders of the Kildare rebels:

1   William Aylmer of Painstown
2   Hugh Ware of Rathcoffey
3   George Lube of Corcoranstown
4   [Joseph] Cormick, brother-in-law to Mr Lube, a young man
5   Bryan McDermott of Hayestown
6   Gary Wilde of Prosperous
7   Thomas Hyland of Kilbride
8   James Dunn of Staplestown
9   Edward Moghern – Patrick Wiliss, Dairyman [?]
10 Wm Fitzgerald of Timahoe
11 Farrell of Woods, a son of Daniel Farrell a man of the nickname Roupera Vouda
12 X Doorly of Rathangan and Lullymore
13 John Reilly, shoemaker, Kilcock
14 Tobin ... of Prosperous[17]

The list illustrates the composition of the leadership at Timahoe which included United Irishmen from Prosperous, north east Kildare and further afield, most noticeably Doorly. William Aylmer was certainly the recognised leader at this point. One account describes his dress as follows: 'a scarlet uniform with a green sash or scarf over his shoulder' another added a 'helmet, military boots, sword and pistols'. Doorly and Lube were also in uniform.[18]

The leadership at Timahoe appears to have exerted positive influence in terms of discipline. John Mitchel observed: 'The men of each barony were together under Sergeants, officers or Corporals'. Some Protestants were killed including an army invalid and a tenant of Sir Fenton Aylmer. Mitchel himself narrowly avoided death. As a barber he proved useful to the camp and was actually tipped a shilling by William Aylmer for his services. Revd Charles Eustace, the son of General Eustace, was informed he was held as a hostage for John Esmonde. He was compelled to write to Lord Mayo explaining his situation. Esmonde himself later asked his former comrades to desist 'as he feared they might injure him'.[19] Eustace helped petition government for the release of Bryan McDermott in 1800, one of his captors. He believed McDermott was 'no more than a mere boy' in 1798.[20] Robert Weeks another prisoner believed Aylmer and Kiernan, 'a gentleman farmer' exerted most influence and had complete control of financial matters. Weeks was initially prevented from escaping by Patrick O'Connor a lawyer from Straffan. This is a small indication that the social composition of the camp was wider than often assumed.[21] One source indicates William Aylmer's leadership was less than inspirational. An anonymous Dublin source, closely linked to north east Kildare both before and during the rebellion was informed in mid June: '... that Mr Aylmer had been censured in the camp for not coming to an engagement one night when they were attacked by the army, this was over-looked as he was tipsey [sic]'. Valentine Lawless believed William's death in South America was connected 'to an ancient love for rum'.[22] The same anonymous source separately states that some members of the camp were 'of the opinion that Mr Aylmer was not acting honest this dispute is lettered'.[23] It is difficult to determine the nature of then dissension in the camp. It may reflect the differing aspirations of the various baronies or even counties which constituted the camp.

In early June Belle Martin, a noted informer, was hired as a housemaid at Charles Aylmer house at Painstown. She had prosecuted members of a republican club in Belfast in 1796 and spent the period August 1796 to May 1798 under government protection at Dublin Castle. It is difficult to see why the Kildare rebels did not recognise or suspect her. Based on her statement (made on 23 June), and her assertion that she was hired three weeks previously, she may have arrived at Painstown as early as 2 June. Her evidence shows William Aylmer used Painstown as a personal base during the rebellion. He normally arrived home at 4 a.m., rested until 3 p.m. when he would march out with his force. A chapel near Painstown was utilised as a rebel headquarters for food and weaponry.[24] Martin undoubtedly kept government well informed of the activities of the north Kildare rebels and indicates their fear of the group. It is possible she was despatched following Fenton Aylmer's letter of 4 June which questioned the possibility of prosecuting the rebel leadership.

The leaders in the north Kildare area undoubtedly looked to Dublin for guidance. Belle Martin noted '... that the concourse of Dublin people who come and go backwards and forwards is very great' including the Dublin United Irishmen John Sweetman who stayed at Painstown for three days.[25] Robert Aylmer, William's brother was in Dublin in early June.[26] Malachi Delany's brother Peter was in the capital during the later rebellion and passed information to his brother possibly in Wexford in June. Boyle also informed government that Aylmer and Michael Reynolds were in contact with 'the Dublin party' via two intermediaries: Demsey a smith from Kildare working in Dublin and John Smyth who was messenger to rebels at Fingal.[27]

The important communication with the capital suggests an attack on Dublin was the ultimate aspiration of the rebels in its vicinity. In mid-June Peter Broc, a Clane Yeoman who participated in the rising in Prosperous, was observed conversing with a Dublin Yeoman on the possibility of attacking the capital.[28] Dublin United Irishmen themselves continued to hope the rebels of the surrounding counties would participate in an assault on the capital.[29]

Attempts also appear to have been made to make contact with rebels or former rebels in county Meath. During June Aylmer's attempts to do so failed to produce results. On the day Belle Martin made her statement she was given a letter by William Aylmer to deliver to Revd Richard Meighan of Moynavaly in county Meath. She was instructed to verbally request the priest to delay his congregation at mass next day, until Aylmer arrived, presumably for possible recruitment, to which Meighan agreed. The car in which she travelled was also loaded with gunpowder hidden under hay. This, she claimed, was examined by the priest. Martin later failed to identify the priest at an 'identity parade'.[30] The contacts with United Irishmen in Dublin and Meath illustrate the fact that north Kildare rebels viewed themselves as part of a wider struggle. They hoped to strengthen their position *viz à viz* an attack on the capital. The battle of Ovidstown destroyed ongoing rebel preparations for any assault.

While Timahoe became the effective centre of rebel activity in the county in June some other areas continued to remain disturbed and roads remained dangerous. In early June almost the whole of Kildare town was destroyed following an attempt to destroy 'his majesty's troops, the inhabitants almost to a man having left the place'.[31] In Monasterevan in the aftermath of the breakdown of rebellion in the baronies of West and East Offaly, Lord Tyrawley busied himself examining rebels. On 11 June he arrested Fr Edward Prendegast who was tried by Court Martial and subsequently executed. Tyrawley wrote to Cooke in Dublin:

> The execution of this man has had a good effect. It was clearly proved that he was at one of the rebel camps encouraging the people with a pistol in his hand and that he gave them absolution tho' they confessed to him that they were United Irishmen. I am glad to be able to add that the other priests in this neighbourhood refused absolution to such people as were U.I. I think the people are heartily sick of rebellion and that it will be very difficult to make them rise again.[32]

The local parish priest, Charles Doran was paid by Tyrawley for his loyal role in 'preventing the country people from joining the rebels'.[33] The death of Prendegast is the best documented case of clerical involvement during the Kildare rebellion.[34] In general Kildare provides less examples of 'rebel priests' than Wexford. Not even Prendegast was reported to be a commander. Priests may have provided important channels of communication between north Kildare rebels and Dublin. A local priest informed the Timahoe rebels that 'all Connaught was in arms'.[35] Revd Andrew Ennis, P.P. of Maynooth and Revd Boyce, P.P. of Celbridge were both suspected of carrying correspondence to and from Dublin.[36] Belle Martin also implicated Ennis and a priest or student from Maynooth College named Pat Reilly, who were at least aware of William Aylmer's activities.[37] Prendegast was possibly executed as an example to dissuade the local populace from mounting a second offensive. The involvement of other Kildare clergy was relatively minor.

In the aftermath of the rebellion, Patrick Duignan, an ultra-loyalist attacked Maynooth College for the role of thirty-six students who he claimed joined the rebellion. At least seventeen it was asserted were expelled for their rebellious activities. His denunciations were directly countered by the president of the college Revd Peter Flood whose term of office extended through the troublesome years from 1798 to 1803. An investigation in May 1798 revealed eight students had become United Irishmen in the period 1793-6. Two others refused to talk and all ten were expelled on 12 May – before the rebellion.[38] One of those expelled, Francis Hearn, later studied at St Patrick's College, Carlow. He was executed for rebel activities in his native Waterford in October 1799. It is not surprising that a rebellion, carried on so successfully in north Kildare would reflect suspicion on the nascent institution. Patrick Corish comments that: 'The connection between Maynooth students and the 1798 insurgents was … very indirect, but that did not stop the Dublin papers'.[39]

Through the first weeks of June Prosperous remained in the hands of the insurgents. On 19 June two separate forces attacked the rebel stronghold. A body of Fifth Dragoons under Captain Pack, despatched from Rathangan, engaged about one hundred rebels outside Prosperous. Most were dressed in Yeomen's uniforms. The rebels were defeated with the loss of twenty to thirty men. Later on the same day a force totalling around 200 was despatched from Naas under Lt.-Col. Stewart: 'I perceived the rebels posted on a hill on the left a large flag was flying on a staff which was pulled down on perceiving our strength and fled into Prosperous and the bog in the rear of it'. Pursuant to orders Stewart was unable to pursue the defeated rebels. On a banner was written: 'Prosperous strength exists in Union and Liberty'.[40] At this point Prosperous probably served as one of a number of outposts which provided easy access to the bog in case of attack.

On the same day probably the largest battle of the rebellion in Kildare was fought at Ovidstown Hill near Hortland House, north west of Timahoe. The location of the battle is confusing, however the presence of thousands of insurgents in north Kildare may indicate hopes for an assault on the capital itself. On 20 June Thomas Boyle reported large numbers of men convening on Blackmore Hill under Michael Reynolds and expressly stated plans for a rising in and attack on Dublin still existed. He also believed another camp was to be established at Tara. Sproule later outlined a plan of attack which existed, to be launched from positions in outer county Dublin.[41] Reynolds may have been in contact with Aylmer's force. His Naas comrade Michael Murphy was definitely in Prosperous by mid-June.[42] It is quite possible plans were underway for an attack on Dublin from the surrounding countryside. In the days before Ovidstown Dublin United Irishmen travelled to the rebel camps in the Bog of Allen. Edward Whiteman, an apprentice from near Chapelizod travelled to Straffan with four others on the night of 18 June. They spent some time in the stables of Joseph Henry where they were joined by twenty men from Lucan and Henry's servant who brought them to the Hortland area.[43]

Lt.-Col. Irvine, commander of a garrison at Trim received information on 18 June that a large body of men were assembling near Kilcock. He gathered a large force in the town consisting of 400 men and two battalion guns, determined to attack.[44] The government forces were encountered by an enormous rebel force who retreated on their approach and lined at the bottom of Ovidstown Hill in the townland of Corcoranstown, the home of George Lube. The approach of troops caused a panic at the camp when it was called to arms. Edward Whiteman was informed 5,000-6,000 rebels were present; army commanders estimated 3,000 insurgents. The rebel commanders included Aylmer, Lube, Ware, Doorly, Kiernan and Walsh. Many of the men wore green cockades and white and green flags were also displayed.[45]

The rebel infantry appear to have led the attack, those with muskets firing from behind hedges. However this initial assault made no impact.[46] Edward Whiteman witnessed the breakdowm of the rebel forces; once more the power of heavy weaponry was demonstrated: 'As soon as the cannon of the army began to fire the pike men ran away, about ten minutes after the attack began, they took off their coats and threw away their pikes'.[47] The rebel officers in command were unable to rally their force and fiasco rapidly devolved into rout resulting in 200 rebel deaths.[48] Whiteman's testimony expressly stated 'none of the men were drunk …'[49] This conflicts with strong local tradition which states many of the men were drunk on the day of the attack from drink stolen (or possibly even received) from Hortland House. The surprise element on the part of the government troops was crucial in the defeat, as was the use of cannon. The ill-preparedness of the rebels possibly indicates they intended massing for something larger, such as an attack on Dublin. Brigadier General Grose was, however, mistaken in his assumption that: 'the engagement has done away with that attack you had designed we should make at Tippahoe' [i.e. Timahoe].[50]

Most of the rebels had little choice but to return to the bogs where they continued to pose a military problem for Dublin Castle. Richard Griffith reported on 30 June 'the rebels … continue to plunder with impunity'. Belle Martin's testimony also demonstrates continued rebel activity in the days after Ovidstown. Her departure from Painstown may reflect the Castle's thinking that the rebels in north Kildare were now broken.[51] Following the battle of Ovidstown, Doorly travelled south to the Athy area, possibly as an emissary, to encourage a second rising. Plans to attack Stradbally collapsed despite apparent initial local support.[52] In the aftermath of Ovidstown relations with the Dublin United Irishmen became strained. Aylmer found his Dublin comrades were prevented from assisting the Kildare rebels: 'He therefore requires his friends to assemble in such numbers as they think will be able to make their way good to join him and by so doing – they will be forgiven for their past neglect'. Otherwise they were to be considered 'as enemies to the cause'. This evidence suggests Aylmer continued to see Dublin as the crucial focus of his army.[53]

By late June the government of the recently appointed Lord Lieutenant Cornwallis began to initiate a change in the Castle's policy towards rebellion. On 29 June an offer of terms of surrender was made whereby rebels would acknowledge their guilt, promise good behaviour and take the oath of allegiance and in turn receive protection.[54] While Cornwallis' offer was not acted upon it appears to have indicated to the Kildare leaders the possibility of concluding an acceptable surrender. On 4 July Fenton Aylmer wrote to Lord Castlereagh informing him Kildare magistrates were to meet to discuss an offer of surrender from the rebels. Charles Aylmer of Painstown intended attending and meeting the rebels the following day to 'settle' with them. The letter illustrates the awkward situation Fenton Aylmer found himself in; by his own admission he 'would much rather attack …'[55]

Castlereagh's reply was based on the recent proclamation. Kildare's rebel leaders must be prepared to sign a full confession, persuade their followers to surrender, give up their arms and swear allegiance. They could hope to have their lives spared 'on condition of transportation'. However absolutely no pardon was to be offered to Doorly for whose capture a reward of £100 was offered. The fate of Doorly remains somewhat mysterious, he was reported to have been later executed in both Westmeath and Longford.[56] The Kildare rebels appear to have stalled on Castlereagh's offer because they felt it necessary to receive official assurances. Charles Aylmer had an influential friend in the marquis of Buckingham who also intervened. According to him a surrender offered through himself to Cornwallis on 5 July failed to take place due to lack of trust.[57] On the same day Fenton Aylmer and Michael Aylmer (of Courtown) were ambushed returning from Naas, outside Clane near Castle Browne. 'The whole fields,' he wrote, 'down to Castle Browne were covered with the villains …' Aylmer prudently decided to retreat to Sallins where he requested reinforcements.[58] Both the *Freeman's Journal* and Musgrave stated William Aylmer was in command of the insurgent force, but Fenton Aylmer makes no mention of his presence.[59]

In consequence forces commanded by Capt. Beare and Major Johnston were despatched from Naas. The latter returned the following day with twenty prisoners taken at Castle Browne. These included Patrick Byrne, steward to Wogan Browne. Johnston reported: Byrne '… acknowledges having entertained Mr William Aylmer at Mr Browne's house knowing him to be a chief of the rebels. He says the prisoners were engaged in Mr Browne's work and could answer for this having no arms'.[60] Joseph Lyons, who was forcibly taken to a rebel camp in the Prosperous area made a statement asserting Patrick Byrne was a prominent rebel in that area.[61] The rebel attack illustrates the continuing effectiveness of the United Irish army in their fugitive campaign. It undoubtedly stalled the negotiation process temporarily. Gosford went so far as to comment: 'I do think every house in Clane should be destroyed, it harbours a host of villains'.[62] Richard Griffith believed the rebels were merely 'emboldened by our weakness'.[63]

Despite numerous assaults on their camps and the disastrous collapse at Ovidstown, hundreds if not thousands of rebels continued to wage a guerrilla war in north Kildare. While negotiations stalled the position of the Kildare rebels was suddenly altered by the arrival of Wexford and Wicklow armies in the county between 8 and 19 July. The winding erratic mission of the south eastern rebels to enflame the people in the counties surrounding Dublin has been the subject of relatively detailed research recently. Ruan O'Donnell and

Daniel Gahan have examined the events from the perspective of the Wicklow and Wexford rebellions respectively.[64] By its nature the subsequent activities of a combined army were carried on through the impulse of the fresh arrivals. Their arrival gave fresh momentum to the rebels in north Kildare and their aims were more far reaching, and indeed unrealistic, than those of Aylmer and his comrades.

On the night of 8 July Wexford and Wicklow insurgents crossed the border into Kildare near Blessington. They followed a twisting route north travelling via Kilcullen and Newbridge and studiously avoiding Naas. They encountered Kildare rebels at Robertstown.[65] The rebel force moved further north to the rebel base at Prosperous. Perceiving a government force on their rear, they drew up on a hill near the town but conflict was avoided when the soldiers drew off.[66] By 10 July John Wolfe was aware that a large body (he estimated 1,200 to 1,500 men) had crossed from Whelp Rock to Kildare.[67] The massing of rebels in north Kildare encouraged fresh desertions from government forces. A group of Fourth Dragoons left their post at Santry intending to join 'Captain Doorly' in Kildare.[68]

The plans of the combined rebel force were unclear to government troops. Samuel Sproule believed the north Kildare and Dublin rebels planned to make a 'desperate attack' on Naas.[69] Daniel Gahan argues the ultimate design of the Wexford-Wicklow group was to connect with the Ulster United Irishmen, whose rebellion was now crushed. Within this context it is difficult to explain why Clonard to the north was targeted. Fr Mogue Kearns one of the Wexford leaders had been a curate in the parish. Perhaps he expected to recover arms and ammunition or simply favoured the move from personal motivations.[70] It is possible some leaders wished to strike west not north. The author of *An impartial narrative* believed Aylmer suggested attacking Clonard with a view to pushing towards Athlone. On 16 July 'a man who was in the camp' informed John Wolfe the 'executive' intended making an attempt on Athlone.[71] Above all Clonard presented a soft target to the large rebel force. From the viewpoint of the Kildare insurgents it also offered easy return access to the bogs.

The rebel force possibly numbering 3,000 men arrived at Clonard on the afternoon of 11 July. The garrison was defended by only twenty-seven Yeomen under Lt. Thomas Tyrrell. The attack was led by 'one Farrell', possibly Andrew, with three hundred men. Rourke and his Dublin contingent also took part in this initial assault which was accompanied by burning part of the town. Rourke was incorrect when he asserted the defenders suffered 'considerable loss'. However the timely arrival of fifty infantry and fifty cavalry from Mullingar and Edenderry probably saved the garrison. After six hours of combat those rebels who had succeeded in penetrating the town were expelled. The rebels lost an estimated sixty men.[72] The defeated force fell back to the house of Lord Harberton at Newbury, near Castlecarbery. The house was plundered as were others in the neighbourhood. Up to 1,000 rebels encamped at nearby Carbery.[73]

On the evening of 11 July Lt.-Col. Gough at Philipstown received information from Major Ormsby that an attack on the town was expected. The following morning Gough with a force of ninety men moved west to Carbery Hill where he discovered the rebels had travelled east. He followed the path of the United Irish army, finally encountering the combined army, numbering 4,000 on Knockderg Hill near Johnstown. Gough was under the impression they were drawn up for battle: '... forming such a line as really astonished me, with many standards flying and everything prepared to give me battle ...' A 'desperate attack' up the hill resulted in confusion among the rebels and their complete dispersion. The rebels had just been preparing for dinner not combat.[74] Gough believed the rebels to be commanded by Aylmer, Doorly, Lube and Mogue Kearns and Fitzgerald of Wexford.[75] The evacuation of the camp and second military defeat in two days resulted in the separation of the combined army. The majority of Kildare men under Aylmer and including Edward Fitzgerald returned to their strongholds in the Bog of Allen.[76] The ensuing 'Meath expedition' was a complete disaster. The rebels were continuously harassed by soldiers and failed to rouse local support.

The disastrous sojourn of the combined United Irish army in north Kildare undoubtedly confirmed Aylmer and his comrades of the necessity of concluding a surrender. Military victory was impossible, there was still no sign of the French and while the Bog of Allen provided a natural defence, it was not impenetrable nor was the warm summer going to last indefinitely. While their Wexford and Wicklow comrades marched further north channels of communication were reopened between government and the Kildare rebels. Once more the collateral branches of William Aylmer's family – the Aylmers of Donadea and Courtown – provided middlemen. A copy of correspondence between the rebels and these go betweens was forwarded to Castlereagh on 16 July. The detail of this flow of letters reveals the difficulties of dealing with rebels in arms.[77]

On 15 July Michael Aylmer received a letter from the 'officers of the barony anxious to restore it to its lost peace and tranquillity'. They were prepared to accept exile to 'their choice of country'. Significantly the letter also contained an apologia stating the leaders – Aylmer, Ware, Lube and Cormick

– attempted to escape to America when the rebellion began but were forced to return 'in their own defence to join their respective places'. They attempted at all times to prevent the destruction of property and expressed sorrow for the desolation of Courtown. Fenton Aylmer replied the same day, sending what he described as a 'memorandum' referring to a letter of Lord Castlereagh dated 12 July. This suggests government may have attempted to maintain contact during the campaign of the combined army. This letter accepted exile not transportation was to be the punishment. It also requested surrender within forty eight hours (i.e. by 14 July) which had elapsed however 'every interest' was to be used 'to protect the time'. Otherwise the conditions outlined by Castlereagh on 5 July still applied. The hill of Ballygordon was suggested as a suitable surrender point.

The rebels replied later on the same day. They wished to know if America could be arranged as a place of exile. They also expressed reservations about Fenton Aylmer's proposed method of surrender (i.e. en masse) given the experience of their comrades on the Curragh. Fenton Aylmer's reply the next day was non-committal. He informed the Kildare leaders the correspondence was forwarded to Dublin where the place of banishment would be decided. A note written by Cornwallis, possibly in reply to Aylmer's letter (16 July) indicated General Lake was willing to accept the 'unconditional surrender' of the rebels.[78]

Around the same time Buckingham was allowed to write a letter to Charles Aylmer of Painstown to help arrange the surrender. He claimed a reply was received from William Aylmer and Edward Fitzgerald which resulted in surrender. The influence of a prominent figure like Buckingham, undoubtedly provided the rebel leaders with the security they required.[79] The negotiations ran into difficulty during the 17-18 July. Cornwallis received two despatches from General Wilford who met Aylmer and Fitzgerald at Sallins.[80] At this meeting an armistice, including all those rebels in arms, was agreed which provoked an angry response from Castlereagh. He expressed disapprobation at Wilford for entering into treaty with rebels who had for almost two weeks 'trifled with government'. The armistice was to be revoked immediately and twenty four hours allowed for submission. In the event of non-compliance rewards were to be offered for the apprehension of Aylmer (£1,000) and the other leaders (£300). Cornwallis also expressed anger at Wilford's conduct in a letter to William Pitt on 20 July, conduct which 'rendered more difficult' the surrender.[81]

The determined attitude of government must have been instrumental in finally producing a surrender – though it did not occur until 21 July. At two o'clock a body of 120 rebels surrendered headed by Aylmer and Fitzgerald. Edward Cooke wrote to William Wickham:

> After some little mismanagement the heads of the Wexford and Kildare rebels submitted this day. Fifteen of them have been dirtying my parlour this evening. I have not yet talked to them. Aylmer the Kildare leader seems to be a silly ignorant, obstinate lad. The surrender was on the condition the lives of the leaders should be saved.[82]

The fifteen who surrendered were escorted to Dublin from Montgomery Mills by Col. Handfield. They were: William Aylmer, Edward Fitzgerald, Joseph Cormick, George Lube, Andrew Farrell, Hugh Ware, Denis Farrell, Pat Mooney, Richard Daly, James Tiernan, Thomas Andoe, Michael Quigly, Pat Hanlon, Peter Cockran and Bryan McDermott.[83] Buckingham refused to have any dealings with leaders after their surrender. He reported 5,000 pikes and firelocks with all the rebel provisions were handed in.[84] The government's patience with the rebels is best explained by their determination to quell the rebellion, best achieved by removing the recognised leaders from the conflict. The intricacies of the surrender clearly demonstrate Dublin Castle's conflict of interests, with one eye on the loyalist population, another on the restoration of tranquillity. Government clearly believed what occurred was a 'surrender' not a 'treaty'.

Those who travelled north were not so lucky. Anthony Perry and Fr Mogue Kearns returned too late to participate in the surrender. They were taken in Kildare and hanged in Edenderry.[85] On 7 August Felix Rourke and three Dublin comrades surrendered to Dundas at Kilcullen, escaping the ultimate fate of Perry and Kearns.[86] Others managed to return to the Wicklow mountains where they continued to plague the government in the years after 1798. While the surrender of 21 July was successful in terminating overt rebellion in Kildare the county was tormented by 'different bands of rebels and robbers' for months afterwards. The problem was particularly acute in north Kildare. Louisa Conolly knew the problem would be significant but hoped 'when *all* are joined against them, that they cannot long be screened'.[87]

The rebellion had a devastating effect on Kildare as a whole but the Leinster family, and their local and national position was particularly damaged. On 4 June Lord Edward had died in prison of wounds inflicted during his arrest.[88] Thomas Reynolds had also implicated (to a much lesser degree) his wife Pamela.[89] Government decided to confiscate Lord Edward's property by means of an act of attainder despite the protests of the duke of Leinster. However they added the names of Cornelius Grogan and Bagnell Harvey to the bill 'that the measure nay not appear personal to the Leinster family'.[90] The extent of the rebellion in Kildare reflected badly on Leinster. Cornwallis blamed the 'fostering hand of Lord Edward Fitzgerald, and the countenance which it received from his weak brother Leinster …'[91] Kildare, of which he owned one-third, was ravaged by the combat and much of his vast estates lay in ruins.[92] Three hundred and ninety-one suffering loyalists from Kildare later claimed £97,979 from the commission appointed to reimburse them. Only Wexford, Wicklow and Mayo produced higher petitions.[93]

Patrick O'Kelly's reactive rebellion forced on a suffering people by an undisciplined solidery is no more convincing than Richard Musgrave's reading of the rebellion as a sectarian rising. Captain Swayne's barbarity at Prosperous is well documented but it does not explain why a ferocious rising occurred in that area while the long-suffering region around Athy hesitated and failed. Three chapels were destroyed, at Kildare, Athy and Stradbally, during May and June.[94] However the minimal role of the Catholic clergy may be one indication of the limited religious motivation. The best documented sectarian murders, particularly those of Brewer, Stamer and Spencer, are best explained in terms of loss of authority and discipline in the United Irish force allowing the expression of sectarian and agrarian forces to be unleashed. Lady Louisa Conolly believed: 'This business is too deep for such a political head as mine to judge of, but I still think that it does not proceed from a religious cause …'[95] It is significant that the two baronies where the United Irishmen were most seriously damaged before the rebellion, Kilkea and Moone and West Narragh and Rheban witnessed the most ineffectual rebel activity in the county. The rebellion in Kildare was United Irish in its origins, timing and leadership, and remained focused on Dublin throughout.

CHAPTER 7

Rebels and robbers

ℰᴐ

1798–1803

The surrender of the Kildare leaders on 21 July 1798 did not mark the end of overt rebellion in the rest of the country. During late August and early September 1,000 French troops under General Jean Humbert conducted an audacious but ultimately ill-fated invasion from Killala, county Mayo. Despite a sympathetic rising in areas where the French operated and a victory over government forces at Castlebar, Humbert was forced to surrender at Ballinamuck on 8 September.[1] Some effort was made to encourage renewed rebel activity in Kildare on the arrival of their overdue allies. William Putnam McCabe, with the financial assistance of Philip Long, a Dublin merchant, unsuccessfully attempted to encourage a second rising, narrowly avoiding capture himself.[2]

The most successful rebel activity of the period was sustained in the Wicklow mountains under Joseph Holt and Michael Dwyer. The surrender of the leading Kildare rebels in July ensured no such campaign would be conducted under a high-profile rebel from the leadership core of the Timahoe camp. This was reinforced by the fact that the surrender emptied the Bog of Allen, which provided most favourable conditions for a prolonged campaign, of its rebel army. Some noted rebel leaders did escape arrest and appear to have remained in the Wicklow-Kildare border area in the post-rebellion period, notably Malachi Delany, Michael Reynolds and Matthew Kenna.

Even before the end of overt rebellion in Kildare lawlessness, plunder and robbery became acceptable and indeed crucial to survival among elements of the United Irish army. Disorder became a recurring feature of the Kildare landscape during the autumn and winter of 1798. The situation was commonly connected to ex-rebels. Sometimes they were considered as 'United Irish' and often as mere highwaymen and robbers with no political import. The unleashing of lawlessness in the aftermath of rebellion is a feature Kildare shared with the other major centres of conflict, for example Wexford.[3] The available evidence suggests no 'white terror' gripped Kildare in late July-August. This is largely explained by the fact that such a reaction already occurred during June in the areas of the county where open rebellion quickly dissipated. This is illustrated in the execution of Fr Edward Prendegast at Monasterevan or Col. Campbell's destructive pacification of south Kildare. The county appears to have enjoyed a measure of tranquillity during August, encouraged by General Dundas' continued leniency.[4]

Sectarianism of a sort attended the months after the rebellion in Kildare. In August the surface calm was threatened by a frustrated plot to massacre the Protestants of Athy. Around the same time the Catholic chapel in the town was burned in an apparent attempt to encourage disaffection. Among those implicated were James Noud, Fr Patrick Kelly and Thomas Fitzgerald of Geraldine recently released from prison. The same information, of a Militiaman Timothy Sullivan and that of a prisoner suggests the United Irishmen in the Athy region continued to meet in committee, were actively engaged in arming or rearming and expected a French invasion in the two years following 1798.[5] 'If the French [i.e. Humbert's invasion force] had gained any considerable advantage,' Thomas Fitzgerald wrote on 10 September, 'a rising was to have taken place between this Sunday and next.'[6] The collieries in the vicinity of Athy appear to have been an important base for some rebel groups.[7]

The situation in south Kildare grew worrying for government during the autumn and winter of 1798. The reports of frightened loyalists reflects their insecurity as much as the existence of plots or intended massacres. In late September the house of Thomas Rawson at Glasealy outside Athy was destroyed by a rebel group of sixteen men under Matthew Kenna and James Murphy. According to one of the participants the group launched the attack from the Glen of Imaal in the Wicklow Mountains. Some of the participants, for example one 'Antrim John', were known to be associated with Holt and Dwyer. The party also murdered four local Protestants during the assault which Musgrave portrays as sectarian. Perhaps revenge was a greater motivating factor.[8] William Goldwin writing to Rawson around the same time stated: 'We are threatened to be attacked (every day) the poor loyalists of Narraghmore and Calverstown are all flying this moment to Athy and the bridge. They are all to be destroyed this night; the villains gave them notice to quit'.[9]

The uncertainty of the situation created an atmosphere which heightened criminal activity, often associated (at least in the minds of loyalists) with continuing rebel activities. The Cork mail coach was a frequent target in the area south of Kilcullen. The robbers were based in the Wicklow Mountains close to the Kildare border. Those who headed a gang which struck in September at Red Gap had military titles – Colonel MacMahon, Captain Neale and Captain Walsh – formerly an attorney, a doctor and a maltster. Samuel Reilly taken prisoner from the coach recorded a perilous journey into the neighbouring mountains with the gang who appear to have been unconnected with either Holt or Dwyer.[10] Maurice Keatinge's comments on the situation are interesting:

> The Cork mail coach has twice been robbed on the border of my estates … I do not absolutely know that it is by the people but I know so far as this that there is a connection between the inhabitants of that country and the robbers who are all both passive and active more or less concerned in the general system of depredation.

He concluded the area could only be 'governed by a military force' and expressly stated that the moral economy which had existed ten years previously between gentlemen and the lower orders had collapsed irretrievably under the 'system'.[11]

North Kildare exhibited the same disturbing features during late 1798. In September an informant writing under the pen name 'A county Kildare Farmer' reported the deplorable state of the Kilcock district. This was Revd Christopher Robinson who sent seven surviving letters to Dublin Castle in May and June. As an ultra-loyalist, Camden's departure deprived him of a sympathetic audience hence his anonymity.[12] A group of six or seven men, including yeoman deserters were 'constantly galloping thro' this country, plundering and making use of every means in their power to rise the country once more and again involve us in misery'. The group lived off the local inhabitants and had been involved in mail coach robbery.[13] Violent death became a common occurrence in the unruly situation. In October six members of a notorious gang of 'rebels and robbers' were killed in an ambush by government forces.[14] Intimidation prevented adequate prosecution of those arrested. In the same month a Mr Cooley, an intended crown evidence at the next assizes, was killed with his eighty-year-old mother.[15] No common leaders emerge from the information sent to Dublin Castle suggesting that the various gangs were working independently. In this atmosphere rebellion and robbery had overlapped.

The activities of one rebel group are accessible through information supplied by a former member in late 1803. In September 1798 the North Cork Militia marched from Blessington to Ballinamuck, county Longford. James

Nagle, a private in the force deserted near the Wood of Allen in Kildare following an argument with a superior officer. He subsequently met five men headed by Michael Doorly. They asked Nagle to join their group and brought him to Lullymore. On his arrival:

> Michael Doorly took a prayer book out of his pocket and swore him: 'to do as they would do, and not to deceive them, and not to part from them till the last drop of his blood would be spilt, unless he should be forced or that they themselves should be forced to quit from each other and be steady and determined and to free his country and liberty for ever'.

His hair was cropped and he was cheered by the crowd gathered in the area.[16] Lullymore provided the ideal situation for a rebel base positioned as it was (like Timahoe) on a dry island surrounded by bog land, to the north of Rathangan. John Doorly, Michael's brother led the rebel attack on and occupation of Rathangan in May 1798. A Doorly was reported active in south Kildare in September 1798 whom Thomas Fitzgerald believed to be 'a brother to the general of that name'.[17]

Marianne Elliot recognised the importance of figures such as Doorly during the period between 1798 and 1803. She comments however: '… there were few signs that Dourly [sic] was creating anything other than a personal mafia, vaguely identified with the United Irish cause'.[18] Members were successfully prosecuted for house and highway robbery. Sectarianism also played a role in the groups identity. It appears from Nagle's testimony that only Catholics were admitted to the group. However they were more than a symptom of the pervading lawlessness of the post-rebellion months. Nagle lived at 'old Doorly's' where he spent his time 'sometimes digging potatoes, sometimes casting bullets, sometimes exercising the men who assembled at Lullymore'. It is clear that the group actively expected another rising. The core of those involved were the extended Doorly family. Nagle himself married locally to Esther Malone of the Wood of Allen. He left the area after nine months and enlisted in the army, serving in both England and later Egypt.[19]

The leading loyalists of the county realised the need for direct action if the county was to be pacified. On 23 October John Wolfe who recently returned from the west of the country with the Kildare Militia sent a circular letter to Michael Aylmer, Thomas Tyrrell, John Cassidy, Thomas Rawson and Theobald Wolfe, requesting information on the state of the county. He revealed the government was prepared to take strong measures and requested specific information on ex-rebels, Yeomanry deserters and possible military stations.[20] The reports received suggested the 'rebels' were actively engaged in preparations for another rising. A group was reported to have taken position on Eagle Hill where they were cutting trees in broad daylight. Theobald Wolfe's report was particularly alarming: '... the system of terror which prevailed before the rebellion is in operation at this *moment*. The mass of the people is so corrupted as to be ripe for any enormity'. Another correspondent Edward Richardson, while conceding the poor situation of the county, realised that a second rising depended on 'certain circumstances' – on Holt's party gaining ground or more importantly French assistance.[21] The need for pacification was rendered necessary not just by the state of the country but by the analogies to be drawn with the years before the outbreak of May 1798 and the perceived inefficiency of the magistracy in that period. In all Wolfe estimated that one hundred prominent rebels were at large in the county.[22]

The cornerstone of Wolfe's plan of pacification was the establishment of over thirty military stations around the county. However it was realised the co-operation of the magistrates (given their local knowledge) with the military was fundamental to the success of the project. These two it was urged should investigate criminal behaviour with a renewed sense of urgency. This involved lists of suspects being compiled, searches for arms and domicillary visits. Wolfe concluded optimistically: 'the county of Kildare will be at peace in three months'.[23] Letters sent from Littlehales, Cornwallis' military secretary, stressed the importance of military action under the presence or 'positive instruction' of a magistrate.[24] No doubt government was mindful of the patchy support of Kildare magistrates during the months before the rebellion, for military action.

It is difficult to ascertain what effect direct action had in Kildare. During the winter the government constantly received reports of an alarmist nature, hence Cornwallis' comment in December that in the suspect counties of Kildare, Carlow, Wicklow and Wexford 'there is every appearance, as I am informed, of an intended insurrection'.[25] Loyalists who had suffered during the 1798 rising were quick to draw parallels with the current situation and found conspiracy everywhere. Michael Aylmer noted in early 1799, 'the system of terror is so successfully practised that unless in case of desertion it is almost impossible to procure a prosecutor'.[26] Based on the reports arriving at Dublin Castle Kildare appears to have tranquillised to some degree during 1799. After January and February the number of alarming reports declined significantly.[27]

The increased vigilance of the military and magistrates may have informed James Nagle's decision to leave Lullymore during 1799. Other factors were also significant. Joseph Holt's surrender in November 1798 must have affected the morale of rebel pockets in south Kildare. More fundamentally the failure of the French, the disorganisation of the United Irishmen and the hardship of life in the mountains, bogs and collieries may have persuaded many to desert the rebels whose existence was the result of uncertainty in the post-rebellion period. The downturn in the number of reports to Dublin Castle also reflects the increased security felt by loyalists in the countryside as they emerged from the winter without any serious attempted rising. This does not mean disturbance ceased completely. North Kildare was troubled by men who quickly became notorious to local magistrates. Thomas Conolly believed a gang including John Kilfoyle, Thomas Tallant, Thomas Rook and Andrew Flood 'have been publicly harboured by all the farmers and some of the *gentlemen* farmers'.[28] During the summer John Wolfe noted circulating reports of the approach of a large group of Orangemen for the purpose of Catholic massacre. The reports caused such consternation that the villagers of the Kill-Johnstown area vacated their houses and slept in the fields.[29] Intimidation and terror continued to fuel the activities of all shades of the spectrum in Kildare.

The union debate which occurred during 1799 and 1800 served to destabilise the existing establishment divisions in Kildare. The Fitzgerald family itself was split. The duke was a firm opponent of the measure, while his brother Lord Robert (MP for Ardfert) supported it. The duke's borough influence was reduced to one anti-union seat, that of James Fitzgerald MP for Kildare town.[30] The pro-union faction in the county included liberals – Col. Keatinge, Thomas Conolly, Fenton Aylmer, Richard Griffith and Lord Cloncurry and loyalists – earl of Mayo, marquis of Drogheda, Richard Nevill and John Cassidy.[31] For some the decision lay in the realm of practicality not constitutional politics. Col. Keatinge, viewed with suspicion since the rebellion, attempted to solicit government support in the next election and a return to his Kildare powerbase in return for his pro-union stance.[32] Lord Cloncurry's overriding concern was the welfare of his son. Valentine Lawless was re-arrested on 14 April 1799 and spent the following twenty-three months in prison. Lawless himself believed this to be the result of his publicly aired anti-union stance. His father died before union was passed, in autumn 1799.[33]

The anti-union group in the county was similarly composed of strange bed-fellows. Not only the duke but the weight of the La Touche family in Kildare opposed the measure. The key anti-unionist at a local level was John

Wolfe who was dismissed as a commissioner of the revenue for his stance. He was the prime organiser of a series of anti-union meetings in the county. Their existence suggest some popular involvement in the issue. However Castlereagh was probably correct in his assertion that: 'The clamour out of doors is principally to be apprehended as furnishing the members within with a plausible pretext for acting in conformity with their own private feelings'.[34]

At the 1802 election the Fitzgerald's re-asserted their political strength following their abstention from the 1797 election. However, the act of union had effectively destroyed the family's political strength nationally. The disappearance of borough seats in Kildare curtailed Leinster family power to just one county seat, filled by Lord Robert Fitzgerald (a unionist). The other was taken by Robert La Touche. Until the 1830 election these two families continued to divide Kildare's parliamentary representation between them. John Wolfe mounted a strong campaign during 1801-2 but again failed to break the stranglehold of these stronger families.[35]

The apparently autonomous nature of the rebel groups which operated in Kildare in late 1798 and 1799 provide evidence of the collapse which occurred in United Irish organisation in the wake of the rebellion. They illustrate however that popular resistance to government and indeed support for the United Irishmen continued to exist. In October 1798 the informer Samuel Sproule reported the 'executive' had met and 'came to a resolution that all should be over and not to act without the French or till the English troops are recalled'.[36] Doorly's group provides a good example of the remnants of radicalism loosely gathered under the United Irish umbrella. A new organisational structure slowly emerged during 1798 and 1799. A paper entitled 'A plan for the organisation of United Irishmen' outlined the failures of the pre-1798 movement: the publicity attracted by its proceedings, robbery of arms and the 'glare and pomp of surrounding nobility'. The new organisation encouraged discipline and political education. The organisational plan was to be as simple as possible; lower societies would meet only once to elect a sergeant; sergeants to choose a captain and captains to choose a colonel. County, provincial and national committees were to be similarly appointed. Thus when the rising was organised information would be passed down the permanent command chain only when necessary.[37]

The second element in the revolutionary equation was the securing of French assistance. It was to this end that United Irish efforts were most strongly directed after 1798. In this context the native organisation was 'an action force designed to implement a specific plan'.[38] If this plan of organisation was effected in Kildare, it fulfilled its purpose exceptionally well since government was unaware of any developed countywide organisation. What appears more probable is that United Irish leaders in the capital maintained some contact with the pockets of residual support in the county.

The early years of the nineteenth century provided the longest period of protracted calm county Kildare had witnessed since before the Defender disturbances of 1795. By early 1802 most of those who surrendered at Sallins on 21 July 1798 had been released. Fenton Aylmer was confident enough to recommend the release of Hugh Ware, Bryan McDermott and John Reilly.[39] Landowners and magistrates were continually vigilant and viewed any fresh disturbance with apprehension. Reports continued to arrive at Dublin Castle. Information received in January 1801 stated Col. Lunn [i.e. Lumm] and a Mr Collogan of Danaughtown (a relative of Thomas Fitzgerald of Geraldine) were to command the Kildare rebels in the event of a French invasion.[40] In the same year John Walsh perceived 'that conspiracies are again forming in this county and its environs'. The disaffected continued to hold arms and meetings for the purpose of fostering rebellion, he believed. Walsh traced the disaffection to the rebellion of 1798. He carefully noted: 'With respect to open treason there remains not the smallest vestige that I can discover. Every man who is not a robber offers his assistance to the civil powers'.[41]

During the summer of 1802 Oliver Nelson of Rathangan, which had suffered particularly harshly in 1798, reported the loyal inhabitants of the town nightly 'expect the rising of the disaffected'. Loyalists were fleeing to Dublin while there was insufficient protection against the attack.[42] Even apparently agrarian disorder was suspicious, for example the attempted murder of Thomas Little and his family near Timahoe in February 1802. The episode underlined the threat posed by 'the most secret system this long time going on …'.[43] A county meeting and proclamation were subsequently produced in an attempt to alleviate the threat from the 'lower orders'.[44] At Naas and Athy radicalism was apparently fuelled by the prospects of a French invasion as well as the actions of a 'foolish soldiery' and the existence of Orangemen.[45] Loyalist thinking in the post rebellion years was continually informed by the memory of 1798.

The crucial point about the period 1798 to 1802 is that political radicalism continued to persist among the lower orders, i.e. those who had filled the lower structures of the pre-rebellion United Irishmen. Michael Doorly's gang at Lullymore provides the best documented example of such a continuity. James Nagle returned to Ireland in late 1801 and having worked in a number of jobs he returned to Lullymore around November 1802. 'Doorly told him there was to be a turn out again and that there were to be meetings there (in Lullymore) both by night and by day'. Nagle actively drilled between four and five hundred men one or two nights a week at Lullymore. The commanders included Michael Doorly and Matthew Donnellan a farmer who headed a group from Clane. Those in Doorly's company alone included men from Rathangan, Prosperous and Clane. Some attended from Carlow and King's County. It is not clear at exactly what point such a relatively extensive force was active at Lullymore but it appears from Nagle's testimony that a conspiracy was initiated in late 1802 if not before.[46]

The release of the United Irish state prisoners in June 1802, in the wake of the Peace of Amiens, added strength to United Irish negotiations in France. While many settled into a life of 'temporary normality' in their adopted home they expected the organisation of an invasion force on the outbreak of war. Robert Emmet's return to Ireland from France in 1802 did not immediately signal the beginning of the native conspiracy.[47] In Kildare Richard Griffith perceived the capacity for a second rising continued to haunt loyalists in early 1803. He wrote to Thomas Pelham:

> But your Lordship has not seen Paddy since the rebellion. He is an altered being. The bare possibility of a general open resistance did not before occur to him – but though foiled and beaten he *now* thinks he *might* have succeeded and he now looks for another opportunity to try his strength with the assistance of France.[48]

The evidence for such a viewpoint was not particularly strong. In the same month Daniel Collison did report the occurrence of seditious meetings in the Maynooth-Moyglare area.[49]

It was in March 1803 that the United Irish conspiracy of that year began in earnest. In Dublin a number of buildings were purchased, particularly in Patrick Street, Thomas Street and Marshallsea Lane, which served as depots for weaponry. The key Kildare conspirator, Michael Quigly, was recruited in France in early February 1803 and arrived in Ireland on 5 March. It appears likely Quigly was chosen both for his obvious readiness to undertake the task and the connections he held with the disaffected in the crucial county of Kildare. On 7 March he was introduced to Emmet who questioned him on the possibility of mobilising a Kildare force for a rising in Dublin. Quigly (who had not visited Kildare in five years) estimated 1,000 men could be mustered on at least two days notice even from the farthest parts of the county. Following the meeting Quigly was given fifteen guineas and sent to

Kildare to establish contact with the interested parties in the county. He was accompanied, on Emmet's approval, by Kildaremen Thomas Wylde, his brother-in-law, John Mahon and Bryan McDermott.[50]

Quigly's journey to Kildare took him all over the north of the county. Essentially he made contact with veterans of '98 and those known to be interested in participating in a fresh rebellion. His mission was quickly made known to Dublin Castle through reports from Sir Fenton Aylmer and Lt.-Col. Michael Aylmer. At Naas he assured the people he met 'that the French had prepared a large armament for the invasion of Ireland – and that they ought to be soon expected'. Meanwhile at Timahoe and Prosperous they were 'joyfully received and promised general support'. Pat Heffernan had reported to Fenton Aylmer that the lower orders were meeting since February, their grievances largely based on economic issues. However Quigly's mission certainly reactivated an interest in a rebellion. On 13 March a crowd of several hundred gathered in the Timahoe area in suspicious circumstances. Fenton Aylmer wrote in the same month: 'From the informations received within a day or two the peasantry of the county Kildare in general are determined to rise when they hear of a French invasion and join the enemy ...'[51] Quigly's journey lasted only a few days and he returned to Dublin on 10 March with optimistic reports of the Kildare situation. He remained hidden in Dublin for the next four months.[52]

Quigly's mission never attempted to re-establish a United Irish organisation on the basis of the pre-1798 model. He simply visited known rebels who in turn informed those in the locality of the intended rising. A number of Kildaremen were brought to the Thomas and Patrick Street depots where preparations were underway. These included: Edward Condon, Bernard Duggan, James Flood, John and William Parrott, one Dunn, Nicholas Stafford, Thomas Wylde, John Mahon, Henry Howley, John Burke, Richard Eustace and Christy Nowlan.[53] The fact that no official structure was reconstituted meant that despite Quigly's publicised visit to Kildare only patchy reports of radical activity in Kildare between March and July reached government. This was compounded by the fact that preparations were concentrated in the depots in the capital.

In March renewed reports of disaffection emerged from the Naas area. French agents and native emissaries were apparently active and meetings were taking place.[54] Information received after the July rising suggested United Irishmen were meeting in the Naas area in preparation for a rising in the months before July. Two active rebels, James and Martin Duff, were engaged in exercising men under their command in June. According to Peter

Hamilton, one Flood of Kilcullen was the 'only man that gave orders to the United sergeants'.[55] Rebel activity was also evident in west Kildare. James Gorman, a limeburner and John Byrne, a whitesmith both from the Kildare town area who were active in 1798 were both swearing in their locality. Numbers in the renewed 'organisation' were rising, particularly in Kildare town itself. Sylvester Kelly and George Rankin were also active organisers. John Cassidy believed Rankin 'possibly secretary to the Kildare rebels' was involved in mail coach robbery and the burning of Kildangan chapel – a measure intended to encourage the people to rise.[56]

Information on radicalism in the Athy area is less revealing. The key conspirators were Nicholas Gray and his brother-in-law, Henry Hughes who had been involved in the rebellion in Wexford. They had only recently settled in Kildare. Patrick O'Kelly, who makes curiously little mention of Kildare's involvement in his account of 1803, claimed the men contributed £2,000 to Robert Emmet.[57] Patrick Whelan of Athy fought under Patrick Dowling in 1798 and was later involved in robberies in both Dublin and Kildare. He believed the county was organised by July 1803 by 'new laws, new tests, new regulations'.[58] Meetings were held in Dublin before the rising which discussed the problem of procuring arms for the Athy region (which undoubtedly presented logistical problems). John Boyle was sent to the town to gather intelligence for the rebels. He was informed it was 'ready to rise'. He was later present at a number of meetings at locations between Athy and Straffan in the weeks before the rising. Discussion included plans to break open Athy jail, attack soldiers stationed on the Curragh and inform the people on rising that the French had landed in England. Boyle's information also suggests a number of 'gentlemen' were involved in the preparations. Positive information of organising was provided by the robbery of a stand of arms from a boat in Athy harbour. Despite the recovery of the small quantity the comparisons with the 1797 robbery were chilling for loyalists.

The nature of the renewed activity meant there was no real organisation to penetrate. Hence the level of activity in county Kildare was probably underestimated. One of the most important preoccupations of the Dublin leaders was the arming of rebels in the surrounding counties. Michael Quigly later claimed this incurred a very real danger of discovery. In July ammunition was secretly delivered to Rathcoffey.[59] Connor Keevan appears to have acted as a messenger between the Dublin rebels and north Kildare.[60] Patrick Hanlon of Hogestown was informed as early as December 1802 that the disaffected 'were making pikes and weapons in all the seaport towns and sending them out into the country'. Rebels in the Timahoe area were well organised and armed before the July rising.[61] Many of the potential rebels were of course armed and indeed organised – Doorly's group is a good example. A large force was organised in the Lullymore area since 1802 and before. Three months previous to the July rising Michael Doorly and John Green told James Nagle they had a six-pound brass cannon which had been sent from Gorey. It was buried to prevent discovery though later searches failed to uncover it. In general the Lullymore rebels were well armed by July. 'They had blunderbusses, muskets, fowling pieces, pikes, poles and pitchforks,' noted Nagle, 'every man had something on his shoulder.' Doorly's United Irishmen had made contact with Emmet at some point and were willing to participate in his planned rebellion.[62]

Radical activity in the county was worrying enough in April to cause a county meeting. This was probably precipitated by the initial mission of Quigly and his associates. The gentlemen entered into resolutions of loyalty and determination to oppose rebellion.[63] The activists of 1803 were noticeably distinct in composition from those of 1798. Marianne Elliot has commented, 'leaders were hand-picked, mostly from a lower social grouping ...'[64] Fenton Aylmer noted in March: '... the farmers in general are adverse to the measure [rebellion] ... The peasantry are determined to elect officers from among themselves and never again trust gentlemen'.[65] Keatinge (himself, implicated by Rawson) also argued the lower orders were the basis of the conspiracy and that the 'farmers' had held aloof. 'This determination of the latter,' he observed, '... I know is very hard to keep.'[66] There is no evidence to suggest William Aylmer was involved in Emmet's conspiracy, he had enlisted in the Austrian army in 1800.[67]

In a sense the conspiracy of 1803 achieved what that of 1798 did not in that it remained largely unknown to government. There was no spate of housebreaking such as accompanied the preparations of 1798. Major General Trench reported on 1 July 1803: 'The counties Kildare, Carlow, Queen's County and Westmeath are in a perfect state of tranquillity and the inhabitants are pursuing habits of industry'.[68] John O'Brien was despatched to the county by government on 13 July to determine its mood. After nine days in Naas, Kilcullen, Athy and Kildare town he reported: 'from all I could learn it would be impossible to induce them [the people] to oppose the government of this country ... the people have the greatest aversion to the French'.[69] Preparations in the Dublin depots continued unabated. The Kildare element appeared to have been consolidated, Dwyer agreed to participation (after Dublin rose) and Thomas Russell arrived in April and travelled north with Hamilton to enlist support. In Dublin itself the professional and trading classes which Emmet conceived of as the backbone of his plan were slow to come forward. The French, and indeed English and Scottish elements remained ill-coodinated.[70]

About 15 July Nicholas Gray arrived in the depot at Thomas Street. He was introduced as the general of the Kildare forces by Emmet. On recommendation three men from the Maynooth area: Thomas Frayne, Owen Lyons and Thomas Kereghan were appointed officers. Lyons had been in constant contact with Quigly, Emmet and the other Dublin leaders. It was agreed a Naas force was to march on Dublin after the rising began while other forces acted in the county itself. The subsequent rising loosely implemented this plan, the rebellion at Maynooth was initially local while that at Naas quickly looked to a march on Dublin as its purpose.[71] Disaster struck in Dublin on 16 July when an explosion occurred in the Patrick Street depot. The next day a party delivering arms was interrupted by a watchman. These events alerted the authorities to the preparations for a possible rising.[72] 23 July was hurriedly settled on as the date for rising. Notification reached Kildare as early as 20 July. Leaders at Naas quickly passed the information on to the surrounding countryside.[73] On the evening of 21 July Thomas Wylde and John Mahon were despatched to Kildare by Quigly or Emmet.[74]

On the morning of the rising a number of Kildare leaders arrived in Dublin anxious to view for themselves the preparations which had been made. According to Quigly:

> ... it appeared that the two men who had been sent [to] Kildare had in order to entice the greater numbers exaggerated considerably in their statements, on discovering the truth nothing could exceed the disappointment of the deputies and disagreement having taken place in consequence between them and Mr Emmet the Kildare men who were coming to town got orders to return and a few men who had actually arrived were sent back.[75]

The two men referred to, who were sent to Kildare were almost certainly Wylde and Mahon. The Kildare leaders obviously expected a much greater level of preparedness. It is not clear who these leaders were or what part of county Kildare they came from. They certainly could not have comprised the total expected force from the county. James Nagle's evidence states Doorly and his group were in Dublin on 23 July and participated in the rising.[76] The confused Dublin 'rising' which occurred that evening was a complete fiasco scuppered by ill-coordination and confused reports. After a hurried march up

Thomas Street the leaders abandoned any hopes of success and Emmet issued countermanding orders.[77]

The confusion in Dublin in turn isolated the Kildare rebellion. It was concentrated in two centres – Maynooth and Naas. Some rebel activity took place elsewhere in the county. Maynooth possibly figured in Emmet's plans specifically to cut off one major route in and out of Dublin. In August the state solicitor James McClelland compiled a report on the 'late insurrection in the county of Kildare' which concentrated on the Maynooth element largely because of the political implications for the duke of Leinster and Maynooth College. It was based on the evidence of the key crown witness Daniel Collison. It does however make some fundamental errors which reflect the narrowness of Collison's information. For example it states 'James Quigly' returned to Ireland in May 1803 and thereafter 'remained principally in Kildare fostering rebellion'.[78] The duke of Leinster and Carter Connolly, a rebel leader, both believed Collison himself was actively involved in the rebellion. The duke of Leinster commented later: 'I can assure you [Marsden] Collison is much deeper concerned in this business than he thinks we are aware of'.[79]

About 8 o'clock on the evening of 23 July about 100 people gathered in Maynooth under the command of Owen Lyons, Thomas Kereghan and Carter Connolly. Connolly, the local schoolmaster, was later certified insane following his imprisonment in the aftermath of the rising.[80] One estimate put the figure as high as 400.[81] Their first act was to imprison two Dragoon Guards who were stationed to ensure the safety of the mail coach. About 10 o'clock a party of the rebels departed in search of arms in the vicinity. The duke of Leinster was informed almost immediately of the activities of the small rebel army. Despite the fact that Carton was well armed the duke decided to offer his weaponry to the rebels and sent a servant, Thomas Cooney, as a messenger for this purpose. He apparently informed them:

> … that the duke's arms were ready for them in the duke's saloon and that refreshment was prepared for his [Lyons'] party – and that the duke desired him to say that he would be glad that Lyons should take his arms least government should say that the party … would not lay a hand on him.

Lyons appears to have cautiously accepted the offer.[82]

About midnight the Longford mail approached the town and the rebels were quickly mobilised into three groups to effect its interception. However the coach managed to pass the first two 'divisions' and the third simply fled. The coach passed through the town with relatively little damage despite the fact that two bullets passed through the carriage.[83] The rebel leaders decided to march to Celbridge where they met Thomas Frayne's contingent. However news of the Dublin failure reached them and plans to march to Rathcoole to link with 'General Fox' were abandoned. A meeting probably took place on Windgate Hill near Celbridge where it was decided to fall back on Rathcoffey.[84] While the leaders dined at Quigly's house they received a message from the duke of Leinster offering an unconditional surrender without an enquiry. The offer was not immediately acted upon instead the rebels continued to search for arms. On their return to Maynooth on Monday 25 July they communicated with the duke through Abbé Darre, a professor of natural philosophy at Maynooth College. The duke consented to a surrender and personally accepted that of twenty men including Thomas Kereghan, in the town.[85]

Elsewhere in north Kildare the rebels were prepared for action. John Wolfe received information on the morning of the rising that rebellion was on the verge of breaking out in Prosperous where it was 'this night to join the party in Dublin'. Next day Patrick Hanlon was informed by a rebel leader, at Timahoe, to be prepared for action and that he and 100 men were ready.[86] Michael Aylmer at Kilcock reported on the same day that rebels had been sighted on the Hill of Lyons and an attack on Kilcock itself was imminent.[87] A report to Dublin Castle stated: 'scarce a person is to be seen about the country on either side [of] the Grand Canal and it is almost certain a great part of the county of Kildare (I mean rebels) will be in arms tomorrow or the next day'.[88] Wogan Browne, however, believed the people of his neighbourhood had refused to cooperate with 'the rabble in Dublin'.[89]

Naas was the other major centre of rebellion in Kildare. The main source of evidence for the Naas rising is a collection of depositions and informations taken in the town between July and October 1803 by the solicitor general, General Trench and John Wolfe. Most of those questioned denied any involvement in the conspiracy. Many admitted their presence in Dublin on the day of the rising but on business. At least 150 men left Naas on 23 July intending to participate in the Dublin rising. Thomas Brophy, a chandler from Naas had, 'not a doubt that there were four times 150 people from the town and neighbourhood of Naas who went to Dublin on 23 July for the town and neighbourhood were deserted'. Most rebels travelled in small groups of up to ten people. Some turned back on the road having heard of the disastrous events in the capital. Others participated in the skirmishes which occurred and a few were suspected dead as a result of the fighting. The majority returned on Saturday and Sunday. Some spent the following nights in the surrounding country for fear of arrest.[90]

No assault was mounted on Naas itself by the rebels. Nevertheless open rebel activity in the area caused panic among loyalists. The Griffiths, Montgomerys and Burghs were all forced to evacuate to the town itself for safety.[91] The movements of Nicholas Gray who was to command the Kildare forces was particularly suspect. He was known to have been in Dublin in the days before the rising. On 24 July he rode towards Naas and Dublin from Athy but turned back on hearing of the disturbances, at Johnstown. It is possible he was to command the United Irish forces gathered at Naas.[92] Further south at Kildare town Thomas Rawson believed 'thousands' had assembled on 24 July and were restrained by their leaders 'with difficulty'. Although nothing had occurred in the south of the county, at Athy Rawson industriously arrested 'every person absent from hence on the fatal Saturday, many are wounded'. He was not mistaken in his perception that the area was organised and that veterans of 1798 were involved.[93]

The evidence provided by a study of the events in county Kildare in 1803 suggests Marianne Elliot's reappraisal of the conspiracy was correct.[94] Thousands of people were involved in the preparations in the spring of 1803. While no formal organisation was reconstituted, the leaders relied on the prospect of a semi-spontaneous rising. At least 1,000 men were prepare to actively participate in the rebellion itself on 23-25 July. The failure of the Dublin element (comparable to the events of 1798) left it completely lacking in direction. It is clear that many of the men of '98 were still warm to the United Irish cause in 1803.[95]

Disaffection continued to exist in the immediate aftermath of the rising but essentially the events of 23-26 July ended the prospect of another attempt in the near future. After the 'Battle of Dublin' James Nagle returned to Doorly's at Lullymore where he continued to drill rebels who assembled in the area. He had met Doorly at Clane the day after the rising itself. Nagle was arrested in October and on his evidence a spate of arrests followed including that of Michael and Thady Doorly. John Wolfe who examined Nagle and the others expressed serious reservations about the worth of the former's information. In early 1804 Wolfe recommended the release of twenty four of the twenty five arrested on his evidence. Only Michael Doorly was held because there was some proof of his involvement in robberies.[96] Admiral Packenham in Leixlip made a large number of arrests in the north of the county in the autumn and winter of 1803.[97] In the Naas area too suspects were rounded up and in September Gray and Hughes were lodged in Athy jail.[98]

The Kildare leaders who had been in Dublin effected their escape to the Wicklow Mountains on 23-24 July. Duggan, Lennon, Stafford, Quigly and John and William Parrott spent five to seven weeks at Rathcoffey and regrouped at Ardfry, county Galway.[99] Their plan was probably to quit the country but in October Quigly, Stafford and the Parrotts were captured. Wylde and Mahon became the objects of an extensive search in which Quigly assisted. Bernard Duggan was finally taken in Dublin in 1805.[100] By the end of October 1803 Quigly agreed to provide government with information and continued to do so after his release in 1806. The prospect of his disclosures was favourable to government at least in 'reducing our doubts and suspicions to certainties'. William Wickham described Quigly as 'by far the cleverest I have yet seen or conversed with of the rebels'.[101] It is almost certainly a retrospective analysis of Quigly's role as the most senior rebel to provide information that informs Helen Landreth's opinion. She tentatively suggests he was in the pocket of government from the start of his mission to Ireland. She argues 'no effort' was made by Marsen to arrest him in March.[102] It is possible Marsden, who shouldered much of the blame for government inactivity before 23 July, believed more could be learned by following Quigly's movements than by arresting him.

The county establishment and government struggled to find a reason for the widespread activity in the county. The magistrates and justices of the peace assembled for the summer assizes in early August, passed declarations of loyalty and condemned the rebellion.[103] Kildare (and neighbouring Meath) were proclaimed with the active support of the duke of Leinster in August.[104] The most puzzling element of the Kildare rising for government was its sporadic nature.[105] Fenton Aylmer asked in late July, 'have any people of consequence been their leaders or what the devil do they want?'[106] James McClelland in compiling his report on Maynooth found such a determined rising in such a relatively small town with no apparent overall strategy 'difficult to account for'. He sought answers in two sources which had remained under suspicion since 1798: Maynooth College and the duke of Leinster. The college it was argued increased 'among the Catholic inhabitants that intemperate spirit which contributed so powerfully to produce in several counties the former rebellion'. It was also believed the rebels were informed the duke was to lead them.[107] The duke for the second time found himself implicated in a rebellion against government. He had in fact written to the viceroy, Hardwicke, on 24 July outlining the situation and requesting 'part of the army' to be despatched. In forwarding the report of the solicitor general to the home secretary Charles Coote, Hardwicke noted that Leinster had no previous knowledge of the rising and had positively acquiesced in the proclamation of the county. As had been the case five years earlier the duke was guilty of what the king himself described as 'extreme weakness'. With the county proclaimed the government of it was essentially in the hands of Dublin Castle.[108]

During the period between the two United Irish rebellions popular radicalism continued to exist among the lower orders. The failure in 1798 ensured the middling and upper classes associated with the liberal-radical cause were separated from militant radicals. They simply had too much to lose. Thomas Wogan Browne, Thomas Fitzgerald and Maurice Keatinge all provided government with reports of radicalism in Kildare between 1798 and 1803. For Dublin Castle Kildare presented a continual problem. During 1804 there were more reports of radical activity than in the years 1800 to 1802.[109] The Lord Lieutenant, Hardwicke, commented after the July rebellion:

> ... I am sorry to say that such has been the state of the county of Kildare since the rebellion of 1798 as to require at all times the particular attention of government, and there is a more general and rooted spirit of disaffection in that county than in any other part of Ireland.[110]

Conclusion

The period from 1790 to 1803 in county Kildare was one of unprecedented political activity and disaffection. The appeal of prominent liberals and Catholic activists to a wide base of public opinion radicalised the lower orders to a greater degree than was previously the case. The introduction of Defenderism to the county in 1795 provided the disaffected of a lower social class with a means of co-ordination. The Defenders when they emerged in Kildare linked particular grievances to wider hopes of a 'just' society now inspired by the prospect of a French assisted revolution. However it was the United Irishmen who most effectively harnessed the radicalism of the county. Their mobilisation created a vast underground army prepared to rise in support of a separate, French inspired, Irish republic. The radical threat forced loyalists to define their position more clearly. Under the impetus of Dublin Castle the relatively small, but nonetheless powerful conservative faction organised themselves practically and coherently. The pre-rebellion divisions between radicalism and loyalism continued to dominate Kildare's political landscape until the rebellion of 1803 and beyond.

Kildare at the end of the eighteenth century was one of the most liberal counties in Ireland. This was largely due to the powerful influence, politically and geographically, of the duke of Leinster. At the beginning of the 1790s the liberal position in Ireland was increasingly influential and institutionalised in the hesitant Irish Whig Club and the short-lived Association of the Friends of the Constitution, Liberty and Peace. The beginning of the French war and increasing radicalism within Ireland, which polarised Irish society, rendered the liberal standpoint increasingly untenable. The dilemma facing Whig politicians is illustrated by the case of the duke of Leinster. His attempt to maintain a middle course in opposition to government led ultimately to, an albeit temporary, abdication of his political authority in 1797. The vocal liberal attitude of many of Kildare's landowners in the 1790s created an atmosphere in which disaffection thrived. Moreover, the division in the county establishment which was exhibited most clearly from 1797 further encouraged the dissemination of United Irish ideals as 'out-of-doors' politics became the acceptable means of expressing political opposition. An understanding of liberal politics in Kildare is crucial to the study of the 1790s and the contexts of both 1798 and 1803.

By 1798 the United Irishmen in Kildare were a powerful revolutionary force with a paper strength of up to 12,000 members. The involvement of Lord Edward Fitzgerald gave the United Irishmen a veneer of respectability. He was crucial in the development of Kildare's United Irish movement based on locally influential figures: George Cummins, Malachi Delany, Matthew Kenna and Michael Reynolds for example. Fitzgerald himself was not a powerful thinker but a military man of position imbued with the ideas of the French revolution. Almost all the leading Kildare United Irishmen were Catholic. Thomas Pakenham comments that: 'Nothing is more striking than the absence from the movement of protestant nationalists in the best controlled and best educated of counties like Kildare'.[1] Those Protestants who were tentatively linked with the organisation by 1798, for example Col. Keatinge or Thomas Wogan Browne, were effectively distanced by the military actions of government in the spring of that year. Prominent liberal figures, such as Thomas Fitzgerald or Daniel Caulfield, were more involved than hitherto thought. Their connection is best explained in the context of the breakdown of effective opposition politics around 1797 and the resulting moral respectability of the United Irishmen as the only remaining option for some liberals.

In understanding the period from 1790 to 1803 an appreciation of the forces of conservatism in Kildare is essential. This is particularly pertinent since the dominant interest was liberal. John Wolfe emerges as the central loyalist figure at a local level. The threat of the United Irishmen ensured loyalist leaders received the support of Dublin Castle as organised disaffection spread. The military reaction in the form of the Yeomanry was insufficient and in a number of cases provided military training for United Irish commanders. In political terms the conservative faction gained ascendancy in Kildare in 1797. Liberals such as Richard Griffith actively rejected the radical cause. In 1798 he commented: 'Good God, how bitterly Mr Grattan and others [will have] to reproach themselves for having wrought the giddy multitude into their excesses'.[2] This did not indicate he had relinquished his original political sympathies. Commenting on the union question in early 1799 he noted 'I confess I am extremely sorry that the union does not bring the Catholics into the pale of the constitution'.[3]

An examination of the period under discussion in the context of politics and politicisation illustrates important connections between the various shades of the political spectrum in Kildare, from Defenderism to high politics. This also provides the context to the rebellions of 1798 and 1803. The precise motivations of particular individuals involved in these risings is more problematic. The rebellion taken as a whole was not a sectarian rebellion forced on the peasantry by a draconian military government. Of those leaders who participated in 1798 many were locally influential; strong farmers, minor gentry and wealthy landowners: Aylmer, Reynolds, Esmonde, Delany and Doorly. Neither was the Kildare rebellion a localised revolt. The politicisation of Kildare throughout the period under discussion is an example of a process which occurred at a national level. The present study illustrates this factor as crucial in examining the background to the 1798 rebellion itself. The rebellion was inspired and organised by the United Irishmen though it unleashed forces of sectarianism where military control was poor. The mobilisation of the county again in 1803 proves that 1798 was not an isolated reaction. Kildare's proximity to the capital ensured its national strategic importance in any plans of rebellion. Wexford in 1798 has been a focus of the recent historical reappraisal of the 1790s period and particularly the rebellion itself. By providing an examination of radicalism and reaction at a county level, in Kildare, this study aims to contribute to the wider debate on Ireland during this turbulent period.

Notes

INTRODUCTION

1   L.M. Cullen, 'Politics and rebellion: Wicklow in the 1790s' in Hannigan and Nolan (eds), *Wicklow: history and society* (Dublin, 1994), pp. 414-18.

2   Stella Tillyard, *Aristocrats: Caroline, Emily, Louisa and Sarah Lennox 1740–1832* (London, 1994), pp. 441-2.

3   NLI Wolfe Papers. Some of the papers in this collection have been copied and catalogued, PRONI T. 3474 Wolfe Papers.

4   Thomas Moore, *The life and death of Lord Edward Fitzgerald*; Thomas Reynolds Jnr, *The life of Thomas Reynolds esq., formerly of Kilkea Castle in the county of Kildare* (2 vols, Dublin, 1839); Valentine Lord Cloncurry, *Personal recollections of the life and times with extracts from the correspondence of Valentine Lord Cloncurry* (Dublin, 1849).

5   See Kevin Whelan, ''98 after '98: The politics of memory' in *The tree of liberty: Radicalism, Catholicism and the construction of Irish identity 1760–1830* (Cork, 1996), pp. 133-75.

6   Richard Musgrave, *Memoirs of the different rebellions in Ireland* (2nd edn, Dublin, 1801); Patrick O'Kelly, *General history of the rebellion of 1798 with many interesting occurrences of the two preceding years also a brief account of the insurrection of 1803 will be subjoined* (Dublin, 1842).

7   Kevin Whelan, ''98 after '98: the politics of memory', pp. 135-40.

8   Musgrave, *Rebellions*, p. 255.

9   Patrick O'Kelly, *General history*, pp. 308-12; Abbé MacGeoghegan, *History of Ireland, ancient and modern, taken from the most authentic records* trans. Patrick O'Kelly (Dublin, 1831, first published 1758); F.S. Bourke, 'Patrick O'Kelly – an historian of the rebellion of 1798' in *Irish Booklover*, vol. xxxviii (June 1941), pp. 37-43, 17-18; Seamus O'Casaide, 'Patrick O'Kelly, the translator of Mac Geoghegan' in *Irish Booklover*, vol. xxxviii (Feb. 1942), pp. 84-6.

10 O'Kelly, *General history*, p. 92.

11 R.R. Madden, *The United Irishmen: their lives and times* (7 vols, Dublin, 1842-6).

12 Fr Patrick Kavanagh, *A popular history of the insurrection of 1798* (4th edn, Cork, 1898), pp. 31-7.

13 Anna Kinsella, 'The nineteenth century interpretation of 1798' (M.Litt., TCD 1992), pp. 15-35; Kevin Whelan, ''98 after '98: the politics of memory', pp. 169-73.

14 Thomas Rawson, *Statistical survey of the county of Kildare, with observations on the means of improvement* (Dublin, 1807).

15 Title page of Duggan's narrative, Duggan's narrative, 1838, W.H. Cogan to R.R. Madden n.d. (TCD Madden Papers 873/26, 29, 30); Madden, *United Irishmen*, 3rd series (3 vols, Dublin, 1846), vol. ii, pp. 96-116, 120-1.

16 Mary Leadbeater, *The Leadbeater papers* (2 vols, London, 1862), vol. i, 'the annals of Ballitore' pp. 211-41.

17 An tAth Seosamh O'Murthuile, 'An t-eiri amach i gCill Dara 1798' in *Feasta*, iml. 1 uimh. 2-12 (Bealtine 1948-Marta

1949), iml. 2, uimh. 1 (Aibrean, 1949); idem, *Kildare 1798 commemoration* (Kildare, 1948).

18 Fr Peadar MacSuibhne, *Kildare in '98* (Naas, 1978).

19 Thomas Pakenham, *The year of liberty: The history of the great Irish rebellion of 1798* (London, 1969), pp. 110-11, 274-5.

20 Marianne Elliot, *Partners in revolution* (New Haven, 1982); idem, *Wolfe Tone: Prophet of Irish independence* (Yale, 1989).

21 L.M. Cullen, 'The 1798 rebellion in county Wexford: United Irishmen organisation, membership and leadership' in Kevin Whelan (ed.), *Wexford: history and society* (Dublin, 1987), pp. 248-95; idem, 'The 1798 rebellion in its eighteenth century context' in P. Corish (ed.), *Radicals, rebels and establishments* (Dublin, 1985), pp. 91-113; for Kevin Whelan's most recent comments see: 'Reinterpreting the 1798 rebellion in county Wexford' in Dáire Keogh and Nicolas Furlong (ed.), *The mighty wave: The 1798 rebellion in county Wexford* (Dublin, 1996), pp. 9-36.

22 Nancy Curtain, 'The transformation of the United Irishmen into a mass based revolutionary organisation' in *I.H.S.*, vol. xxiv, no. 5 (1985), pp. 463-92; L.M. Cullen, 'The internal politics of the United Irishmen' in David Dickson, Dáire Keogh and Kevin Whelan (eds), *The United Irishmen: Republicanism, radicalism and reaction* (Dublin, 1993), pp. 176-96; Michael Durey, 'The Dublin Society of the United Irishmen and the politics of the Carey-Drennan dispute' in *Historical Journal*, vol. xxvii (1994), pp. 89-112

23 N. Curtin, *The United Irishmen: Popular politics in Ulster and Dublin 1791-1798* (Oxford, 1994), p. 7; J.S. Donnelly, 'Propagating the cause of the United Irishmen' in *Studies*, vol. lxix, no. 273, (1981), pp. 5-23; Kevin Whelan, 'The republic in the village' in *The tree of liberty*, pp. 59-96; Mary Helen

Thuente, *The harp re-strung: The United Irishmen and the rise of Irish literary nationalism* (Syracuse, 1994); For an argument against the effectiveness of United Irish politicisation see Tom Dunne, 'Popular ballads, revolutionary rhetoric and politicisation' in David Dickson and Hugh Gough (eds), *Ireland and the French Revolution* (Dublin, 1990), pp. 139-55.

24 L.M. Cullen, 'The political structures of the Defenders' in Gough and Dickson (eds), *Ireland and the French Revolution* (Dublin, 1990), pp. 117-38; Thomas Bartlett, 'Select documents xxxviii: Defenders and Defenderism in 1795' in *I.H.S.*, vol. xxiv, no. 95 (1985), pp. 373-94; Tom Garvin, 'Defenders, ribbonmen and others: Underground political networks in pre-famine Ireland' in *Past and Present*, no. 96 (1982), pp. 133-55; David Millar, *Defenders and peep of day boys* (Belfast, 1990).

25 A.P.W. Malcolmson, *John Foster: The politics of Anglo-Irish ascendancy* (Oxford, 1978); Ann C. Kavanaugh, *John Fitzgibbon, earl of Clare: A study in personality and politics* (Dublin, 1997).

26 Thomas Bartlett, 'Defence, counter-insurgency and rebellion: Ireland 1790-1803' in Bartlett and Jeffery (eds), *A military history of Ireland* (Cambridge, 1996), pp. 247-93; Dáire Keogh, 'The French disease': The Catholic church and radicalism in Ireland 1790-1800 (Dublin, 1993); Kevin Whelan, 'United and disunited Irishmen: the state and sectarianism in the 1790s' in *The tree of liberty*, pp. 99-130.

27 T. Bartlett, ' "The masters of the mountains" the insurgent careers of Joseph Holt and Michael Dwyer, county Wicklow, 1798-1803' in Hannigan and Nolan (eds), *Wicklow: History and society*, pp. 379-410; Daniel Gahan, ' "The Black Mob" and the "Babes in the Wood": Wexford in the wake of the rebellion 1798-1806' in *Journal of the Wexford Historical Society*,

no. 13 (1990-1), pp. 92-110; Marianne
Elliot, *Partners in revolution*, pp. 214-
322.

28 T. Bartlett, '"The masters of the
mountains" the insurgent careers of
Joseph Holt and Michael Dwyer,
county Wicklow, 1798-1803', p. 408.

29 Padraig O'Snodaigh, 'Notes on the politics of Kildare at the end of the 18th
century' in *Kildare Arch. Soc. Jn*, vol. xvi
(1981-2), pp. 264-71.

30 John Lindsay, *The shining life and death
of Lord Edward Fitzgerald* (London,
n.d.); Ida Taylor, *The life of Lord
Edward Fitzgerald 1763-1798* (London,
1903); Patrick Byrne, *Lord Edward
Fitzgerald* (London, 1955).

31 Stella Tillyard, *Citizen Lord: Edward
Fitzgerald 1763-1798* (London, 1997), p.
x.

32 Revd John Brady, 'Lawrence O'Connor
– a Meath schoolmaster' in *Irish
Ecclesiastical Record*, vol. xlix (1937),
pp. 281-7; Martin Tierney, 'William
Aylmer 1772-1820' in *Irish Sword*, vol.
iv, no. 23 (1963), pp. 103-7; Seamus
Cummins, 'Pike heads and the
calico printer: Leixlip in '98' in *Kildare
Arch. Soc. Jn*, vol. xvi (1985-6), pp. 418-
31.

33 L.M. Cullen, 'Politics and rebellion:
Wicklow in the 1790s', pp. 411-501;
Ruan O'Donnell, 'The 1798 rebellion in
county Wicklow' in Hannigan and
Nolan (eds), *Wicklow: History and
society* (Dublin, 1994), pp. 341-78; Sr
Mary Duggan, 'County Carlow 1791-
1801: A study in era of revolution'
(M.A., UCD, 1969); Padraig
O'Snodaigh, *'98 and Carlow: A look at
the historians* (Carlow, 1979); J.G.O.
Kerrane, 'The background to the 1798
rebellion in county Meath' (M.A.,
UCD, 1971); Seamus O'Lionsigh, 'The
rebellion of 1798 in county Meath' in
Riocht na Midhe, vol. iii-v (1966-71);
Daniel Gahan, *Wexford 1798, the people's
rising* (Dublin, 1995).

CHAPTER I
KILDARE COUNTY, 1790

1 Arthur Young, *A tour in Ireland 1777-
1779* (2 vols, 1780, Shannon 1970), vol. i,
p. 424.

2 Edward Wakefield, *An account of
Ireland statistical and political* (2 vols,
London, 1812), vol. i, p. 41.

3 Rawson, *Statistical survey*, p. 52.

4 Marc de Bombelles, *Journal des voyage
en Grande Bretagne et Irlande, 1784*, ed.
Jaques Gury (Oxford, 1989), p. 233.

5 William Fitzgerald to Emily
Fitzgerald, Carton 4 Dec. 1777 (NLI
Leinster Papers MS 617) [Brian Vesy
Fitzgerald in a typescript version of the
letters asserts this was incorrectly dated
and should be dated 1787, see NLI MS
13022.]

6 Leinster to Lord Temple, Dublin, 17
Apr. 1788 and Frescati, 16 June 1788
(PRONI Leinster Papers
D.3078/3/4/14,16).

7 Stella Tillyard, *Aristocrats*, p. 357; R.B.
McDowell, *Ireland in the age of
imperialism and revolution 1760-1801*
(Oxford, 1979), pp. 339-42.

8 Tillyard, *Aristocrats*, p. 358.

9 Young, *Tour in Ireland*, p. 30.

10 The countess of Drogheda (ed.), *The
family of Moore*, p. 127; *DNB* (London,
1894), vol. 38, p. 344.

11 See Diary of Edward Stratford (second
earl of Aldborough), 1792 (NLI
Stratford Papers MS 19,164).

12 L.M. Cullen, 'Politics and Rebellion:
Wicklow in the 1790s', p. 421.

13 Valentine Lord Cloncurry, *Personal
recollections*, pp. 19, 21.

14 Miss M.F. Young, 'The La Touche
family of Harristown, county Kildare'
in *Kildare Arch. Soc. Jn*, vol. vii (1912-14),
pp. 33-40

15 Sir F.J. Aylmer, *The Aylmers of Ireland*
(London, 1931), p. 225.

16 A.A. Horner, 'The pre-famine
population of some Kildare towns' in
Kildare Arch. Soc. Jn, vol. xiv (1964-70),
pp. 443-51. These figures are based on

data from the *Journal of the Irish house of commons* (Dublin, 1796-1800), the accuracy of which is questionable; note the divergence between Horner's figures for Kildare town and those of J.H. Andrews arrived at using a contemporary map.

17 Richard Lucas, *A general directory of the kingdom of Ireland*, vol. ii (Dublin, 1788), pp. 103-5.

18 J.H. Andrews, *Kildare* (Irish Historic Towns Atlas no. 1, Dublin, 1986); Horner, 'The pre-famine population of some Kildare towns', p. 451.

19 de Bombelles, *Journal des voyages*, pp. 233-5.

20 de Montbret, 'An 18th- century French traveller in county Kildare', pp. 385-6.

21 Campbell, *A philosophical survey*, p. 95; de Bombelles, *Journal de voyage*, pp. 260-1.

22 Young, *Tour in Ireland*, vol. i, p. 419.

23 Rawson, *Statistical survey*, p. 2.

24 Ibid., p. 7.

25 Young, *Tour in Ireland*, vol. i, p. 423; Brian J. Cantwell, 'Notes on Young's Tour 1777-1779' in *Kildare Arch. Soc. Jn*, vol. xiii (1946-63), p. 136.

26 James Kelly, 'Prosperous and Irish industrialisation in the late eighteenth century' in *Kildare Arch. Soc. Jn*, vol. xvi (1985-6), p. 442; see also A.K. Longfield, 'Prosperous 1776-1798' in *Kildare Arch. Soc. Jn*, vol. xiv (1964-70), pp. 212-31.

27 de Bombelles, *Journal de voyage*, p. 244.

28 V.T.H. and D.R. Delany, *The canals of the south of Ireland* (Plymouth, 1966), pp. 46-7.

29 Ibid., p. 77.

30 Rawson, *Statistical survey*, p. 41.

31 K.H. Connell, *The population of Ireland 1750-1845* (Oxford, 1950), chapter one.

32 This figure is taken from the Dundas Papers. The author, based on the hearth money returns of 1788 (which Bushe also used) reaches the population figure by using the following figures for the number of people in a house: in houses of one

hearth, 6.25, two hearths 5.625, new houses 4.25 and paupers houses 5.2 (NLI Dundas Papers 54/31).

33 Rawson, *Statistical survey*, pp. 2, 23.

34 Viscount Castlereagh, *Memoirs and correspondence of Viscount Castlereagh*, ed. Marquis of Londonderry (12 vols, London, 1848-53), vol. iv, pp. 149, 135.

35 Connell, *Population*, pp. 24-5.

36 Wakefield, *An account of Ireland*, vol. ii , pp. 630-1.

37 Mason, *A statistical account*, vol. iii, p. xlix.

38 E.M. Johnston, 'The state of the Irish House of Commons in 1791' in *R.I.A Proc.*, vol. 59, sec. C, no. 1 (1957-9), p. 30.

39 *FJ*, 27 May 1790.

40 Falkland, *Parliamentary representation, being a political and critical review of all the counties, cities and boroughs of the kingdom of Ireland with regard to this presentation by Falkland* (Dublin, 1790), p. 42; Johnston, 'State of the Irish House of Commons in 1791', pp. 24-5.

41 Falkland, *Parliamentary representation*, p. 42.

42 Ibid., p. 42

43 See Alexander Taylor, *A map of the county of Kildare 1783* (reprint Dublin, 1983).

44 See Minute Book of the Corporation of Harristown 1714-90 (PRONI Leinster Papers D.3078/4/2).

45 Thos. U. Sadlier, 'Kildare members of parliament 1559-1800' in *Kildare Arch. Soc. Jn*, vol. vii (1912-14), pp. 312-14.

46 Falkland, *Parliamentary representation*, p. 42; Minute Books of Naas Corporation, 1665-1842 (TCD MSS 2251-2254).

47 Johnston, 'State of the Irish house of commons in 1791', p. 30.

48 Ibid., p. 30.

49 John Ribton Garstin, 'The high sheriffs of the county Kildare' in *Kildare Arch. Soc. Jn*, vol. ii (1896-99), p. 204.

50 Rawson, *Statistical survey*, p. 36.

51 Grand Jury presentment lists; Lent 1791, 1792, 1795, 1796, 1799, 1801,

1802; Summer 1793, 1796, 1797, 1800, 1802.

52 *The Gentleman's and Citizen's Almanack*, 1795, 1798.

53 Pakenham, *The year of liberty*, p. 60, in a footnote he lists the Fitzgeralds, Conollys, Keatinges, Brownes and Lawlesses.

54 Wakefield, *An account of Ireland*, vol. ii, p. 612.

55 Regency resolutions of Co. Kildare, 12 March 1789 (NLI Wolfe Papers unsorted collection).

CHAPTER 2
POLITICS AND POLITICISATION, 1791-95

1 R.B. McDowell, *Ireland in the age of imperialism and revolution*, pp. 351-461; W.E.H. Lecky, *A history of Ireland in the eighteenth century* (5 vols, London, 1892), vol. iii, pp. 1-211.

2 'Naas Volunteers 1779' in *Kildare Arch. Soc. Jn*, vol. xi (1930-33), pp. 468-9, information on other corps is not available; James Spencer, Rathangan, to John Wolfe, 25 Feb. 1779 (NLI Wolfe Papers); 'Rules and resolutions of the Anna Liffey Club' in *Kildare Arch. Soc. Jn*, vol. xii (1935-45), pp. 124-7.

3 R. Dudley Edwards, 'The minute book of the Catholic Committee 1773-1792' in *Archivium Hibernicum*, vol. ix (1942), pp. 43, 45, 46, 89, 92, 103.

4 Ibid., pp. 103, 117.

5 Ibid., pp. 95, 98.

6 Ibid., pp. 118, 120.

7 Thomas Bartlett, *The fall and rise of the Irish nation: The Catholic question 1690–1830* (Dublin, 1992), pp. 127-8.

8 Edwards, 'The minute book of the Catholic committee 1773-1792', pp. 125, 133-4, 166-7.

9 *FJ*, 27 Dec. 1791.

10 *DEP*, 7 Jan. 1792.

11 *DEP*, 31 Jan. 1792.

12 *DEP*, 7 Feb. 1792.

13 P. O'Snodaigh, 'Notes on the politics of Kildare at the end of the 18th century' in *Kildare Arch. Soc. Jn*, vol. xvi p. 270. He mistakenly dates the address as 1793.

14 William Drennan, *The Drennan letters*, ed. D.A. Chart (Belfast, 1931), p. 71.

15 *FJ*, 17 Dec. 1791.

16 *DEP*, 29 Mar. 1792; Thomas Fitzgerald Papers, 1798 (NAI Reb. Papers 620/42/18). This incident does not seem to mark the reunion of the leading Catholic activists of the county, O'Reilly and Michael Aylmer of Lyons signed the Kenmareite address of thanks in May 1792 (*DEP*, 12 May 1792).

17 *DEP*, 29 Mar. 1792.

18 Theobald Wolfe Tone, *The autobiography of Theobald Wolfe Tone 1763–1798*, ed. R. Barry O'Brien (2 vols, London, 1893), vol. i, pp. 94, 126-7.

19 Bartlett, *The fall and rise of the Irish nation*, pp. 150-1; *FJ*, August-September 1792, *passim*.

20 Curtin, *The United Irishmen*, pp. 49-50.

21 *A full and accurate report of the debates in the parliament of Ireland in the session 1793; On the bill for the relief of his Majesty's Catholic subjects* (Dublin, 1793), pp. xii-xxvi.

22 *DEP*, 8 Dec. 1792.

23 Fitzgerald (ed.), *The earls of Kildare*, second addenda, pp. 267-8; Tillyard, *Citizen Lord*, pp. 133-9.

24 Duke of Leinster to Richard Griffith, 10 December 1792 in Fitzgerald (ed.), op. cit., pp. 268-71.

25 *DEP*, 24 Dec. 1792; NAI Reb. Papers, 620/19/125.

26 R.B. McDowell, 'Proceedings of the Dublin Society of United Irishmen' in *Analecta Hibernica*, vol. xii (1949), p. 58; W.J. MacNeven (ed.), *Pieces of Irish history* (New York, 1807), pp. 64-5.

27 *DEP*, Jan.-Feb. 1793 *passim*.

28 *DEP*, 21, 28 Feb., 2 Mar., 27 Apr. 1793; *The Freeman's Journal* reported its demise on 15 Oct. 1793.

29 *DEP*, 25 July 1793; *FJ*, 23 July 1793.

30 *FJ*, 4 May 1793.

31 *County of Kildare Summer Assizes August the 4th 1793* (n.p., 1794). The Catholics were: Thomas Fitzgerald, John Esmonde, Michael Aylmer, James Archibald, Dominic Wm. O'Reilly and Richard Dease. Lord Edward Fitzgerald was foreman.

32 *DEP*, 25 July 1793.

33 James Alexander, *Some account of the first apparent symptoms of the late rebellion in the county of Kildare, and an adjoining part of the King's County with a ... narrative of some of the most remarkable passages in the rise and progress of the rebellion in the county of Wexford* (Dublin, 1800), p. 18.

34 Printed pamphlet dated Rathcoffey, 1 May 1793 (NAI Reb. Papers 620/20/19).

35 McDowell, 'Proc. of the Dublin Soc. of United Irishmen', pp. 79, 80, 87, 92.

36 *Autobiography of Theobald Wolfe Tone*, vol. i, pp. 126-7.

37 Thomas Russell, *Journals and memoirs of Thomas Russell 1791-5*, ed. C.J. Woods (Dublin, 1991), p. 138.

38 Alexander, *Some account*, pp. 13-22.

39 Ibid., p. 14.

40 Ibid., pp. 14-15.

41 Ibid., p. 19.

42 Leadbeater, *The Leadbeater papers*, vol. i, p. 198.

43 Alexander, *Some account*, p. 19.

44 Henry McAnally, *The Irish Militia 1793-1816* (Dublin, 1949), p. 54.

45 *DEP*, 24 Apr. 1793; *FJ*, 20 Apr. 1793; McAnally, op. cit., p. 54.

46 Thomas Bartlett, 'An end to the moral economy: the Irish militia disturbances of 1793' in *Past and Present*, no. 99 (1983), pp. 49-53; *DEP*, 26 July 1793; Musgrave, *Rebellions*, p. 66.

47 Alexander, *Some account*, p. 15.

48 Ibid., pp. 15-16.

49 Ibid., p. 18.

50 McAnally, *Irish Militia*, p. 54; repeated by P. O'Snodaigh, 'Notes on the Volunteers, Militia, Yeomanry and Orangemen of county Kildare in the 18th century' in *Kildare Arch. Soc. Jn*, vol. xv (1971-6), p. 44.

51 Fitzgerald (ed.), *The earls of Kildare*, second addenda, p. 274.

52 *Drennan letters*, p. 143; Fitzgerald (ed.), op. cit., p. 274; *FJ*, 28 May 1794.

53 *DEP*, 17 June 1794; *FJ*, 19 June 1794.

54 McDermott (ed.), *Memoirs of Lord Edward Fitzgerald*, p. 186.

55 Leadbeater, *The Leadbeater papers*, vol. i, p. 200.

56 *FJ*, 26 July 1794. On 15 June 1793 a meeting of the 'Associations of Kilcullen, Castledermot and Narraghmore' had convened following a disturbance at Kilcullen market. Resolutions were passed condemning 'illegal combinations' and vowing to protect farmers. This fracas was not connected with the militia [*DEP*, 18 June 1793].

57 *DEP*, 18 Aug. 1794.

58 Bartlett, 'An end to the moral economy: the Irish Militia disturbances of 1793', p. 44.

59 *DEP*, 5 Aug. 1794; T. Graves 'Officers of the Kildare Militia 1794-1817' in *Kildare Arch. Soc. Jn*, vol. xii (1935-45), pp. 194-6; Fitzgerald (ed.), *The earls of Kildare*, second addenda, p. 274.

60 Militia Ireland, Kildare 1793-1798 (PRO WO 13/2923); *FJ*, 2 Oct. 1794.

61 N. Curtin, 'The transformation of the United Irishmen into a mass based revolutionary organisation 1794-6', pp. 463-92; L.M. Cullen, 'The internal politics of the United Irishmen', pp. 176-96.

62 Fitzgerald (ed.), *The earls of Kildare*, second addenda, p. 275; *FJ*, 29 Jan. 1795.

63 *DEP*, 27 Jan. 1795; *FJ*, 17 Feb. 1795.

64 *DEP*, 19 Feb. 1795. The Catholics were: Dominic Wm. O'Reilly, Patrick Latten, Daniel Caulfield, Gerald Aylmer, Charles Aylmer, John Cassidy (secretary), James Hussey, Thomas Ryan, Walter Dowdall, Richard Dease, Captain Hussey, John Esmonde, Thomas Dillon and Thomas Fitzgerald (chairman).

65 *DEP*, 19 Feb. 1795.

66 *DEP*, 5 Mar. 1795. The paper later stat-

ed the meeting was attended by people of all religious persuasions and not only Catholics as had been reported elsewhere [*DEP*, 7 Mar. 1795].

67 *DEP*, 5, 7 Mar. 1795.

68 *DEP*, 28 Mar. 1795; *Walker's Hibernian Magazine* (1795, part i, Jan.-June) pp. 272-3.

69 Ibid.

70 McDowell, *Ireland in the age of imperialism and revolution*, pp. 443-4, 470-3; Nancy Curtin, 'The transformation of the United Irishmen into a mass based revolutionary organisation 1794-6', especially pp. 468-76. Her arguments apply largely to Dublin and Ulster.

71 *DEP*, 25 July 1795, seems to indicate a division over the use of military force [favoured by a faction headed by La Touche] to dispel a riot caused by a 'drunken vagrant' which Keatinge effectively dealt with. It may have been at Kilcullen, see above footnote 56.

72 Harristown borough was sold to the La Touche family in 1793 and the duke seems to have been in financial difficulty during this period. See P. O'Snodaigh, 'Notes on the politics of Kildare in the late 18th century', p. 271. He dates the decline to the start of the decade. Not only were Kildare politics affected by the decline of the duke's influence, but his own increasingly minority position accelerated this development.

CHAPTER 3
'TO BE TRUE TO THE FRENCH'

1 Jim Smyth, *The men of no property*, pp. 33-51.

2 'County Meeting, Naas, 9 Nov. 1778' (NLI Wolfe Papers).

3 David Miller, 'The Armagh Troubles 1784-95', in S. Clark and J.S. Donnelly Jr (ed.), *Irish peasants: Violence and political unrest 1780–1914* (Manchester, 1983), pp. 155-91.

4 L.M. Cullen, 'The political structures of the Defenders', p. 118; Jim Smyth, *The men of no property*, pp. 45-51.

5 See Jim Smyth, *The men of no property*, pp. 52-78.

6 J.G.O. Kerrane, 'The background to the 1798 rebellion in Co. Meath' (M.A., UCD, 1971), pp. 25-37.

7 Printed in Bartlett, 'Defenders and Defenderism', p. 391; Kerrane 'Meath', pp. 52-7; see J. Smyth *The men of no property*, pp. 115-16.

8 Deirdre Lindsay believes there was 'some connection' between Fitzwilliam's removal and the upsurge in Defenderism. See D. Lindsay, 'The Fitzwilliam episode revisited' in D. Dickson, D. Keogh and K. Whelan (eds), *The United Irishmen: Republicanism, radicalism and reaction* (Dublin, 1993), p. 205.

9 'Trial of Lawrence O'Connor and Michael Griffin for High Treason' in *Walker's Hibernian Magazine*, 1795, vol. ii (July-Dec.), p. 351. The fullest trial report is contained in this volume, pp. 351-5, 425-34.

10 For biographical details see, Revd John Brady, 'Lawrence O'Connor – A Meath Schoolmaster' in *Irish Ecclesiastical Record*, vol. xlix (Jan.-June 1937), pp. 281-7.

11 An official statement of what occurred can be found in a proclamation issued from a county meeting held at Naas, 24 July 1795. See *FJ*, 28 July 1795. The proclamation is reproduced in Francis Plowden, *An historical view of the state of Ireland* (2 vols, London, 1803), vol. ii, appendix no. xcvii, pp. 235-9.

12 Letter of —— Nevill to 'My Dear Marquis', describing incidents involving Defenders in county Kildare n.d. [mid 1795] (NLI MS 15,060).

13 *FJ*, 28 July 1795.

14 Nevill to My Dear Marquis, n.d. (NLI MS 15,060).

15 Bartlett , 'Defenders and Defenderism in 1795', p. 394.

16 *FJ*, 15 Aug. 1795; Revd John Brady, 'A rebel schoolmaster' in *Irish Booklover*, vol. xxviii, no. 4 (Feb. 1942), p. 92.

17 Lady Louisa Conolly to Thomas Conolly, endorsed 20 July 1795 (PRONI Mc Peake Papers T.3048/B/14); Stella Tillyard, *Aristocrats*, pp. 373-4.

18 Camden to Portland, 15 July 1795 (PRO HO 100/58/136-7).

19 *FJ*, 24 July 1795; Camden later enclosed the resolutions of the meeting in a letter to Portland, Camden to Portland, 24 July 1795 (PRO HO 100/58/157-60).

20 *FJ*, 28 July 1795.

21 *FJ* and *DEP*, July-Aug. 1795 *passim*.

22 Oath of the 'principal inhabitants of Kilcock' against Defenderism, 21 July 1795 (NAI Reb. Papers 620/22/18).

23 *DEP*, 25 July 1795, 143 names are listed.

24 *FJ*, 8, 11 Aug., 26 Sept. 1795.

25 *FJ*, 18 Aug. 1795.

26 *FJ*, 22 Aug. 1795.

27 John Walsh to ——, 20 Aug. 1795 (NAI Reb. Papers 620/22/34).

28 John Walsh, Kilcock, to Sackville Hamilton, 5 Oct. 1795 (NAI Reb. Papers 620/22/44).

29 *Walker's Hibernian Magazine*, 1795, vol. ii (July-Dec.), pp. 352, 354, 425.

30 Ibid., pp. 430-1.

31 Ibid., p. 431.

32 Lecky, *Ireland in the eighteenth century*, vol. iii, p. 392.

33 M.R. Beames, 'Peasant movements, Ireland 1785-1795' in *Journal of Peasant Studies*, vol. ii, no. 4 (1975), p. 506.

34 See T. Bartlett's comments in 'An end to the moral economy: the anti-militia riots of 1793', pp. 194-5; Plowden noted the importance of this event, see Plowden *An historical view of the state of Ireland*, vol. ii, part 1, p. 537.

35 *DEP*, 28 July 1795.

36 Elliot, *Partners in revolution*, p. 58.

37 *Walker's Hibernian Magazine*, 1795, vol. ii (July-Dec.), p. 354.

38 Ibid., pp. 433-4; Camden to Portland, 9 Sept. 1795 (PRO HO 100/58/335-44).

39 J. Bird, Under Sheriff, Co. Kildare to

—— , 27 Mar. 1803 [*sic* 1796] (NAI Reb. Papers 620/23/54).

40 *The martyr of liberty, a poem on the heroic death of L. O'Connor, executed at Naas, in Ireland, on a charge of high treason, Sept. 7th 1796. [sic] Addressed to all the Irish. By an English brother printed for the United Irishmen. 1798* (Dublin, 1798). A hand-written note on the National Library copy states it may have been composed by Thomas Moore while at college. Brady contended the note was in R.R. Madden's handwriting. See John Brady 'Lawrence O'Connor – A Meath schoolmaster', p. 287. *The Freeman's Journal* reported O'Connor had requested his heart be sent to the Dublin United Irishmen, *FJ*, 5 Sept. 1795.

41 The press also latched onto O'Connor's case. See *FJ*, 18 July, 15 Aug., 17 Aug., 5 Sept., 15 Sept. 1795; *DEP*, 19 Sept. 1795.

42 *FJ*, 25 July 1795; Camden to Portland, 29 July 1795 (PRO HO 100/58/171-7).

43 Fitzgerald (ed.), *The earls of Kildare*, second addenda, p. 280.

44 Camden to Portland, 25 Sept. 1795 (PRO HO 100/58/335-44).

45 Robert Harding, Cork, to Edward Cooke, 10 Dec. 1796 (NAI SOC 1015/28).

46 John Wolfe to Edward Cooke, 16 Oct. 1796 (NAI Reb. Papers 620/26/114).

47 John Walsh to Thomas Pelham, 4 Dec. 1796. Enclosed: Edward Byrne and Patrick Connor, Cove of Cork, to Revd Mr Franson, Colgaugh, near Kilcock. (also addressed to Mr Wade and Mr Watson) 14 Nov. 1796 (NAI Reb. Papers 620/26/109 (4)).

48 Eleven men were tried for the crime in early March, *FJ*, 1 Mar., 3 Mar. 1796; Musgrave refers to Hanlon as a magistrate, Musgrave, *Rebellions*, p. 142.

49 A copy of the document in John Walsh's hand omits Wogan Browne's name, perhaps a politically motivated oversight. This copy is enclosed with the original (NAI Reb. Papers 620/26/109 (4)).

50 Edward Byrne and Patrick Connor, Cove of Cork to Revd Mr Franson, Colgaugh, near Kilcock, 14 Nov 1796 (NAI Reb. Papers 620/26/109 (4)). They noted, 'we wrote to Mr Sheriff Aylmer but we had nothing from him.'

51 John Wolfe to Edward Cooke, 27 Dec. 1795 (NAI Reb. Papers 620/22/57).

52 McDermott (ed.), *The memoirs of Lord Edward Fitzgerald*, pp. 162-5

53 On the location of the residence, see L. Boylan, 'Kildare Lodge, Lord Edward Fitzgerald's house' in *Kildare Arch. Soc. Jn*, vol. xvi, no.1 (1977-8) pp. 26-34 and Tillyard, *Citizen Lord*, pp. 174-9, 306-7.

54 McDermott (ed.), *The memoirs of Lord Edward Fitzgerald*, p. 204

55 L.M. Cullen, 'The internal politics of the United Irishmen', pp. 188-92; T.A. Emmet, W.J. MacNeven and A. O'Connor, *Memoire or detailed statement of the origins and progress of the Irish union* (London, 1802), p. 9.

56 James Alexander, *Some account*, p. 22.

57 R.B. McDowell, 'The personnel of the Dublin Society of United Irishmen' in *I.H.S.*, vol. ii (1940), p. 46, 33, 39; NAI Prisoners Petitions and Cases 482, Memorial of George Lube to Lord Lieutenant, 16 May 1800. The petition is included in a letter from John Lube, Summerhill (George's brother) to Edward Cooke 16 May 1800; Miles Byrne, *The memoirs of Miles Byrne*, edited by his widow (1863, Shannon, 1972), p. 275.

58 John Walsh, Kilcock, to Edward Cooke, 27 June 1796 (NAI Reb. Papers 620/23/196).

59 Sir Fenton Aylmer, Donadea, to ——, 28 Aug. 1796 (NAI SOC 1015/23).

60 Lord Aldborough to Edward Cooke, 9 Aug. 1796 (NAI Reb. Papers 620/24/97).

61 Camden to Portland, 6 Aug. 1796 (NAI Reb. Papers 620/18/11/1).

62 'Autobiographical memoir of James Hope' in Madden, *United Irishmen*, 3rd series, vol. i, pp. 238-9.

63 Ibid., p. 257.

64 *The report from the secret committee of the house of commons with an appendix* (Dublin, 1798), pp. 57-8.

65 John Corry, *Odes and elegies, descriptive and sentimental with the patriot a poem; by John Corry* (Newry, 1797).

66 *The report from the secret committee of the house of commons with an appendix*, pp. 80-1.

67 Information of B, Oct. 1796, (i.e. Thomas Boyle of Drumcondra) (NAI Reb. Papers 620/18/3).

68 [M.B.St.L. Keatinge], *On the defence of Ireland* (Dublin, 1795), pp. 35-6. William Drennan noted government's anger at the publication, see *The Drennan letters* (Belfast, 1931), pp. 230, 276.

69 Maurice Keatinge to ——, 6 Sept. 1796, Lord Aldborough to Edward Cooke, 19 Sept. 1796 (NAI Reb. Papers 620/25/133); Sir Fenton Aylmer to ——, 26 Aug 1796 (NAI Reb. Papers 620/24/158).

70 Two letters, Thomas Fitzgerald to duke of Leinster, n.d. [late 1796] (NAI Reb. Papers 620/42/18 Thomas Fitzgerald Papers 1798).

71 *A list of the officers of the several district corps of Ireland together with the date of their respective commissions and an alphabetical index*, Dublin Castle, 26th Jan. 1797 (Dublin, 1797); Oliver Snoddy, 'The Volunteers, Militia, Yeomanry and Orangemen of Co. Kildare in the 18th century' in *Kildare Arch. Soc. Jn*, vol. xv (1971-76), pp. 46-8.

72 Richard Griffith, Millicent, to John Wolfe, 13 Oct. 1796 (NLI Wolfe papers).

73 John Wolfe, Forenaughts, to Edward Cooke, 5 Jan. 1797 (NAI Reb. Papers 620/28/44).

74 John Wolfe to Edward Cooke, 5 Jan. 1797 (NAI Reb. Papers 620/28/51); L.M. Cullen comments on the episode in 'Politics and rebellion: Wicklow in the 1790s', pp. 441-2.

75 Emmet et al., *Memoire or detailed statement of the origins and progress of the Irish union*, p. 11.

76 Leadbeater , *The Leadbeater papers*, vol. i, p. 207.

77 John Wolfe to Edward Cooke, 10 Dec. 1796 (NAI Reb. Papers 620/26/114).

78 John Wolfe to John Beresford, 3 Jan. 1797 (NAI Reb. Papers 620/28/27).

79 John Wolfe to Edward Cooke, 5 Jan. 1797 (NAI Reb. Papers 620/28/44).

80 John Walsh, Kilcock, to Thomas Pelham, 25 Jan. 1797 (NAI Reb. Papers 620/28/145).

81 Rev Thomas F. Knipe to Thomas Pelham, 23 Feb. 1797 (NAI Reb. Papers 620/28/292).

82 Warrant of Thomas Conolly for the arrest of James Murphy for administering illegal oaths, 29 May 1797 (NAI Reb. Papers 620/30/228).

83 *The report from the secret committee of the house of commons with an appendix*, p. 133.

84 E. Boyle to Edward Cooke, 12 May 1797 (NAI Reb. Papers 620/30/61).

85 Information of B, Apr. 1797 (NAI Reb. Papers 620/18/3).

86 Gerard Campbell, *Pamela and Edward Fitzgerald*, pp. 111-12; Tillyard, *Citizen Lord*, pp. 208-11.

CHAPTER 4
LIBERAL FAILURE,
MAY 1797–MAY 1798

1 *FJ*, 2 May 1797.

2 T.B and T.J. Howell, *A complete collection of state trials* (33 vols, London, 1809-28), vol. xxvii, pp. 1127-34. For T.F. Knipe's Orange associations see p. 64; *FJ*, 11 May 1797.

3 Extract of a letter from Edenderry, dated 7 May in *FJ*, 11 May 1797, possibly the work of William Lambert.

4 Stephen Sparks, Castlecarbery, to Thomas Pelham, 14 May 1797 (NAI Reb. Papers 620/30/66); William Lambert to —— , Edenderry, 10 May 1797. Enclosed: Examination of Stephen Hyland of New Chapel in the county Kildare, 10 May 1797 (NAI Reb. Papers 620/30/47).

5 *FJ*, 20, 23 May 1797.

6 36 Geo. III c.20 An act to more effectively suppress insurrections and prevent the disturbance of the publick [*sic*] peace.

7 John Tyrell to Thomas Pelham, 26 Apr. 1797 (NAI Reb. Papers 620/29/315). A copy reply states government's intention to proclaim.

8 List of justices of the peace assembled at Naas, 8 May 1797 who signed the memorial for proclaiming the barony of Carbery (NLI Wolfe Papers). The list has thirty-three names, while Wogan Browne stated in a letter to Pelham that thirty-five magistrates had been present (Wogan Browne to Thomas Pelham, 9 May 1797 NAI Reb. Papers 620/30/46). The list contains the names of the twenty-one memorialists, perhaps Wolfe omitted abstentions.

9 Sir Fenton Aylmer to —— , 8 May 1797 (NAI Reb. Papers 620/30/38). He seems to suggest the meeting took place on 7 May.

10 L.M. Cullen, 'Politics and rebellion: Wicklow in the 1790s', p. 443.

11 Wogan Browne to Thomas Pelham, 9 May 1797 (NAI Reb. Papers 620/30/46).

12 (Copy of) duke of Leinster to Camden, 25 April 1797 (PRO HO 100/69/238-9); Fitzgerald (ed.), *The earls of Kildare*, second addenda, p. 291. This work dates the letter 26 April.

13 *DEP*, 2 May 1797.

14 *FJ*, 1 June 1797.

15 *DEP*, 13 May 1797.

16 *DEP*, 23 May 1797.

17 James Gordon, *History of the rebellion in Ireland in the year 1798* (Dublin, 1801), p. 251; Richard Griffith to John Wolfe, 5 May 1797 (NLI Wolfe Papers).

18 *DEP*, 27 May 1797.

19 Thomas Pelham to Wogan Browne and Hon. V.B. Lawless, Dublin Castle, 25 May 1797 in W.J. Fitzpatrick, *The life, times and contemporaries of Lord Cloncurry*, p. 132; Cloncurry, *Personal recollections*, pp. 52-3.

20   *FJ*, 20 May 1797; W.J. Fitzpatrick, *The life, times and contemporaries of Lord Cloncurry*, p. 132; Valentine Lord Cloncurry, *Personal recollections*, p. 52.

21   Richard Nevill to —— , 28 May 1797 (NAI Reb. Papers 620/30/221). The enclosed handbill was a shorter version of the liberal press statement also dated 26 May, see *DEP*, 27 May 1797.

22   Wogan Browne to Thomas Pelham, 29 May 1797. Enclosed: one handbill and three newspaper cuttings (NAI Reb. Papers 620/30/237).

23   'To the kings most excellent majesty. The humble petition of the governor, magistrates, freeholders and inhabitants of the county of Kildare' (NAI Reb. Papers 620/53/35 one copy, 620/54/41 five copies); C.H. Teeling, *History of the Irish rebellion of 1798 and sequel to the history of the Irish rebellion of 1798* (Shannon, 1972, IUP reprint of 1876 edition), pp. 162-4.

24   Stephen Sparks, Castlecarbery, to Mr Pelham, 15 June 1797. Petition enclosed (NAI Reb. Papers 620/31/103).

25   J.W. [McNally] to —— , 29 May 1797 (NAI Reb. Papers 620/10/121/62); *The Press*, 16 Dec. 1797 repeated this assertion.

26   Cloncurry, *Personal recollections*, p. 51; C.H. Teeling, *History of the Irish rebellion of 1798*, p. 162.

27   *DEP*, 10 Oct. 1797; *FJ*, 16 Oct. 1797 'A few observations on the Co. Kildare petition.'

28   Camden to Portland, [correspondence between Leinster and Camden enclosed] 28 Apr, 19 May 1797 (PRO HO 100/69/236-245, 324-9); an edited version was published in Fitzgerald (ed.), *The earls of Kildare*, second addenda, pp. 291-4, 305-6.

29   'Lady Lucy's Diary' in Gerald Campbell, *Edward and Pamela Fitzgerald*, p. 119.

30   Leinster to Carhampton, Leinster House, 9 May 1797 in Fitzgerald (ed.), *The earls of Kildare*, second addenda, pp. 294-5.

31   Carhampton to Leinster, Royal Hospital, 17 May 1797, Leinster to Carhampton, n.d., in Fitzgerald (ed.), *The earls of Kildare*, pp. 296-305.

32   *The report from the secret committee of the house of commons with an appendix*, p. 255.

33   Michael Aylmer to Thomas Pelham, 24 May 1797. Enclosed: Lord Carhampton to Michael Aylmer and (copy) Pelham to Aylmer, 26 May 1797 (NAI Reb. Papers 620/30/172).

34   Tenison Graves, 'Officers of the Kildare militia 1794-1817', p. 194; Fitzgerald (ed.), *The earls of Kildare*, second addenda, p. 306; *FJ*, 10 June 1797.

35   J. Carlisle to John Wolfe, Leinster Street, n.d. [May or June 1797] (NLI Wolfe Papers).

36   Tenison Graves, 'Officers of the Kildare militia 1794-1817', pp. 194-6.

37   *The parliamentary register or history of the proceedings and debates of the house of commons of Ireland* (17 vols, Dublin, 1782-1801), vol. xvii, p. 570.

38   Fitzgerald (ed.), *The earls of Kildare*, second addenda, p. 311.

39   Ibid., p. 312.

40   *DEP*, 18 July 1797; Cloncurry, *Personal recollections*, p. 54.

41   *Belfast Newsletter*, 31 July 1797 in G.C. Bolton, *The passing of the Irish act of union* (Oxford, 1966), p. 153

42   *DEP*, 20, 22, 25 July 1797.

43   *DEP*, 27 July 1797.

44   *DEP*, 3 Aug. 1797; Cloncurry, *Personal recollections*, p. 54.

45   Robert Graydon to John Wolfe, 27 July 1797, William Grattan to [John Wolfe], 27 July 1797 (NLI Wolfe Papers); *DEP*, 1 Aug. 1797.

46   John Wolfe to —— , 28 July 1797 (NAI OP 34/8).

47   L.M. Cullen, 'Politics and rebellion: Wicklow in the 1790s', p. 421.

48   *DEP*, 18 July 1797; Mary Leadbeater, *The Leadbeater papers*, vol. i, pp. 209-10.

49   Thos U. Sadlier, 'Kildare members of parliament 1559-1800' in *Kildare Arch.*

Soc. Jn, vol. vii (1912-14), pp. 314-16, vol. xiii (1915-17), pp. 73-5, 489-501, vol. xx (1920-22), pp. 166-73.

50 Fitzgerald (ed.), *The earls of Kildare*, second addenda, pp. 312-13.

51 Cloncurry, *Personal recollections*, p. 57; Fitzpatrick, *The life, times and contemporaries of Lord Cloncurry*, pp. 128, 142.

52 *FJ*, 11, 27 May 1797.

53 Richard Cane, Maynooth, to Thomas Pelham, 27 May 1797 (NAI Reb. Papers 620/30/210).

54 Richard Nevill to —— , 21 May 1797 (NAI Reb. Papers 620/30/138).

55 John Wolfe to Thomas Pelham, 23 May 1797 (NAI Reb. Papers 620/30/156).

56 John Wolfe, Balbriggan, to Edward Cooke, 23 June 1797, marked 'private' (NAI Reb. Papers 620/31/141).

57 [Theobald Wolfe] to John Wolfe, n.d. [1797] (NLI Wolfe Papers).

58 John Ravell Walsh, Strawberry Lodge, near Naas to —— , 6 June 1797 (NAI Reb. Papers 620/31/45).

59 Maurice Tracey, Carlow, to Thomas Pelham, 26 May 1797 (NAI Reb. Papers 620/30/198).

60 Robert Cornwall to —— , 29 Aug. 1797 (NAI Reb. Papers 620/34/18).

61 Benjamin O'Neale Stratford to —— , 9 June 1797 (NAI Reb. Papers 620/31/65).

62 Lord Aldborough, Castledermot, to Thomas Pelham, 29 Sept. 1797 (NAI Reb. Papers 620/32/147).

63 *FJ*, 29 Aug 1797; J. Pollock, Philipstown, to —— , 30 Aug. 1797 (NAI Reb. Papers 620/32/89).

64 *County [Kildare] at large Summer Assizes 1797* (Carlow, 1797).

65 See p. 45.

66 *The Press*, 16 Nov. 1797 contained a full trial report. *FJ*, 29 Aug. 1797; *DEP*, 26 Sept. 1797.

67 J. Pollock, Philipstown to —— , 30 Aug. 1797 (NAI Reb. Papers 620/32/89).

68 *FJ*, 14 Oct. 1797 included a full trial report; Fitzpatrick, *The life, times and contemporaries of Lord Cloncurry*, pp. 137-41; *The Press*, 19 Nov. 1797.

69 J. Pollock, Philipstown, to —— , 30 Aug. 1797 (NAI Reb. Papers 620/32/89); O'Kelly, *General history*, p. 22.

70 Arthur Wolfe to Edward Cooke, 24 Aug. 1797. Eight enclosures, including: Robert Day, Philipstown, to Arthur Wolfe, 19 Aug. 1797 (NAI Reb. Papers 620/34/14).

71 Richard Nevill to —— , 2 Nov. 1797 (NAI Reb. Papers 620/33/7).

72 John Wolfe to Edward Cooke, 20 Nov. 1797 (NAI Reb. Papers 620/33/82). The quote is taken from an enclosure in Wolfe's hand which he urged should be burned so the 'hand' was not recognised.

73 John Wolfe to Edward Cooke, 20 Nov. 1797 (NAI Reb. Papers 620/33/82).

74 Capt. Richard L. Swayne to Gen. Eustace, 21 Dec. 1797 (NAI Reb. Papers 620/33/172).

75 Richard Nevill to —— , 10 Dec. 1797. Enclosed: a pamphlet entitled 'To the men of property of the Co. Down' (NAI Reb. Papers 620/33/139)

76 Lord Downshire, Edenderry, to Edward Cooke, 9 Dec. 1797 (NAI Reb. Papers 620/33/135); Thomas J. Rawson to John Wolfe, 10 Dec. 1797 (NLI Wolfe Papers).

77 A. Weldon, Athy, to John Wolfe, 24 Dec. 1797 (NLI Wolfe Papers).

78 R. Abercromby, Royal Hospital, to Thomas Pelham, 12 Dec. 1797. Enclosed: two letters from Gen. Dundas transmitting two letters with nine depositions from Brigadier General Wilford relative to the Athy packet boat robbery (NAI Reb. Papers 620/33/147); Patrick O'Kelly, *General history*, p. 27.

79 Thomas Pope, Athy, to William Green, 10 April 1798 (NAI Reb. Papers 620/36/156).

80 Reynolds, *Life*; Thomas Reynolds, Kilkea Castle, county Kildare, information before the Privy Council, 1798 (NAI Reb. Papers 620/3/32/23). This testimony was reproduced in *The report from the secret committee of the*

house of commons with an appendix, pp. 165-74.

81 Reynolds, *Life*, vol. i, pp. 181-2.

82 Ibid., vol. i, p. 183.

83 Ibid., pp. 183-6; Thomas Reynolds ... information before the Privy Council, 1798 (NAI Reb. Papers 620/3/32/23).

84 Reynolds, *Life*, vol. i, pp. 185-6; Thomas Reynolds ... information before the Privy Council, 1798 (NAI Reb. Papers 620/3/32/23).

85 *The report from the secret committee of the house of commons with an appendix*, p. 136.

86 R.B. McDowell and E. Curtis (eds), *Irish historical documents* (Dublin, 1943, reprinted 1977), pp. 238-42.

87 Thomas Reynolds ... information before the Privy Council, 1798 (NAI Reb. Papers 620/3/32/23).

88 O'Kelly, *General history*, p. 26.

89 J. Pollock, Philipstown, to —— , 30 Aug. 1797 (NAI Reb. Papers 620/32/89).

90 Information of B [Thomas Boyle], n.d. (NAI Reb. Papers 620/18/3).

91 Information about Lord Edward Fitzgerald headed 'Leixlip Business', n.d., Information about Lord Edward Fitzgerald, Tanner and Bird, n.d. (TCD Sirr Papers 869/9 ff. 7-8, 92-3); Seamus Cummins, 'Pike heads and the calico printer: Leixlip in 98' in *Kildare Arch. Soc. Jn*, vol. xvi (1985-86) pp. 418-31.

92 Madden, *United Irishmen*, 3rd series, vol. iii, pp. 296-360; L.M. Cullen, 'Politics and rebellion: Wicklow in the 1790s', pp. 449-51.

93 Thomas Reynolds ... information before the Privy Council, 1798 (NAI Reb. Papers 620/3/32/23).

94 Lord Tyrawley, Monasterevan to —— , 8 June 1798. Enclosed: Information of James Molloy of Springfield, n.d. [late May/early June 1798] (NAI Reb. Papers 620/56/191).

95 Thomas Reynolds ... information before the Privy Council, 1798 (NAI Reb. Papers 620/3/32/23).

96 Reynolds, *Life*, vol. i, pp. 186-90.

97 W.J. Fitzpatrick, *The sham squire and the informers of 1798* (Dublin, third edition, 1895), pp. 227-46. For Cope's statement see pp. 230-3.

98 Thomas Reynolds ... information before the Privy Council, 1798 (NAI Reb. Papers 620/3/32/23); Reynolds, *Life*, vol. i, pp. 205-7, 212-15.

99 Examination of George Cummins, 13 March 1798 (NAI Reb. Papers 620/36/9a).

100 Thomas Reynolds ... information before the Privy Council, 1798 (NAI Reb. Papers 620/3/32/23).

101 Reynolds, *Life*, vol. i, p. 213.

102 Untitled [account of searches carried out by John Wolfe, 10 Jan. 1798] (NLI Wolfe Papers).

103 Thomas Reynolds ... information before the Privy Council, 1798 (NAI Reb. Papers 620/3/32/23).

104 Information of James Kelly, Co. Kildare, 14 May 1798, Information of John Chandler, Shrowland, Parish of Athy, 17 May 1798 (NAI Reb papers 620/37/66, 98).

105 Col. Campbell to Edward Cooke, 15 May 1798 (NAI Reb papers 620/37/66).

106 Col. Campbell to Lord Castlereagh, 29 Apr. 1798. Enclosed: *A short answer to a brief caution to the Roman Catholics of Ireland by A Liberty Boy* (Dublin, 1792), 'United Irishmen of Dublin 7 June 1793' (NAI Reb papers 620/36/216); Thomas Fitzgerald Papers, 1798 (Reb. Papers 620/42/18).

107 Thomas Fitzgerald Papers, 1798. An 'Orange Oath', hand-written (NAI Reb papers 620/42/18).

108 Thomas Fitzgerald Papers, 1798. Information of Thomas Fitzgerald, 10 May 1798 (NAI Reb papers 620/42/18). For Fitzgerald's account of the interview see: T. Fitzgerald esq ... to James Bernard Clinch esq., 20 Dec. 1802 in Madden, *United Irishmen*, 3rd series, vol. ii, pp. 340-4.

109 Thomas Fitzgerald to J. Parnell, 23 Mar. 1798, Thomas Fitzgerald to —— , 21 July 1798 (NAI Reb. Papers 620/36/59a, 620/37/118).

110 O'Kelly, *General history*, pp. 41-2

111 Thomas Reynolds ... information before the Privy Council, 1798 (NAI Reb. Papers 620/3/32/23); Reynolds, *Life*, vol. i, p. 214; Examination of Patrick Germaine, 10 May 1798, Information of Philip Germaine, 10 May 1798, Examination of Luke Brannick, 10 May 1798 (NAI Reb. Papers 620/37/48, 620/37/49, 620/37/50).

112 Camden to Portland, 11 March 1798 (PRO HO 100/75/207).

113 Kildare county gentlemen contemplating co-operation with the people, as meeting to be held, n.d. (NAI Reb. Papers 620/51/118).

114 *Drennan letters*, p. 274; R.R. Madden, *United Irishmen*, 2nd edn, 4 vols (1858-60), vol. ii, p. 405; Teeling, *History of the Irish rebellion of 1798*, p. 81.

115 Cloncurry, *Personal recollections*, pp. 177-8.

116 Richard Nevill to —, 21 May 1797 (NAI Reb. Papers 620/30/38).

117 Cloncurry, op. cit., p. 167; William Sampson, *Memoirs* (New York, 1807) does not mention Aylmer; Tenison Graves, 'Officers of the Kildare Militia 1794-1817', p. 195.

118 Teeling, *History of the Irish rebellion of 1798*, pp. 84-5

119 *The report from the secret committee of the house of commons with an appendix*, p. 177.

120 Reynolds, *Life*, vol. i, pp. 195-6; Musgrave, Rebellions, p. 203.

121 Thomas Rawson to [Wolfe], 6 Jan. 1798 (NLI Wolfe Papers).

122 Capt. Richard L. Swayne to Major General Needham, 1 Jan. 1798, Dundas to Abercromby, 4 Jan. 1798 (NAI Reb. Papers 620/35/1, 620/35/17); *The Press*, 13 Jan. 1798.

123 Reynolds, *Life*, vol. i, p. 195; Musgrave, *Rebellions*, pp. 197-8; Dundas to Pelham 2 Feb. 1798 [*sic* – March], Dundas to Pelham, n.d. (NAI SOC 3160/1-2); J. Barrington, Naas, to Edward Cooke, 22 Mar. 1798, Solicitor general to —, Naas, 22 Mar. 1798 (Reb. Papers 620/36/47, 620/52/120)

124 Richard Nevill to —, 10 Dec. 1797 (NAI Reb. Papers 620/33/139).

125 Thomas J. Rawson to John Wolfe, 10 Dec. 1797 (NLI Wolfe Papers).

126 Thomas Rawson to John Wolfe, n.d. 'Thursday evening' (NLI Wolfe Papers).

127 Ibid., also letters dated 10 Dec. 1797, 24 Dec. 1797 and 6 Jan. 1798 (NLI Wolfe Papers).

128 A. Weldon to Col. Wolfe, 18 Jan. 1798. Weldon had opposed the use of proclamation the previous October, Weldon to Wolfe, 24 Oct. 1797 (NLI Wolfe Papers).

129 Thomas Rawson to John Wolfe, n.d. 'Sunday morning' (NLI Wolfe Papers).

130 [copy of] John Wolfe to Thomas Pelham, 21 Jan. 1798 (NLI Wolfe Papers). The sentiments are repeated in a letter to Edward Cooke of the same day, John Wolfe to Edward Cooke, 21 Jan. 1798 (NAI Reb. Papers 620/35/52).

131 Sir Fenton Aylmer to John Wolfe, 23 Jan. 1798 (NLI Wolfe Papers).

132 [copy of] John Wolfe to Sir Fenton Aylmer, 23 Jan. 1798 (NLI Wolfe Papers).

133 [copy of] John Wolfe to Thomas Pelham, 27 Jan. 1798 (NLI Wolfe Papers).

134 An account of the several parts of the kingdom of Ireland that have been proclaimed, n.d. (PRO HO 100/77/346-351).

135 Mary L. Duggan, 'County Carlow 1791-1801 a study in an age of revolution' (M.A. UCD 1969) pp. 125-43.

136 Aiken McClelland, *The formation of the Orange Order* ([Belfast, 1971]), p. 13.

137 J.H., J.D., C.W. and D.J. to J.W. Kane Blackwood, 4 Mar. 1798 (NAI Reb. Papers 620/36/1); L.M. Cullen, 'Politics and rebellion: Wicklow in the 1790s', pp. 471-2.

138 Copy of a list of members of the Orange Lodge 176, Dublin City, 1798 (NLI MSS 5398); William Blacker and

Robert H. Wallace, *The formation of the Orange Order 1795-98*, ed. Cecil Fitzpatrick (Belfast, 1994), pp. 117-18; Duggan, 'County Carlow 1791-1801', pp. 131-3.

139 Rawson floated the idea to Wolfe in early April, Thomas Rawson to John Wolfe, 1 Apr. 1798 (NAI Reb. Papers 620/36/109); *DEP*, 24 Apr. 1798.

140 Thomas Rawson to John Wolfe, 9 Nov. 1798 (NLI Wolfe Papers).

141 See p. 69.

142 *FJ*, 4 Apr. 1798; *Castlereagh correspondence*, vol. i, p. 164.

143 Camden to Portland, 5 Apr. 1798 (PRO HO 100/80/173-4).

144 'Notice to the inhabitants of Kildare' dated Kildare, 3 Apr. 1798 in *Castlereagh correspondence*, vol. i, pp. 169-70 and PRO HO 100/80/177-8.

145 *Castlereagh correspondence*, vol. i, pp. 186-7; Pakenham, *The year of liberty*, pp. 64-5. Pakenham provides an account of disarming in Kildare see pp. 66-75.

146 *Drennan letters*, p. 273.

147 Reynolds, *Life*, vol. i, pp. 216-17.

148 Ibid., pp. 218-19, 223.

149 Ibid., pp. 223-31.

150 O'Kelly, *General history*, p. 41; Thomas Fitzgerald to ——, 21 July 1798 (NAI Reb. Papers 620/37/118); T. Fitzgerald esq ... to James Bernard Clinch esq., 20 Dec. 1802 in Madden, *United Irishmen*, 3rd series, vol. ii, pp. 340-4; *DEP*, 14 May 1798.

151 Information of Patrick Whelan, 1804 (NAI Reb. Papers 620/50/38/67).

152 O'Kelly, *General history*, pp. 40-1; E. Kelly, Monasterevan, to John Carleton, 2 May 1798 (NAI Reb. Papers 620/37/6).

153 *DEP*, 14 May 1798; Evidence of Lt. Caulfield, n.d. [1798] (NAI Reb. Papers 620/17/34).

154 *Drennan letters*, p. 274; Madden, *United Irishmen*, 1st series (Dublin, 1842) vol. ii, p. 152.

155 William Farrell, *The autobiography of William Farrell of Carlow*, ed. Roger McHugh (Dublin, 1949), p. 75.

156 O'Kelly, *General history*, p. 42; Leadbeater, *The Leadbeater papers*, vol. ii, p. 216.

157 T. Fitzgerald esq ... to James Bernard Clinch esq., 20 Dec. 1802 in Madden, *United Irishmen*, 3rd series, vol. ii, pp. 340-4.

158 Campbell to Edward Cooke, 14 May 1798, Campbell to ——, 15 May 1798 (NAI Reb. Papers 620/37/67, 620/37/78).

159 Letter from Baltinglass to Edward Cooke, 14 May 1798 (NAI Reb. Papers 620/3/32/5).

160 Leadbeater, *The Leadbeater papers*, vol. ii, pp. 213-16.

161 Lewis Morgan, Monasterevan, to John Lees, 2 May 1798. Enclosed: —— to John Lees, Kilcullen, 9 May 1798 (NAI Reb. Papers 620/37/8); *Castlereagh correspondence*, vol. i, p. 185.

162 *Castlereagh correspondence*, vol. i, pp. 188-9.

163 Camden to Portland, 11 May 1798 (PRO HO 100/76/170-7).

164 General Dundas to Edward Cooke, 16 May 1798 (NAI Reb. Papers 620/37/90).

165 Louisa Conolly to William Ogilvie, 21 May 1798 in McDermott (ed.), *The memoirs of Lord Edward Fitzgerald*, p. 326.

166 Bernard Duggan's narrative (TCD Madden Papers 873/30).

167 Musgrave, *Rebellions*, pp. 234-5.

168 Madden, *United Irishmen*, 3rd. series, vol. ii, pp. 97-8. This contradicts Walter (Watty) Cox's account of Swayne, the archetypal pitchcapper, *The Irish Magazine*, vol. iii, (1810) pp. 49-50.

169 Examination of Luke Brannick, 8 May 1798, Examination of John Pendred, n.d. (620/52/75), Examination of Patrick Germaine, 10 May 1798 (Reb. Papers 620/37/48), Examination of Philip Germaine, 10 May 1798 (Reb. Papers 620/37/49), Examination of Luke Brannick, 10 May 1798 (Reb. Papers 620/37/50), Examination of David Fardy, 5 May 1798 (Reb. Papers

620/37/25), Copy of information of Philip and Patrick Germaine, n.d. (Reb. Papers 620/52/75)

170 Information of James Kelly, Co. Kildare, 14 May 1798, Information of John Chandler, Shrowland, Parish of Athy, 17 May 1798 (NAI Reb papers 620/37/66, 98).

171 Thomas Reynolds ... information before the Privy Council, 1798 (NAI Reb. Papers 620/3/32/23); Reynolds, *Life*, vol. i, p. 212; Madden, *The United Irishmen*, second edn, vol. 1, p. 417.

172 Reynolds, *Life*, vol. 1, pp. 213-15.

173 Ibid., vol. 1, pp. 220-4; Madden, *The United Irishmen*, second edn, vol. 1, pp. 414-15.

174 O'Kelly, *General history*, pp. 33, 35.

175 *The report from the secret committee of the house of commons with an appendix*, pp. 233-4, Instructions drawn up by the committee of Leinster 19 April 1798. The measures are summarised by Ruan O'Donnell, 'General Joseph Holt and the Rebellion of 1798 in county Wicklow' (M.A., UCD 1991), pp. 72-3.

176 Musgrave, *Rebellions*, app. xv, p. 61.

177 Ibid.; List of United Irish returns in Leinster received from Sirr, n.d. (NAI Reb. Papers 620/37/29).

178 See p. 60.

179 Statement issued by T.J. Rawson, Glasealy, 27 January 1798. Printed in Musgrave, *Rebellions*, appendix xv, p. 65.

180 Return of arms, a smith at Celbridge (NAI Reb. Papers 620/52/105).

181 O'Kelly, *General history*, p. 43.

182 Madden, *United Irishmen*, 3rd series, vol. ii, p. 101.

183 *The report from the secret committee of the house of commons with an appendix*, p. 320.

184 O'Kelly, *General history*, p. 43.

185 Gosford to General Craig, Naas, 15 July 1798 (NAI Reb. Papers 620/39/76).

186 Thomas Reynolds ... information before the Privy Council, 1798 (NAI Reb. Papers 620/3/32/23).

CHAPTER 5
THE 1798 REBELLION IN COUNTY KILDARE, 24 MAY–30 MAY

1 The most detailed accounts of the Kildare rebellion are provided by Musgrave, *Rebellions*, pp. 233-300, 526-30 and O'Kelly, *General history*, pp. 57-96, 192-3, 262-8. Other useful nineteenth century accounts include: Gordon, *History of the rebellion in Ireland in the year 1798*, pp. 83-102, 213-14; Rawson, *Statistical survey*, pp. v-xxiv; Teeling, *The history of the Irish rebellion of 1798*, pp. 83-6, 93-5, 235-8, 275-83, 289; W.H. Maxwell, *History of the Irish rebellion of 1798* (first published 1845, London, 1903), pp. 60-83; Kavanagh, *A popular history of the rebellion of 1798*, pp. 25-52. For the most recent accounts see: S. O'Muirtile, *Kildare 1798 commemoration* (Kildare, 1948); P. MacSuibhne, *Kildare in '98* (Naas, 1978); T. Pakenham, *The year of liberty*, pp. 107-36, 158-9, 274-7; McDowell, *Ireland in the age of imperialism and revolution 1760-1801*, pp. 616-22, 635-6.

2 Thomas Graham, '"An union of power?" The United Irish Organisation: 1795-1798' in Dickson, Keogh and Whelan (eds), *The United Irishmen: Radicalism, republicanism and reaction* (Dublin, 1993), p. 251; idem., 'Dublin in 1798: the key to the planned insurrection' in Keogh and Furlong (eds), *The mighty wave: The 1798 rebellion in Wexford* (Dublin, 1996), pp. 65-78.

3 *The report from the secret committee of the house of commons with an appendix*, p. 146.

4 S. Sproule to J. Lees, received 1/2 past 4, 23 May [1798] (NAI Reb. Papers, 620/51/118); Graham, '"An union of power?" The United Irish organisation: 1795-1798', p. 253.

5 Lord Gosford, Naas, to General Lake (copy), 24 May 1798 (NAI Reb. Papers, 620/27/152); Warrant for the arrest of

Michael Reynolds ... for 'treasonable
practices' signed by Castlereagh, 6 May
1798 (TCD Sirr Papers 869/6 f.2).
6 Musgrave, *Rebellions*, p. 233.
7 Lord Gosford, Naas, to General Lake
   (copy), 24 May 1798 (NAI Reb. Papers,
   620/27/152).
8 Ibid.; Musgrave, *Rebellions*, pp. 233-4;
   O'Kelly, *General history*, pp. 58-9.
9 O'Kelly, *General history*, pp. 58-9.
10 Madden, *United Irishmen*, 3rd series,
   vol. ii, p. 98.
11 Musgrave, *Rebellions*, p. 235.
12 Madden, *United Irishmen*, 3rd series,
   vol. ii, p. 98.
13 Musgrave, *Rebellions*, pp. 234-5.
14 Affidavit of Thomas Davis of
   Prosperous, 16 Sept. 1798 (TCD MS
   871 Depositions 1798 f. 81). Printed in
   Musgrave, *Rebellions*, appendix xv, pp.
   67-8.
15 Musgrave, *Rebellions*, pp. 234-5; Richard
   Griffith, Naas, to Thomas Pelham, 4
   June 1798 (BL, Pelham Papers Add.
   MS 33,105 ff.380-5).
16 Madden, *United Irishmen*, 3rd series,
   vol. ii, pp. 99-100.
17 Musgrave, *Rebellions*, p. 237.
18 Ibid., pp. 236-9; Information of Jane
   Davis, Prosperous, wife of Thomas
   Davis now Cook St Dublin, 20 Oct.
   1798, Information of John Williams of
   the city of Dublin, captain of the late
   120th regiment of foot, 20 Oct. 1798,
   Information of Mary Eldon, wife of
   Nicholas Eldon, Oct 1798 (NAI Reb.
   Papers 620/40/174).
19 Musgrave, *Rebellions*, p. 240.
20 Richard Griffith, Naas, to Thomas
   Pelham, 4 June 1798 (B.L., Pelham
   Papers Add. MS 33,105 ff.380-5).
21 Madden, *United Irishmen*, 3rd series,
   vol. ii, p. 104.
22 Ibid., pp. 100-4; Musgrave, *Rebellions*,
   p. 242; Richard Griffith, Naas, to
   Thomas Pelham, 4 June 1798 (BL,
   Pelham Papers Add. MS 33,105 ff. 380-
   5); NLI L.O. Folder 6 (1798) 27 Official
   Bulletin, Dublin Castle, 13-14 June
   1798.
23 Musgrave, *Rebellions*, pp. 258-9.

24 Ibid., pp. 259-60; O'Kelly, *General history*, pp. 67-8; Rawson, *Statistical
   survey*, p. vii.
25 Musgrave, *Rebellions*, p. 260; O'Kelly,
   General history, p. 68; Rawson,
   Statistical survey, pp. viii-x; NLI L.O.
   Folder 6 (1798) 10 Printed Pamphlet:
   Gen. Dundas to Castlereagh, 25 May
   1798.
26 For the rebellion in west Wicklow see
   Ruan O'Donnell, 'The 1798 rebellion in
   county Wicklow' in Hannigan and
   Nolan (eds), *Wicklow: History and
   society* (Dublin, 1994), pp. 346-50.
27 Musgrave, *Rebellions*, p. 243.
28 O'Donnell, 'The 1798 Rebellion in
   county Wicklow', pp. 347-8.
29 Ibid., p. 349.
30 Luke Cullen Papers, p. 29 (NLI MS
   9762).
31 O'Donnell, 'The 1798 Rebellion in
   county Wicklow', p. 349.
32 Information as to Baltinglass, 29 May
   1798 (NAI Reb. Papers 620/37/211A).
33 Examinations of Joseph Dale of
   Fonstown, Joseph Whitaker, James
   McKeever, John Jeffries, Mary Jeffries,
   Catherine Lucas, Thomas Corry,
   William Cope, Darby Kehoe, and
   Robert Cooke, all of Narraghmore, n.d.
   (NAI Reb Papers 620/51/58) probably
   sworn on 26 May 1798, see Musgrave,
   Rebellions, p. 277.
34 T. Rawson to John Wolfe, 9 Nov. 1798
   (NLI Wolfe Papers); Musgrave,
   Rebellions, pp. 275-6.
35 List of East Narragh Yeomanry and
   their roles during the rebellion [in
   Rawson's hand], n.d. [late 1798] (NLI
   Wolfe Papers).
36 Leadbeater, *The Leadbeater papers*, vol.
   i, p. 218; Musgrave, *Rebellions*, pp. 275-6;
   T. Rawson to John Wolfe, 9 Nov. 1798
   (NLI Wolfe Papers).
37 Leadbeater, *The Leadbeater papers*, vol.
   i, p. 218.
38 Ibid., vol. i, pp. 219-20; Lord
   Aldborough to William Elliot, 27 May
   1798 (NAI Reb. Papers 620/37/182);
   Diary of Edward Stratford, 1798 (NLI
   MS 19,165)

printed in E.M. Richardson, *Long forgotten days (leading to Waterloo)* (London, 1928), chapter xxii.

39   Leadbeater, *The Leadbeater papers*, vol. i, p. 222.

40   T. Rawson to John Wolfe, 9 Nov. 1798 (NLI Wolfe Papers); Musgrave, *Rebellions*, p. 277; O'Kelly, *General history*, pp. 66-7.

41   O'Kelly, *General history*, pp. 66-7; Leadbeater, *The Leadbeater papers*, vol. i, p. 222.

42   Lord Aldborough to William Elliot, 5 June 1798. Two enclosures: list of rebels, Revd C. Robinson, Baltinglass, to Lord Aldborough, Dublin, 3 June 1798 (NAI Reb. Papers 620/38/51).

43   Leadbeater, *The Leadbeater papers*, vol. i, pp. 222-3; Musgrave, *Rebellions*, p. 278; T. Rawson to John Wolfe, 9 Nov. 1798 (NLI Wolfe Papers); Rawson, *Statistical survey*, p. xxiv.

44   Musgrave, *Rebellions*, pp. 248-9, 251.

45   Ibid., p. 245.

46   Ibid., p. 246; Statement of charges preferred against James Magee by Elizabeth Crawford (NAI Reb. Papers 620/7/74/36); Petition of Elizabeth Crawford to the committee for relief of suffering loyalists (TCD MS 871 Depositions 1798 f. 57).

47   Musgrave, *Rebellions*, p. 247.

48   Lord Tyrawley, Monasterevan, to —— , 8 June 1798. Enclosed: Information of James Molloy of Springfield, n.d. (NAI Reb. Papers 620/56/191).

49   O'Kelly, *General history*, p. 267; Gordon, *History of the rebellion in Ireland in the year 1798*, pp. 80-1.

50   O'Kelly, *General history*, pp. 267-8.

51   Musgrave, *Rebellions*, pp. 248-9; Major General Asgill to Lake, 27 May 1798. Enclosed: Major Latham, Mountmellick, to —— , 26 May 1798 (NAI Reb. Papers 620/37/179).

52   Musgrave, *Rebellions*, pp. 248-9; O'Kelly, *General history*, pp. 267-8; *FJ*, 7 June 1798.

53   Musgrave, *Rebellions*, p. 249; Printed communiqué … extract from a letter from Col. Campbell to General Dundas, Athy, 27 May 1798 (TCD Madden Papers 873/835).

54   O'Kelly, *General history*, pp. 70-2.

55   Examination of Joseph Dale of Fonstown, n.d. [*c.*26 May 1798] (NAI Reb Papers 620/51/58).

56   For the rebellion in Carlow see Duggan, 'Carlow 1791-1801', chapter vii; P. MacSuibhne, *'98 in Carlow* (Carlow, 1974).

57   Leadbeater, *The Leadbeater papers*, vol. i, p. 244.

58   Musgrave, *Rebellions*, pp. 251-2.

59   Asgill to Lake, 27 May 1798. Enclosed: Latham, Mountmellick to —— , 26 May 1798 (NAI Reb. Papers 620/37/179), Edenderry officers to Castlereagh, 27 May 1798 also states 5,000 Defenders were involved in the attack (Reb. Papers 620/18/11/6).

60   O'Kelly, *General history*, p. 85.

61   Ibid., p. 88; Musgrave, *Rebellions*, p. 252.

62   Musgrave, *Rebellions*, pp. 252-4; Reynolds, *Life*, vol. ii, pp. 281-3; Edenderry officers to Castlereagh, 27 May 1798 (NAI Reb. Papers 620/18/11/6).

63   O'Kelly, *General history*, p. 90.

64   William Dundas to William Wickham, 26 Mar 1799. Enclosure: William Cruise to William Dundas, 22 Mar. 1799 (PRO HO 100/46/9-11).

65   Statement of Revd Charles Eustace, 7 June [1798] (NAI Reb. Papers 620/51/59).

66   For the Meath rebellion see: J.G.O. Kerrane, 'The background to the 1798 rebellion in county Meath' (M.A. UCD 1971), pp. 110ff; Seamus O'Lionsigh, 'The rebellion of 1798 in Meath', in *Riocht na Midhe*, vol. iii-v (1966-71).

67   W. Wilson, P.O. Maynooth to —— , 24 May 1798 (NAI Reb. Papers 620/37/142).

68   Col. Gordon to —— , 26 May 1798 (NAI Reb. Papers 620/37/167).

69   Statement of Revd Charles Eustace, 7 June [1798] (NAI Reb. Papers 620/51/59).

70 Lousia Conolly's 'attempt to keep a journal of the rebellion, too full of misery to continue it.' n.d. [late May 1798] (PRONI Mc Peake Papers T. 3048/B/21); Louisa Conolly to William Ogilvie, 1 June 1798 in McDermott (ed.), *The memoirs of Lord Edward Fitzgerald*, p. 337; Pakenham, *The year of liberty*, p. 133; Seamus Cummins, 'Pike heads and the calico printer Leixlip in '98', pp. 422-3.

71 Kerrane, 'Meath', p. 133; O'Lionsigh, 'Rebellion in Meath', pp. 40-5; Musgrave, *Rebellions*, pp. 296-7; Lambert to —— , 27 May 1798 (NAI Reb. Papers 620/37/180).

72 Teeling, *History of the Irish rebellion of 1798*, pp. 94-5.

73 Pakenham's map of the 'midlands front' on the 26 May clearly illustrates the short term success of the United Irishmen in Kildare, *The year of liberty*, p. 132.

74 Musgrave, *Rebellions*, p. 261.

75 Ibid., p. 268.

76 Examination of Pat Delemar, Prosperous, 8 June 1798 (NAI Reb. Papers 620/38/95). He was court martialed and sentenced to death as 'a rebel in arms' in May 1801, Court martial of Pat Delemar at Leixlip, 11 May 1801 (NAI Reb. Papers 620/10/107/4).

77 Thomas Munkittrick to Edward Cooke, 5 June 1798 (NAI Reb. Papers 620/38/58); [J. Jones], *An impartial narrative of the most important engagements which took place between his majesty's forces and the rebels during the Irish rebellion, 1798* (3rd edn, 2 parts, Dublin, 1799), part ii, pp. 128-37.

78 O'Kelly, *General history*, pp. 73-7.

79 Rawson, *Statistical survey*, p. ix.

80 O'Kelly, *General history*, pp. 77-8; Beresford to Lord Auckland, 30 May 1798 in *Auckland correspondence*, vol. iii, pp. 432-6.

81 Musgrave, *Rebellions*, pp. 261-2; Gordon, *History of the rebellion*, p. 99.

82 O'Kelly, *General history*, p. ii; F.S. Bourke, 'Patrick O'Kelly – An historian

of the rebellion of 1798' in *Irish Booklover*, vol. xxviii (Apr. 1941-May 1942), pp. 37-9. Bourke suggests his mistake was made in haste; *FJ*, 19 July 1858.

83 Teeling, *History of the Irish rebellion of 1798*, p. 237

84 Camden to [Portland], 29 May 1798 (PRO HO 100/80/339-342).

85 Richard Griffith, Naas, to Thomas Pelham, 4 June 1798 (B.L., Pelham Papers Add. MS 33,105 ff.380-5); Rawson, *Statistical survey*, p. ix.

86 Camden to [Portland], 29 May 1798 (PRO HO 100/80/339-342).

87 Musgrave, *Rebellions*, p. 262. He suggests the rebels at Barnhill (the Kildare town camp) sued for peace at the same time as Knockallen, i.e. 27 May.

88 O'Kelly, *General history*, pp. 81-2.

89 Duff to [Lake], 29 May 1798 (NAI Reb. Papers 620/37/211). The sentence in square brackets is crossed out.

90 Gordon, *History of the rebellion*, p. 100. Musgrave's account is close to Duff's, *Rebellions*, p. 262.

91 O'Kelly, *General history*, p. 84.

92 Capt. John Wakely, Lt. Thomas James, 2nd Lt. Shaw Cartland and two others to Castlereagh, Edenderry, 27 May 1798. Enclosed: Major Latham to Capt. Wakely, n.d., Major Latham to Capt. Wakely, 25 May 1798, Castlereagh [Camden?], n.d. [c.26 May 1798], Camden to —— , 27 May 1798 (NAI Reb. Papers 620/18/11/6).

93 Lt.-Col. Dunne, Tullamore, to General Lake, 29 May 1798 (NAI Reb. Papers 620/37/209); Musgrave, *Rebellions*, pp. 255-6.

94 R. Marshall to Brig. Gen. Knox, 30 May 1798 (NLI MS 56 Gen. Lake Correspondence 1796-9).

95 Lt.-Col. Longfield, Rathangan, to General Dundas, 29 May 1798 (NAI Reb. Papers 620/37/208); Musgrave, *Rebellions*, pp. 256-7. A letter written on 7 June states Longfield was an officer in the North Cork Militia, Longfield

96 O'Kelly, *General history*, p. 89.
97 Leadbeater, *The Leadbeater papers*, vol. i, pp. 227-8.
98 Ibid., vol. i, pp. 228-30; Musgrave, *Rebellions*, p. 278; T. Rawson to J. Wolfe, 9 Nov. 1798, [Rawson] to —— , n.d. [probably late 1798] (NLI Wolfe Papers).
99 Leadbeater, *The Leadbeater papers*, vol. i, pp. 230-5, 240. On Dr Johnson's United Irish connections see p. 60.
100 Ibid., pp. 246-7; M.J. Curran, 'Hugh Cullen and the Gibbet Rath massacre' and 'Cardinal Cullen: biographical matters' in *Reportorium Novum*, vol. i, no. 1 (1955), pp. 213-27, 242-4; Desmond Bowen, *Paul Cardinal Cullen and the shaping of modern Irish Catholicism* (Dublin, 1983), pp. 2-4.
101 E. Linde to Mrs Linde, 1 June 1798 (NAI Reb. Papers 620/38/15); Cooke to —— , 1 June 1798 (PRO HO 100/81/3-5); Musgrave, *Rebellions*, p. 263.
102 Leadbeater, *The Leadbeater papers*, vol. i, pp. 240-1; Musgrave, *Rebellions*, p. 279; Col. Campbell to Gen. Dundas, 2 June 1798 (NAI Reb. Papers 620/38/23).
103 Col Campbell to Gen. Dundas, 2 June 1798 (NAI Reb. Papers 620/38/23).
104 Musgrave, *Rebellions*, p. 279.

CHAPTER 6
THE 1798 REBELLION IN COUNTY
KILDARE, 1 JUNE–21 JUNE

1 C.H. Teeling, *The history of the Irish rebellion of 1798*, p. 95.
2 Musgrave, *Rebellions*, pp. 266-7.
3 O'Kelly, *General history*, p. 90.
4 Ibid., p. 90; For a short biographical sketch see: Martin Tierney, 'William Aylmer 1772-1820' in *The Irish Sword*, vol. vi (1963-4), pp. 103-7.
5 Sir F.J. Aylmer, *The Aylmers of Ireland*, p. 214; Richard Aylmer, 'The imperial service of William Aylmer 1800-1814', unpublished paper (1996); Dr Aylmer kindly provided me with a copy of

William Aylmer's enlistment in the Austrian army.
6 *The Times*, 26 Mar. 1846; Miles Byrne, *The memoirs of Miles Byrne, edited by his widow* (Shannon, 1972, first published 1863), pp. 175-7.
7 Fenton Aylmer, Harrogate, Yorkshire, to Marsden, 29 July 1803 (NAI Reb. Papers 620/64/21).
8 Fenton Aylmer, Kilcock, to —— , 4 June 1798 (NAI Reb. Papers 620/38/44).
9 Musgrave, *Rebellions*, pp. 270-1.
10 Ibid., pp. 271-2; Copy of a petition from Michael Aylmer of Courtown, Co. Kildare, for compensation for losses suffered in the rebellion of 1798 (NLI MS 8281).
11 Fenton Aylmer, Kilcock. to —— , 4 June 1798 (NAI Reb. Papers 620/38/44).
12 Oliver Barker, Clonard, to John Lees, 6 June 1798 (NAI Reb. Papers 620/38/73); Musgrave, *Rebellions*, pp. 268-9; [J. Jones], *An impartial narrative*, part i, pp. 9-10.
13 Musgrave, *Rebellions*, pp. 283-4.
14 Richard Griffith to Thomas Pelham, 23 June 1798 (BL Pelham Papers Add. MS 33,105 ff.445-8).
15 Madden, *United Irishmen*, 3rd series, vol. ii, p. 105.
16 Oliver Barker, Clonard, to John Lees, 6 June 1798 (NAI Reb. Papers 620/38/73).
17 List of county Kildare leaders of rebels, 4 July 1798 [in the hand of Sir Fenton Aylmer] (NAI Reb. Papers 620/39/18).
18 Examination of Belle Martin, Co. Meath, 23 June 1798, Examination of John Laffan, 4 July 1798 (NAI Reb. Papers 620/38/222, 620/39/19).
19 Statement of Revd Charles Eustace, 7 June [1798] (NAI Reb. Papers 620/51/59).
20 Statement of Charles Eustace, 4 Aug. 1800 (NAI Reb. Papers 620/9/100/18).
21 Information of Robert Weeks, Co. Kildare, by A. Knox [probably late June 1798] (NAI Reb. Papers 620/51/65), Examination of John Laffan, 4 July 1798 (Reb. Papers 620/39/19), Information of John Mitchel of

Dublin, Barber, 8 June 1798 (Reb. Papers 620/38/93).

22 Information about Lord Edward Fitzgerald headed 'Leixlip business', n.d. [probably mid-June 1798] (TCD Sirr Papers 869/9 ff. 7-8); Lord Cloncurry, *Personal recollections*, p. 168. The assertion was later corrected by Gerald, William's brother: Gerald Aylmer to Lord Cloncurry, Painstown, 8 Oct. 1849 in W.J. Fitzpatrick, *The life, times and contemporaries of Lord Cloncurry*, pp. 539-40.

23 Information about Lord Edward Fitzgerald, n.d [probably June or July 1798] (TCD Sirr Papers 869/9 ff. 10-11).

24 Examination of Belle Martin, Co. Meath, 23 June 1798 (NAI Reb. Papers 620/38/222).

25 Ibid.

26 Fenton Aylmer, Kilcock, to ——, 4 June 1798 (NAI Reb. Papers 620/38/44).

27 B information, n.d. [June 1798], Info of B, n.d. [c.10 July 1798], Info of B, Wed. 27 [June 1798] (NAI Reb. Papers 620/18/3).

28 Court martial of Peter Broc, 10 July 1798 (TCD MS 872 Proceedings of courts martial, 1798 ff. 45-56).

29 Information of William McConkery, 6 June 1798 (NAI Reb. Papers 620/38/67).

30 Examination of Belle Martin, Co. Meath, 23 June 1798 (NAI Reb. Papers 620/38/222); Richard Hayes, 'Priests in the independence movement of '98' in *Irish Ecclesiastical Record*, 5th series, vol. lxvi (1945), pp. 266-7.

31 Duff, Monasterevan, to Hewitt, 8 June 1798. Enclosed Col. Thurles, Monasterevan, to Duff, 8 June 1798 (NAI Reb. Papers 620/38/88). Walter Cox dated the burning of the chapel to 4 June, *The Irish Magazine*, vol. i (1808), p. 25.

32 Tyrawley to Cooke, 13 June 1798 (NAI Reb. Papers 620/56/192); Musgrave, *Rebellions*, pp. 249-50.

33 List of persons receiving money owing to sufferings in the rebellion, n.d. [1798 or after] (NAI Reb. Papers 620/52/9).

34 *The Irish Magazine*, vol. viii (1815), p. 248 notes the flogging to death of a Carmelite named Reeny in 1798.

35 Statement of Revd Charles Eustace, 7 June [1798] (NAI Reb. Papers 620/51/59).

36 Mr Keogh, Eccles St, to ——, n.d. [1798] (NAI Reb. Papers 620/551/255); Hayes, 'Priests in the independence movement of '98', pp. 261, 264.

37 Examination of Belle Martin, Co. Meath, 23 June 1798 (NAI Reb. Papers 620/38/222).

38 Patrick Duignan, *A fair representation of the present political state of Ireland* (London, 1799), pp. 216-20; Peter Flood, *A letter from the Revd Peter Flood D.D ... relative to a pamphlet entitled 'A fair ...'* by Patrick Duignan L.L.D. etc. (Dublin, 1800), pp. 3-8.

39 Patrick Corish, *Maynooth College 1795-1995* (Dublin, 1995), pp. 19-21.

40 Lt.-Col. Stewart, Naas, to Lord ——, 19 June 1798 (NAI Reb. Papers 620/38/182); Cornwallis to Portland, 21 June 1798 (Reb. Papers 620/18/9/1 [and PRO HO 100/81/49-50]).

41 Info. of B, 20 June [1798] (NAI Reb. Papers 620/18/3), Capt. H. Morison to Lord Rossmore, 20 June 1798 (Reb. Papers 620/38/192), S. Sproule to John Lees, 25 June 1798 (Reb. Papers 620/38/232).

42 Gosford to Capt. ——, Naas, 11 July 1798. Enclosure: Information of Joseph Lyons, 9 July. 1798 (NAI Reb. Papers 620/39/52).

43 Information of Edward Whiteman, 20 June [1798 not 1797] (NAI SOC 3089).

44 Musgrave, *Rebellions*, pp. 285-6; O'Kelly, *General history*, pp. 92-5.

45 Information of Edward Whiteman, 20 June [1798] (NAI SOC 3089); Brig.-Gen. Grose, Kilcock, to ——, 20 June 1798 (Reb. Papers 620/38/193); O'Kelly, *General history*, p. 93.

46 Information of Edward Whiteman, 20 June [1798] (NAI SOC 3089); Musgrave, *Rebellions*, p. 285; O'Kelly, *General history*, p. 94.

47 Information of Edward Whiteman, 20
June [1798] (NAI SOC 3089), see also
George Holdcroft, Kill, to —— , 21 June
1798 (Reb. Papers 620/38/205).

48 O'Kelly, *General history*, p. 94; Brig.-
Gen. Grose, Kilcock, to —— , 20 June
1798 (NAI Reb. Papers 620/38/193).

49 Information of Edward Whiteman, 20
June [1798] (NAI SOC 3089).

50 Brig. Gen. Grose, Kilcock, to —— , 20
June 1798 (Reb. Papers 620/38/193).

51 Richard Griffith to Thomas Pelham, 30
June 1798 (BL, Pelham Papers Add.
MS 33,105 ff.453-4); examination of
Belle Martin, Co. Meath 23 June 1798
(NAI Reb. Papers 620/38/222).

52 O'Kelly, *General history*, p. 91.

53 —— to Alex Worthington, 25 June 1798,
Information received from B (NAI
Reb. Papers 620/38/233).

54 Pakenham, *The year of liberty*, p. 271; *FJ*,
5 July 1798.

55 Sir Fenton Aylmer to —— , 4 July 1798
enclosed: (copy) reply of Lord
Castlereagh, 5 July 1798 (NAI Reb.
Papers 620/39/23). original reply (Reb.
Papers 620/3/49/1); *FJ*, 17 July 1798.

56 O'Kelly, *General history*, p. 91; B to —— ,
n.d. [late 1798?] (NAI Reb. Papers
620/18/3); W.H. Maxwell, *History of the
Irish rebellion*, p. 68.

57 Marquis of Buckingham to Lord
Grenville, 23 July 1798 in H.M.C.,
*Report on the MSS of J.B. Fortescue
preserved at Dropmore* (London, 1905),
vol. iv, pp. 264-5.

58 Lt.-Gen. Craig to —— , Dublin, 6 July
1798, enclosed: Gosford to Lake, Naas,
4 July 1798, Fenton Aylmer, Sallins, to
Gosford, n.d. [5 July 1798] (NAI Reb.
Papers 620/39/26).

59 Musgrave, *Rebellions*, p. 272; *FJ*, 17 July
1798.

60 Lt.-Gen. Craig to —— , Dublin, 6 July
1798, enclosed: Gosford to Lake, Naas,
4 July 1798, Fenton Aylmer, Sallins, to
Gosford, n.d. [5 July 1798] (NAI Reb.
Papers 620/39/26).

61 Gosford to Capt. —— , Naas, 11 July
1798, enclosure: Information of Joseph

Lyons, 9 July 1798 (NAI Reb. Papers
620/39/52).

62 Lt.-Gen. Craig to —— , Dublin, 6 July
1798, enclosed: Gosford to Lake, Naas,
4 July 1798, Fenton Aylmer, Sallins, to
Gosford, n.d. [5 July 1798] (NAI Reb.
Papers 620/39/26).

63 Richard Griffith, Naas, to Thomas
Pelham, 11 July 1798 (BL, Pelham
Papers Add. MS 33,105 ff. 4-8).

64 Ruan O'Donnell, 'General Joseph Holt
and the rebellion of 1798 in county
Wicklow' (M.A. UCD 1991), pp. 183-
90; idem., 'The rebellion of 1798 in
county Wicklow', pp. 364-5; Daniel
Gahan, *The people's rising, Wexford 1798*
(Dublin, 1995), pp. 278-97.

65 O'Donnell, 'Rebellion', p. 364; Gahan,
People's rising, pp. 282-3, 286.

66 Gahan, *People's rising*, p. 283; Felix
Rourke to Mary Finaghy, 27 July 1798
in Madden, *United Irishmen*, 2nd edn,
vol. iv, p. 547.

67 John Wolfe to Edward Cooke, 10 July
[1798] (NAI Reb. Papers 620/52/47).

68 Court martial of Patrick Gorman,
Carlow, 14 May 1798 (NAI Reb. Papers
620/5/58/22).

69 S. Sproule to J. Lees, 10 July 1798 (NAI
Reb. Papers 620/39/44).

70 Gahan, *People's rising*, p. 284.

71 *An impartial narrative*, pp. 3-4, 12; John
Wolfe to Edward Cooke, 16 July 1798
(NAI Reb. Papers 620/39/93); O'Kelly,
General history, pp. 192-3.

72 *An impartial narrative*, pp. 12-20; Felix
Rourke to Mary Finaghy, 27 July 1798
in Madden, *United Irishmen*, 2nd edn,
vol. iv, p. 547; Cornwallis to Portland, 15
July 1798 (NAI Reb. Papers 620/39/80);
Cooke to Wickham, 12 July 1798 (PRO
HO 100/81/243).

73 Lord Harberton to —— , 14 July 1798,
enclosed: B.F., Newbury, to Viscount
Harberton, 14 July 1798 (NAI Reb.
Papers 620/4/33/1).

74 Col. Vereker, Rathangan, to
Castlereagh, 21 July 1798, enclosed: Lt.-
Col. Gough to Col. Vereker, 14 July

1798 (NAI Reb. Papers 620/4/36/1); *FJ*, July 1798.

75 Col. Vereker, Rathangan, to Castlereagh, 21 July 1798, enclosed: Lt.-Col. Gough to Col. Vereker, 14 July 1798 (NAI Reb. Papers 620/4/36/1); *FJ*, July 1798.

76 Felix Rourke to Mary Finaghy, 27 July 1798 in Madden, *United Irishmen*, 2nd edn, vol. iv, p. 547; O'Donnell 'General Joseph Holt', p. 186; Information of Bartholemew Connolly and Edward McLaughlin, 14 July 1798, Confession of Oliver Nelson, 15 July 1798 (NAI Reb. Papers 620/39/73,75).

77 Sir Fenton Aylmer to Castlereagh, Maynooth, 16 July 1798, four original enclosures: [Kildare rebels] to [Michael] Aylmer, 15 July 1798 [Fenton Aylmer] to [Kildare rebels], Maynooth, 15 July 1798, [Kildare rebels] to Sir Fenton Aylmer, 15 July 1798 [Fenton Aylmer] to [Kildare rebels], Maynooth, 16 July 1798, also enclosed: Note from the Lord Lieutenant relative to affairs at Naas, n.d. [*c.*17-21 July 1798] (NAI Reb. Papers 620/4/36/2).

78 Ibid.

79 Marquis of Buckingham to Lord Grenville, 23 July 1798 in *Fortescue MSS*, vol. iv, pp. 264-5.

80 Marquis of Cornwallis, *Correspondence of Charles, first marquis of Cornwallis*, ed. Charles Ross (3 vols, London, 1859), vol. ii, pp. 366-7. Wilford confirmed Buckingham's intervention.

81 Castlereagh to Wilford, 19 July 1798 (NAI Reb. Papers 620/3/47/4); Cornwallis to Pitt, 20 July 1798 in *Cornwallis correspondence*, vol. ii, p. 368.

82 Edward Cooke to William Wickham, 21 July 1798 (PRO HO 100/77/268-9).

83 *FJ*, 24 July 1798; Gilbert (ed.), *Documents relating to Ireland*, p. 19.

84 Marquis of Buckingham to Lord Grenville, 23 July 1798 in *Fortescue MSS*, vol. iv pp. 264-5.

85 Gahan, *People's rising*, p. 297.

86 Dundas to Castlereagh, 8 Aug. 1798 (NAI Reb. Papers 620/39/58).

87 Thomas Tyrrell to John Wolfe, n.d. [late 1798] (NLI Wolfe Papers); Louisa Conolly to Castlereagh, 25 July 1798 (NAI Reb. Papers 620/3/51/2).

88 Stella Tillyard, *Aristocrats*, pp. 388-97.

89 Information of Thomas Reynolds before the Privy Council ... 1798 (NAI Reb. Papers 620/3/32/23), Particulars of evidence to shew [*sic*] that Lord Edward Fitzgerald has been actively engaged in the treasons carried on in this country, n.d. (620/3/31/3).

90 Castlereagh to Wickham, 31 July 1798, Leinster to Cornwallis, Brompton, 6 Aug. 1798, Cornwallis to Leinster, 11 Aug 1798 in *Cornwallis correspondence*, vol. ii, pp. 379, 384-5.

91 Cornwallis to Maj.-Gen. Ross, 13 July 1798 in *Cornwallis correspondence*, vol. ii, p. 363.

92 Lousia Conolly to the duke of Richmond, 18 June 1798 (PRONI McPeake Papers T. 3048/B/27); G.C. Bolton, *The passing of the Irish act of union*, p. 183.

93 *Commons journal of Ireland*, vol. xix, pt. 1 (1800), pp. cciv-ccxxvii, ccccxcviii.

94 *The Irish Magazine*, vol. i (1808), p. 25.

95 Louisa Conolly to duke of Richmond, 18 June 1798 (PRONI McPeake Papers T. 3048/B/27).

CHAPTER 7
REBELS AND ROBBERS, 1798–1803

1 Elliot, *Partners in revolution*, pp. 214-40.

2 Statement of Michael Quigly, 30 June 1805 (NAI Reb. Papers 620/14/187/11); Madden, *United Irishmen*, 3rd series, vol. ii, pp. 108-9.

3 Daniel Gahan, 'The "Black Mob" and the "Babes in the Wood": Wexford in the wake of the rebellion 1798-1806' in *Journal of the Wexford Historical Society*, vol. 13 (1990-1), pp. 92-110.

4 Dundas to Castlereagh, 8 Aug. 1798 (NAI Reb. Papers 620/39/158).

5 Musgrave, *Rebellions*, appendix xv, pp. 64-5.

6 Thomas Fitzgerald to Sir John Parnell, 10 Sept. 1798 (NAI Reb. Papers 620/46/34).

7 Sir John Parnell to Castlereagh, 21 Oct. 1798, enclosed: J. Weldon to Parnell, 21 Oct. 1798 (NAI Reb. Papers 620/40/180).

8 S. Morgan to J. Lees, 26 Sept. [1798] (NAI Reb. Papers 620/40/107), Thomas Rawson to Littlehales, 18 Nov. 1800, enclosed: Information of James Cranny, Athy Jail, n.d (Reb. Papers 620/58/81); Musgrave, *Rebellions*, pp. 280-1; Charles Dickson, *The life of Michael Dwyer with some account of his companions* (Dublin, 1944), pp. 327-9.

9 William Goodwin, Kilcullen, to Captain Rawson, 26 Sept. 1798 (NAI Reb. Papers 620/40/112).

10 'Journal of Mr Samuel Reilly ... September 1798' in *Journal of the Cork Historical and Archaeological Society*, vol. ii, series 2 (1896), pp. 428-42; Dundas to Castlereagh, 19 Sept. 1798 (NAI Reb. Papers 620/40/75); Leadbeater, *The Leadbeater papers*, vol. i, pp. 250-8, 266-87.

11 Col. Keatinge to —— , 9 Oct. 1798 (NAI Reb. Papers 620/40/143).

12 See L.M. Cullen, 'Politics and rebellion: Wicklow in the 1790s', pp. 466-7.

13 A County Kildare Farmer to Cornwallis, 18 Sept. 1798 (NAI Reb. Papers 620/40/69); Musgrave, *Rebellions*, p. 284.

14 Thomas Tyrrell, Clonard, to —— , 21 Oct. 1798 (NAI Reb. Papers 620/40/172).

15 T. Conolly, Castletown, to T. Kemmis, 27 Oct. 1798 (NAI Frazer MSS 1/41); Michael Aylmer to [Marsden], 8 Jan. 1799 (Reb. Papers 620/46/7).

16 Information of James Nagle, 19 Dec. 1803 (NAI Reb. Papers 620/11/138/48). Published by P. MacSuibhne, *Kildare in '98*, pp. 227-40. He dates the initial events to autumn 1799. Also Information of James Nagle, 29 Oct. 1803 (Reb. Papers 620/50/27).

17 Critchey to Sir John Parnell, 11 Sept 1798, enclosed: J. Belling to —— , n.d. (NAI Reb. Papers 620/40/36), Thomas Fitzgerald to Parnell, 10 Sept. 1798 (620/40/34).

18 Elliot, *Partners in revolution*, p. 245.

19 Information of James Nagle, 19 Dec. 1803 (NAI Reb. Papers 620/11/138/48).

20 John Wolfe to Michael Aylmer, Thomas Tyrrell, John Cassidy, Thomas Rawson and Theobald Wolfe (copy), 23 Oct. 1798 (NLI Wolfe Papers).

21 John Johnston Darrah to John Wolfe, 28 Nov. 1798, Edward Richardson to John Wolfe, 29 Oct. 1798, Theobald Wolfe to John Wolfe, 5 Nov., 18 Nov. 1798 (NLI Wolfe Papers).

22 (Draft) John Wolfe to Castlereagh, Nov. 1798 (NLI Wolfe Papers).

23 Two lists of military stations [Nov. 1798] (NLI Wolfe Papers).

24 Littlehales to Dundas, 29 Dec. 1798, Littlehales to Wolfe, 29 Dec. 1798, Memorial of directions to be sent to the troops stationed in Kildare county for the purpose of restoring the county to quiet, n.d. [late 1798] (NLI Wolfe Papers).

25 Cornwallis to Portland, 21 Dec. 1798 in *Castlereagh correspondence*, vol. iii, pp. 20-1.

26 Michael Aylmer, Kilcock, to [Marsden], 8 Jan. 1799 (NAI Reb. Papers 620/46/7).

27 John Wolfe, Tarbart Batteries, to Cooke, 13 Jan. 1799 (NAI Reb. Papers 620/46/11).

28 Thomas Conolly to —— , 21 May 1799, Thomas Conolly to Marsden, 17 Sept. 1799, enclosed Thomas Conolly to ——, 20 Sept. 1799 (NAI Reb. Papers 620/56/63, 73).

29 John Wolfe to Cooke, n.d. [6 Aug. 1799?] (NAI SOC 3379).

30 John Roche Ardill, *The closing of the Irish parliament* (Dublin, 1907), pp. 91-101.

31 Richard Nevill to —— , 4 Apr. 1800 (NAI Reb. Papers 620/58/31); (copy) Thomas Conolly to John Montgomery,

21 Apr. 1800 (TCD Conolly Papers 3974-84/1322).

32 Maurice Keatinge, Cheshire to —— , 23 June [1799], 30 Sept. 1799 (NAI OP 73/4).

33 Cloncurry, *Personal recollections*, p. 85; Fitzpatrick, *The life and times of Lord Cloncurry*, pp. 224-42; *Thoughts on the projected union between Great Britain and Ireland* (Dublin, 1797), published in Cloncurry, op. cit., pp. 490-510.

34 Over one hundred letters relating to anti-union meetings in Kildare, 1799-1800 (NLI Wolfe Papers); Castlereagh to Portland, 5 Jan. 1799 in *Cornwallis Correspondence*, vol. iii, p. 31; Ardill, *The closing of the Irish parliament*, pp. 91-101.

35 Brian Walker (ed.), *Parliamentary election results 1801-1922* (Dublin, 1978) N.H.I. ancilliary publications, vol. ii, p. 220; Letters relating to John Wolfe's election campaign, 1801-2 (NLI Wolfe Papers).

36 Sproule to Lees, 19 Oct. 1798 (NAI Reb. Papers 620/40/172).

37 Plan for the organisation of United Irishmen, 1799? (NAI Reb. Papers 620/8/72/2); Elliot, *Partners in revolution*, pp. 247-8.

38 Elliot, *Partners in revolution*, pp. 243-81.

39 Sir Fenton Aylmer to Marsden, 2 Feb. 1802 (NAI Reb. Papers 620/61/4).

40 Alderman James, 25 Jan. 1801 (NAI SOC 3440).

41 John Walsh, Kilcock to Lord Lieutenant 18 July 1801, enclosed: 'Parish of Raddinstown' address, John Walsh, Dungannon, to Maj.-Gen. Barnet, 10 Apr. 1801 (NAI SOC 1020/23).

42 Oliver Nelson to —— , 27 June 1802 (NAI Reb. Papers 620/63/11).

43 Duke of Leinster to Littlehales, 18 Mar. 1802, enclosure: Sir Fenton Aylmer to duke of Leinster, 28 Feb. 1802 (NAI Reb. Papers 620/61/5). John Wolfe to —— , 29 Apr. 1802, John Wolfe to —— , 15 Mar. 1802 (SOC 1021/9, 11)

44 Duke of Leinster to —— , 9 Mar. 1802

(NAI Reb. Papers 620/62/44), Richard Nevill to Marsden, 23 Apr. 1802 (Reb. Papers 620/63/2).

45 Mr Pollock to —— , 17 June 1802, enclosed: Information of O.B., 14 June 1802 and four other letters.

46 Information of James Nagle, 19 Dec. 1803, 29 Oct. 1803 (NAI Reb. Papers 620/11/138/48, 620/50/27).

47 Elliot, *Partners in revolution*, p. 278.

48 Richard Griffith to Thomas Pelham, 19 Feb. 1803 (BL Pelham Papers Add. MSS 33,110 ff. 246-9).

49 Daniel Collison to Aldermen James, 6 Feb. 1803 (NAI Reb. Papers 620/64/145).

50 General statement from Michael Quigly's various examinations, letters etc., n.d. (NAI Reb. Papers 620/11/135), Statement of Michael Quigly, 30 June 1805 (Reb. Papers 620/14/187/11), R. Musgrave to W.C. Flint, 14 Sept. 1803 (Reb. Papers 620/11/130/38). See Helen Landreth's account of Quigly's arrival and Kildare mission in *The pursuit of Robert Emmet*, pp. 135-41.

51 Fenton Aylmer to —— , [Mar.] 1803, Fenton Aylmer to —— , 20 Mar. 1803, enclosed: Fenton Aylmer to —— , n.d. [Mar. 1803] (NAI Reb. Papers 620/64/2, 7).

52 General statement from Michael Quigly's various examinations, letters etc., n.d. (NAI Reb. Papers 620/11/135), Major Sirr to —— , Apr. 1803 (Reb. Papers 620/67/59).

53 Bernard Duggan's narrative (TCD Madden Papers 873/30); Information of John Fleming, 3 Sept. 1803 (NAI Reb. Papers 620/11/138/13).

54 (Copy) Maj.-Gen. Trench to Gen. Payne, Naas, 17 Mar. 1803 (NAI Reb. Papers 620/66/135).

55 Depositions and informations, Naas, 1803 pp. 53-65 (R.I.A. MS 12 M 8).

56 William Mills, Kildare town, to Marsden, n.d. [pre-23 June 1803] (NAI Reb. Papers 620/66/45), John Cassidy to Marsden, 21 Aug 1803 (Reb. Papers 620/11/130/19), John Cassidy to marquis

of Drogheda, 15 Aug. 1803 (Reb. Papers 620/12/141/12).

57 Memorial of Nicholas Gray, 19 Nov. 1799 (NAI Reb. Papers 620/48/22), Revd W.W. Pole to —— , 1803 (Reb. Papers 620/66/173); O'Kelly, *General history*, p. 287; Elliot, *Partners in revolution*, p. 162.

58 Information of Patrick Whelan, 1804 (NAI Reb. Papers 620/50/38/57).

59 General statement from Michael Quigly's various examinations, letters etc., n.d. (NAI Reb. Papers 620/11/135); O'Kelly, *General history*, p. 293.

60 Deposition of Connor Keevan, 19 Oct. 1803 (NAI SOC 3529).

61 John Wolfe to [Rawson], 15 Jan. 1804 (NAI Reb. Papers 620/13/178/4).

62 Information of James Nagle, 19 Dec. 1803 (NAI Reb. Papers 620/11/138/48); John Wolfe to Wickham, 6 Jan. 1804 (SOC 1030/39).

63 J.J. Henry to Marsden, 7 Apr. 1803 (NAI Reb. Papers 620/65/70).

64 Elliot, *Partners in revolution*, p. 303.

65 Fenton Aylmer to —— , [Mar.] 1803 (NAI Reb. Papers 620/64/2).

66 Thomas Rawson to Marsden, 21 Aug. 1803 (NAI Reb. Papers 620/66/209), Col. Keatinge, Leominister, to —— , 20 August 1803 (Reb. Papers 620/11/130/8).

67 Landreth, *The pursuit of Robert Emmet*, p. 253; Martin Tierney, 'William Aylmer 1772-1820', p. 105; Richard Aylmer, 'The imperial service of William Aylmer 1800-1814', unpublished paper (1996).

68 Maj.-Gen. Trench to William Wickham, 1 July 1803 (NAI Reb. Papers 620/67/134).

69 John O'Brien to Marsden, 25 July 1803 (NAI Reb. Papers 620/66/96), a John O'Brien was unsuccessfully prosecuted for administering United Irish oaths at the summer assizes in 1797.

70 Lt.-Col. Aylmer to Wickham, 8 Oct. 1803, enclosed: Information of Thomas Frayne, 5 Oct 1803 (NAI Reb. Papers 620/11/130/44); Elliot, *Partners in*

revolution, pp. 304-7; Landreth, *The pursuit of Robert Emmet*, pp. 140-84.

71 Statement of Michael Quigly, 30 June 1805 (NAI Reb. Papers 620/14/187/11), Information of Carter Connolly, July 1803 (Reb. Papers 620/11/129/5); Landreth, *The pursuit of Robert Emmet*, p. 165.

72 Elliot, *Partners in revolution*, p. 309.

73 Depositions and informations, Naas, 1803 pp. 3-5, 206-12, 290, 298 (R.I.A. MS 12 M 8); Landreth, *The pursuit of Robert Emmet*, pp. 170-1; H.H. Bourke to Castlereagh, 22 July 1803 (NAI Reb. Papers 620/64/104).

74 General statement from Michael Quigly's various examinations, letters etc., n.d. (NAI Reb. Papers 620/11/135).

75 Ibid.

76 Information of James Nagle, 29 Oct. 1803 (NAI Reb. Papers 620/50/27).

77 See Elliot's succinct account of the Dublin rising in *Partners in revolution*, pp. 310-11; Miles Byrne, *Memoirs of Miles Byrne*, pp. 364-74.

78 (Copy) James McClelland, to William Wickham, 26 Aug. 1803 (PRO HO 100/112/369-377); Information of Daniel Collison, 26 July 1803 (NAI Reb. Papers 620/11/129/7); Landreth's account of the Kildare rising is based on McClelland's report, *The pursuit of Robert Emmet*, pp. 226-30.

79 Duke of Leinster to Marsden, 30 July 1803, duke of Leinster to Littlehales, 3 Aug. 1803 (NAI Reb. Papers 620/65/170,1), Information of Carter Connolly, July 1803 (Reb. Papers 620/11/129/5).

80 Petition of Ann Russell (Conolly's aunt) to Lord Lieutenant, n.d. [c.Oct. 1803] (NAI Reb. Papers 620/12/141/28).

81 W.H. Irvine to —— , 25 July 1803 (NAI Reb. Papers 620/65/97).

82 (Copy) James McClelland to William Wickham, 26 Aug. 1803 (PRO HO 100/112/369-377).

83 Ibid.; Edward Lees to Marsden, [25 July] 1803 (NAI Reb. Papers 620/65/192).

84 (Copy) James McClelland to William Wickham, 26 Aug. 1803 (PRO HO 100/112/369-377); Information of Mary Lindsay, n.d. (NAI Reb. Papers 620/65/193).

85 (Copy) James McClelland to William Wickham, 26 Aug. 1803 (PRO HO 100/112/369-377).

86 John Wolfe Information, 23 July 1803 (NAI Reb. Papers 620/67/198), John Wolfe to [Rawson], 13 Jan. 1804 (Reb. Papers 620/13/178/4).

87 Lt.-Col. Aylmer, Kilcock. to —— , 24 July 1803 (NAI Reb. Papers 620/64/23).

88 Ald. R. Manders to Col. Alexander, 25 July 1803 (NAI Reb. Papers 620/66/8).

89 Wogan Browne to Marsden, 29 July, 3 Aug. 1803 (NAI SOC 1025/22,23), Fenton Aylmer, Harrogate, Yorkshire. to Marsden, 29 July 1803 (Reb. Papers 620/64/21)

90 Depositions and informations, Naas, 1803 (R.I.A. MS 12 M 8).

91 John Greene to Marsden, 24, 25, 26 July 1803 (NAI Reb. Papers 620/66/32-4)..

92 Revd W.W. Pole to —— , 1803 (NAI Reb. Papers 620/66/173), Thomas Rawson to Marsden, 13 Oct. 1803 (Reb. Papers 620/50/22), Thomas Rawson to Marsden, 25 Sept. 1803, enclosed William Sutton to Rawson, 10 Sept. 1803, Information of Thomas Corcoran, n.d. [1803] (Reb. Papers 620/66/210).

93 Thomas Rawson to Marsden, 21 Aug. 1803 (NAI Reb. Papers 620/66/210); Thomas Rawson to John Wolfe, 15 Aug. 1803 (NLI Wolfe Papers).

94 Elliot, *Partners in revolution*, pp. 282-322.

95 See 'Alphabetical list of suspected persons covering the period 1798 to 1803', marked 'prepared after 1803' (NAI Reb. Papers 620/12/217). Many of the Kildare suspects were involved in both 1798 and 1803.

96 Information of James Nagle, 19 Dec. 1803, 29 Oct. 1803 (NAI Reb. Papers 620/11/138/48, 620/50/27), John Wolfe to William Wickham, 6 Jan. 1803 (SOC 1030/29).

97 Adm. Packenham to Marsden, 13, 28 Sept. 1803 and five letters, dated 1803 (NAI Reb. Papers 620/66/113-5, 119-22).

98 Maj.-Gen. Trench to various, Aug. to Sept. 1803 (NAI Reb. Papers 620/67/136-9, 142-3), Trench to Marsden, 1 Nov. 1803 (Reb. Papers 620/12/141/36).

99 Examination of Nicholas Stafford, 4 Dec. 1803 (NAI Reb. Papers 620/11/138/45); Madden, *United Irishmen*, 3rd series, vol. ii, p. 110; Earl of Hardwicke *The viceroy's post bag: Correspondence hitherto unpublished of the earl of Hardwicke, first Lord Lieutenant after the union*, ed. Michael Mac Donagh (London, 1904), p. 437.

100 E. Boyle to —— , 21 Oct. 1803 (NAI Reb. Papers 620/11/130/48) Papers of B. Doogan [*sic*], 1805 (Reb. Papers 620/14/186/6); Madden, *United Irishmen*, 3rd series, vol. ii, pp. 121-4.

101 Micheal Quigly, Kilmainham Jail, 24 Oct. 1803 (NAI Reb. Papers 620/50/38/55), Quigly to Dr Trevor, 29 Oct. 1803 (Reb. Papers 620/12/141/35), Information of Micheal Quigly, 1804, 1805, 1806 and 26 July 1808 (Reb. Papers 620/13/177/1-17, 620/14/187, 620/199/1-10, 205); MacDonagh, *The viceroy's post bag*, pp. 436-8, 452-3.

102 Landreth, *The pursuit of Robert Emmet*, pp. 138-40.

103 *FJ*, 9 Aug. 1803.

104 *FJ*, 25 Aug. 1803.

105 Wogan Browne to Marsden, 3 Aug. 1803 (NAI SOC 1025/23).

106 Fenton Aylmer to Marsden, 29 July 1803 (NAI Reb. Papers 620/64/21).

107 (Copy) James McClelland to William Wickham, 26 Aug. 1803 (PRO HO 100/112/369-377).

108 Hardwicke, *The viceroy's post bag*, pp. 384-7

109 See NAI SOC 1030/5, 9-11, 13-15, 22-23, 40-54, 56-9, 110

110 Hardwicke, op. cit., pp. 385-6.

CONCLUSION

1 Thomas Pakenham, *The year of liberty*, p. 110.
2 Richard Griffith to Thomas Pelham, 4

June 1798 (BL Pelham Papers Add. MSS 33,105 f. 384).
3 Richard Griffith to Thomas Pelham, 15 Jan. 1799 (BL Pelham Papers Add. MSS 33,106 ff. 169-72).

Bibliography

BIBLIOGRAPHIES AND GUIDES

Bourke, F.S., 'The rebellion of 1803: an essay in bibliography' in *Bibliographical Society of Ireland Publications*, vol. v, no. 1 (1933).

Dickson, David, 'Bibliography' in Moody and Vaughan (eds), *A new history of Ireland, vol. iv, Eighteenth Century Ireland 1691–1800* (Oxford, 1986), pp. 713-95.

Hayes, Richard J., *Manuscript sources for the history of Irish civilisation* (11 vols, Dublin, 1965).

—, *Sources for the history of Irish civilisation: articles in Irish periodicals* (9 vols, Boston, 1970).

Kavanagh, Michael, *A contribution towards a bibliography of the history of county Kildare in printed books* (Newbridge, 1977).

—, 'Kildare bibliography' in *Kildare Arch. Soc. Jn*, vol. xviii, part ii (1994-5), pp. 247-55.

Lyons, Mary Ann, 'Maynooth: a select bibliography of printed sources' in *I.H.S.*, vol. xxix, no. 116 (1995), pp. 441-74.

Simms, Samuel, 'A select bibliography of the United Irishmen, 1791-8' in *I.H.S.*, vol. i, no. 2 (1938), pp. 158-80.

PRIMARY SOURCES: MANUSCRIPT

Public Record Office, London
HO 100 Home Office Papers
WO 13 War Office Papers

British Library, London
Add. MSS 33,105-10 Pelham Papers

National Archives, Dublin
Frazer MSS
Official Papers (second series)
Prisoners Petitions and Cases
Rebellion Papers
State of the Country Papers (first and second series)
Westmorland Correspondence

National Library, Dublin
MSS 54A-55 Melville (Dundas) Papers
MS 56 Lake Correspondence
MSS 611-7, 635, 2123 Leinster Papers
MSS 9330-46 Mary Leadbeater's diaries 1790-1809
MS 5398 Membership of the Grand Orange Lodge, Dublin
MS 8281 Copy of a petition from Michael Aylmer of Courtown, Co. Kildare, for
    compensation for losses suffered in the Rebellion of 1798
MS 9762 Luke Cullen Papers
MS 15060 Letter of [Richard] Nevill to 'My Dear Marquis' 21 July 1795
MSS 19164-5 Stratford Papers
Wolfe Papers (unsorted)

Trinity College Library, Dublin
MSS 869 Sirr Papers
MSS 871-2 Depositions and Courts Martial, 1798
MSS 873 Madden Papers
MS 1472 Luke Cullen Papers
MSS 3974-3984 Conolly Papers
MSS 2251-2254 The Council Books of Naas Corporation 1665-1842

Royal Irish Academy, Dublin
MS 12 M 8 Depositions and information relating to various persons connected with
    Robert Emmet's rising dated Naas, 1803

Public Record Office, Northern Ireland
D. 3078 Leinster Papers
T. 2825 Castletown Papers
T. 3048 Mc Peake Papers

PRIMARY SOURCES: NEWSPAPERS AND OFFICIAL DOCUMENTS

Anthologica Hibernia.
Dublin Evening Post.
Faulkner's Dublin Journal.
Freeman's Journal.
Howell, T.B & T.J. (eds), *A complete collection of state trials* (33 vols, London, 1809-28)
Journal of the house of commons of the kingdom of Ireland 1613-1800 (20 vols, Dublin,
    1796-1800).
Journal of the house of lords, Ireland 1634-1800 (8 vols, Dublin, 1779-1800).
The Gentleman's and Citizen's Almanack.
The Irish Magazine, and monthly asylum for neglected biography.
*The parliamentary register, or history of the proceedings and debates of the house of com-
    mons of Ireland 1781-1797* (17 vols, Dublin, 1782-1801).
The Press.
The report of the secret committee of the house of commons with an appendix (Dublin, 1798).
Walkers Hibernian Magazine.

PRIMARY SOURCES: CONTEMPORARY WORKS AND PAMPHLETS

A County Meath freeholder, *A candid and impartial account of the disturbances in the County Meath in the years 1792, 1793 and 1794* (Dublin, 1794).

Alexander, James, *Some account of the first apparent symptoms of the late rebellion in the County of Kildare and an adjoining part of the King's County with a ... narrative of some of the most important passages in the rise and progress of the rebellion in the county of Wexford* (Dublin, 1800).

A list of officers of several regiments and battalions upon the establishment of Ireland (Dublin, 1797).

A list of the counties of Ireland and the respective Yeomanry corps in each, 1st June 1798 (Dublin, 1798).

An impartial narrative of the most important engagements which took place between his majesty's forces and the rebels during the Irish rebellion carefully collected from authentic letters (3rd edn, 2 parts, Dublin, 1799).

Anonymous, *Society of United Irishmen of Dublin established November ix mdccxci* (Dublin, 1794).

Archer, Forster, 'Some impressions of Kildare in 1801', ed. Padraig de Brun in *Kildare Arch. Soc. Jn*, vol. xvi (1983-4), pp. 340-1.

Auckland, William, Lord, *The journal and correspondence of William, Lord Auckland*, ed. Bishop of Bath and Wells (4 vols, London, 1861-2).

Barrington, Jonah, *Historic memoirs of Ireland* (2 vols, London, 1835).

Bartlett, Thomas, 'Select documents xxxviii: Defenders and Defenderism in 1795' in *I.H.S.*, vol. xxvi, no. 95 (1985), pp. 373-94.

Beaufort, D.A., *Memoir of a map of Ireland* (London, 1792).

Bibliographical anecdotes of the founders of the late Irish rebellion impartially written by a candid observer (Ireland, 1801).

Bibliotheca Browniana: a catalogue of the valuable and extensive library of the late Wogan Brown[e] esq. of Castle Brown[e] (Dublin, 1814).

Blacker, William and Wallace, Robert H., *The formation of the Orange Order 1795-98: the edited papers of Colonel William Blacker and Colonel Robert H. Wallace*, ed. Cecil Fitzpatrick (Belfast, 1994).

Burke, Edmund, *Reflections on the revolutions in France*, ed. Conor Cruise O'Brien (London, 1986, first published 1790).

Bushe, G.P., 'An essay towards ascertaining the population of Ireland' in *R.I.A. Trans.*, vol. iii (1789), pp. 145-55.

Byrne, J., *An impartial account of the late disturbances in the County of Armagh* (Dublin, 1792).

Campbell, Thomas, *Philosophical survey of the south of Ireland* (Dublin, 1778).

Cornwallis, Marquis of, *Correspondence of Charles First Marquis of Cornwallis*, ed. Charles Ross (3 vols, London, 1859).

County Kildare grand jury presentments [Lent 1791, 1792, 1795, 1796, 1799, 1801, 1802, Summer 1793, 1796, 1797, 1800, 1803].

Cloncurry, Lord Valentine, *Personal recollections of the life and times, with extracts from the correspondence of Valentine Lord Cloncurry* (Dublin, 1849).

Corry, John, *Odes and elegies descriptive and sentimental with the Patriot, a poem* (Newry, 1797).

de Bombelles, Marc, *Journal de voyage en Grande Bretagne et en Irlande 1784*, ed. Jacques Gury (Oxford, 1989).

de Latocnaye, *A Frenchman's walk through Ireland 1796-7* trans. John Stevenson (Belfast, 1984, first published 1917).

de Montbret, Coquebert, 'An eighteenth century traveller in County Kildare', ed. Sile Ní Cinneide in *Kildare Arch. Soc. Jn*, vol. xv (1974), pp. 376-86.

Drennan, William, *The Drennan letters 1776-1819*, ed. D.A. Chart (Belfast, 1931)

Duignan, Patrick, *A fair representation of the present political state of Ireland* (Dublin, 1799).

Edwards, R. Dudley (ed.), 'The minute book of the Catholic Committee' in *Archivium Hibernicum*, vol. ix (1942), pp. 1-173.

Emmet, T.A., MacNeven, W.J., and O'Connor, A., *Memoire or detailed statement of the origin and progress of the Irish union* (London, 1802).

Farrell, William, *Carlow in '98: The autobiography of William Farrell of Carlow*, ed. Roger McHugh (Dublin, 1949).

Fitzgerald, Brian (ed.), *Correspondence of Emily duchess of Leinster* (3 vols, Dublin, 1949-57).

Flood, Revd Peter, *A letter from the Revd Peter Flood D.D ... relative to a pamphlet entitled 'A fair representation of the present political state of Ireland' by Patrick Duignan L.L.D.* (Dublin, 1800).

Gilbert, J.T. (ed.), *Documents relating to Ireland 1795-1804* (Dublin, 1893).

Gordon, James, *History of the rebellion in Ireland in the year 1798* (Dublin, 1801).

Grattan, Henry, *Memoirs of the life and times of the Rt. Hon. Henry Grattan by his son* (5 vols, London, 1839-46).

Hancock, Thomas, *The principles of peace exemplified in the conduct of the Society of Friends of Ireland during the rebellion of the Year 1798* (London, 1826).

Hardwicke, earl of, *The viceroy's postbag: correspondence hitherto unpublished of the earl of Hardwicke, first Lord Lieutenant after the union*, ed. Michael MacDonagh (London, 1904).

H.M.C., *The manuscripts of J.B. Fortescue Esq. preserved at Dropmore* (10 vols, London, 1892-1927).

Holt, Joseph, *The memoirs of Joseph Holt*, ed. T.C. Croker (2 vols, London, 1838).

Johnston, E.M. (ed.), 'The state of the Irish house of commons in 1791' in *R.I.A. Proc.*, vol. 59, sect. c, no. 1 (1957-9), pp. 1-56.

[Keatinge, Maurice], *On the defence of Ireland* (Dublin, 1795).

Leadbeater, Mary, *The Leadbeater papers, a selection from the manuscripts and correspondence of Mary Leadbeater* (2 vols, Dublin, 1862).

List of Yeomanry corps on a county basis (Dublin, n.d.).

Lucas, Richard *A general directory of the kingdom of Ireland* (Dublin, 1788).

McDermott, Martin (ed.), *The memoirs of Lord Edward Fitzgerald by Thomas Moore with a preface and many supplementary particulars* (London, 1897).

McDowell, R.B. (ed.), 'The personnel of the Dublin Society of United Irishmen' in *I.H.S.*, vol. ii, no. 5 (1940-1), pp. 12-53.

—, 'Select Documents: United Irish Plans of parliamentary reform' in *I.H.S.*, vol. iii, no. 9 (1942), pp. 39-59.

—, 'Proceedings of the Dublin Society of United Irishmen' in *Analecta Hibernica*, vol. 17 (1949), pp. 3-143.

MacLaren, Archibald, *A genuine account of the capture and death of Lord Edward Fitzgerald. An impartial description of the battles of Dunboyne, Naas, Hacketstown, Tara Hill, Kildare, Owlart [sic] etc* (Bristol, 1799).

MacNeven, William James, *Pieces of Irish history* (New York, 1807).

Mason, W. Shaw, *A statistical account or parochial survey of Ireland* (3 vols, Dublin, 1819).

Maxwell, W.H., *History of the Irish rebellion in 1798* (London, 1845).

Musgrave, Richard, *Memoirs of the different rebellions in Ireland* (2nd edn, Dublin, 1801).

Newenham, T., *A view of the natural, political and commercial circumstances of Ireland* (London, 1809).

O'Kelly, Patrick , *General history of the rebellion of 1798 with many interesting occurrences of the two preceding years also a brief account of the insurrection in 1803 will be subjoined* (Dublin, 1842).

Paine, Thomas, *The Thomas Paine reader*, ed. Michael Foot and Issac Kramnick (London, 1987, first published 1772-1805).

Plowden, Francis, *An historical view of the state of Ireland* (2 vols, London, 1803).

Rawson, Thomas James, *Statistical survey of the County of Kildare, with observations on the means of improvement* (Dublin, 1807).

Refausse, Raymond, 'The visitation notebook of Charles Lindsay, Bishop of Kildare 1804-1808' in *Kildare Arch. Soc. Jn*, vol. xvii (1987-91), pp. 121-47.

'Journal of Samuel Reilly … Sept. 1798' in *Journal of the Cork Historical and Archaeological Society*, ser. 2, vol. ii, (1896), pp. 428-42.

Reynolds, Thomas Jnr, *Life of Thomas Reynolds esq. formerly of Kilkea Castle in the County of Kildare, by his son* (2 vols, London, 1839).

Richardson, W., *History of the origin of the Irish Yeomanry* (Dublin, 1801).

Rowan, Archibald Hamilton, *Autobiography of Archibald Hamilton Rowan*, ed. W. Drummond (Dublin, 1840).

'Rules and resolutions of the Anna Liffey club' in *Kildare Arch. Soc. Jn*, vol. xii (1935-45), pp. 124-27

Russell, Thomas, *Journals and memoirs of Thomas Russell 1791-5*, ed. C.J. Woods (Dublin, 1991).

Sampson, William, *Memoirs* (New York, 1807).

[Scott, Revd John], *Parliamentary Representation, being a political and critical review of all the counties, cities and boroughs of the Kingdom of Ireland with regard to this presentation by Falkland* (Dublin, 1790).

—, *Review of the principal characters in the Irish house of commons* (Dublin, 1789).

Shackelton, Betsy, *Ballitore and its inhabitants seventy years ago by Betsy Shackelton* (Dublin, 1862).

Taylor, John, *A map of the county of Kildare, 1783* (Dublin, 1983).

Teeling, Charles Hamilton, *History of the Irish rebellion of 1798 and sequel to the histo-*

ry of the Irish rebellion (Shannon, 1972, IUP reprint of 1876 edn, first published 1828, 1832).

The martyr of liberty : a poem of the heroic death of Lawrence O'Connor, executed at Naas in Ireland on a charge of High Treason, Sept. 7th 1796 (Dublin, 1798).

[Tone, Theobald Wolfe], *An argument on behalf of the Catholics of Ireland* (Dublin, 1791).

Tone, Theobald Wolfe, *The autobiography of Theobald Wolfe Tone 1763-1798*, ed. R. Barry O'Brien, (2 vols, London, 1893).

Volunteers of the United Kingdom, 1803, ordered by the house of commons to be printed 9th and 13th Dec. 1803 (London, 1803).

Wakefield, Edward, *An account of Ireland statistical and political* (2 vols, London, 1812).

Castlereagh, Viscount, *Memoirs and correspondence of Viscount Castlereagh*, ed. Marquis of Londonderry (12 vols, London, 1848-53).

Vindication of the cause of Catholics of Ireland adopted at a meeting at Taylor's Hall, Backlane December 7 1792 (Dublin, 1793).

Young, Arthur, *A Tour in Ireland* (2 vols, Shannon, 1972, first published 1780).

SECONDARY SOURCES: PUBLISHED WORKS ON IRELAND, 1790-1803

Beames, M.R., 'Peasant movements in Ireland 1785-1795' in *Journal of Peasant Studies*, vol. ii, no. 4 (1975), pp. 502-6.

Bartlett, Thomas, 'An end to the moral economy: the Irish militia disturbances of 1793' in *Past and Present*, no. 99 (1983), pp. 41-64.

—, 'Indiscipline and disaffection in the armed forces in Ireland in the 1790s' in P.J. Corish (ed.), *Radicals, rebels and establishments* (Belfast, 1985), pp. 115-34.

—, 'A people made rather for copies than originals the Anglo-Irish 1760-1800' in *International History Review* (Feb., 1990), pp. 11-25.

—, 'The rise and fall of the Protestant nation' in *Eire-Ireland*, vol. xxvi (1991), pp. 7-18.

—, *The fall and rise of the Irish nation: The Catholic question 1690-1830* (Dublin, 1992).

—, '"Masters of the mountains": The insurgent careers of Joseph Holt and Michael Dwyer, County Wicklow 1798-1803' in Hannigan and Nolan (eds), *Wicklow: History and society* (Dublin, 1994), pp. 379-410.

—, 'Defence, counter insurgency and rebellion: Ireland 1793-1803' in T. Bartlett and K. Jeffery (eds), *A military history of Ireland* (Cambridge, 1996), pp. 247-93.

— and Hayden, D., *Penal era and golden age* (Belfast, 1979)

Bolton, G.C., *The passing of the Irish act of union* (Oxford, 1966).

Bourke, F.S., 'Patrick O'Kelly – an historian of the rebellion of 1798' in *Irish Booklover*, vol. xxviii (June, 1941), pp. 37-43.

Boylan, Lena, 'Kildare lodge, Lord Edward Fitzgerald's house' in *Kildare Arch. Soc. Jn*, vol. xvi (1977-8), pp. 26-35.

Brady, John, 'Lawrence O'Connor – a Meath schoolmaster' in *Irish Ecclesiastical Record*, vol. xlix (1937), pp. 281-7.

—, 'A rebel schoolmaster (Lawrence O'Connor, executed at Naas in 1795)' in *Irish Booklover*, vol. xxvi (Nov.-Dec. 1938), p. 61.

Byrne, Edward, *Lord Edward Fitzgerald* (London, 1955).

Campbell, Gerard, *Edward and Pamela Fitzgerald* (London, 1904).

Christianson, Gale E., 'Secrets societies and agrarian violence in Ireland 1790-1840' in *Agricultural History*, vol. 46 (1972), pp. 369-84.

Connolly, Sean, *Priests and people in pre famine Ireland* (Dublin, 1982).

—, 'Violence and order in eighteenth century Ireland' in Flanagan, P., Ferguson, P., and Whelan, K. (eds), *Rural Ireland 1600-1900* (Dublin, 1987), pp. 42-61.

—, 'Adjustment and aftermath' in Vaughan, W.E. (ed.), *A new history of Ireland vol. v Ireland after the union I: 1801-1870* (Oxford, 1989), pp. 1-23.

—, *Religion, law and power: The making of Protestant Ireland 1660-1760* (Oxford, 1992).

Costello, Con, 'Naas and the country in general, from 1800-'48' in *Kildare Arch. Soc. Jn*, vol. xiii (1961-63), pp. 423-42.

—, 'Wolfe Tone and Naas' in *Kildare Arch. Soc. Jn*, vol. xiv (1968), p. 261.

Cox, L., 'Westmeath in the 1798 period' in *Irish Sword*, vol. ix (1969-70), pp. 1-15.

Cullen, Luke, *Insurgent Wicklow* (Dublin, 1948).

Cullen, L.M., 'The 1798 rebellion in its eighteenth century context' in Corish (ed.), *Radicals, rebels and establishments* (Belfast, 1985), pp. 91-113.

—, 'Catholics under the penal laws' in *Eighteenth Century Ireland*, vol. i (1986), pp. 23-36.

—, 'The 1798 rebellion in Wexford: United Irish organisation, membership, leadership' in Whelan (ed.), *Wexford: History and society* (Dublin, 1987), pp. 248-95.

—, 'The political structures of the Defenders' in Gough and Dickson (eds) *Ireland and the French Revolution* (Dublin, 1990), pp. 117-38.

—, 'Late eighteenth century politicisation in Ireland: problems in its study and its French links' in Bergeron and Cullen (eds), *Culture et pratiques politiques* (Paris, 1991).

—, 'The internal politics of the United Irishmen' in Dickson, Keogh and Whelan (eds), *The United Irishmen* (Dublin, 1993), pp. 176-96.

—, 'Politics and rebellion in Wicklow in the 1790s' in Hannigan and Nolan (eds), *Wicklow: History and society* (Dublin, 1994), pp. 411-501.

C[ullen], M.J., 'Hugh Cullen and the Curragh massacre, May 1798' in *Reportorium Novum*, vol. i, no. 1 (1955), pp. 242-6.

—, 'Cardinal Cullen: biographical materials' in *Reportorium Novum*, vol. i, no. 1 (1955), pp. 213-27.

Cummins, Seamus, 'Pike heads and the calico printer: Leixlip in '98' in *Kildare Arch. Soc. Jn*, vol. xvi (1985-86), pp. 418-31.

Curtayne, Alice, 'The Battle of Prosperous' in *Souvenir of the blessing and official opening of Caragh New Church* (Naas, 1960).

Curtin, Nancy, 'The transformation of the United Irishmen into a mass based organisation 1794-6' in *I.H.S.*, vol. xxiv, no. 96 (1985), pp. 463-92.

—, *The United Irishmen: Popular politics in Ulster and Dublin 1791-1798* (Oxford, 1994).

Dickson, Charles, *The life of Michael Dwyer* (Dublin, 1944).

Dickson, David, *New foundations: Ireland 1660-1800* (Dublin, 1987).

—, Keogh, Dáire and Whelan, Kevin (eds), *The United Irishmen: Republicanism, radicalism and reaction* (Dublin, 1993).

Doyle, Sean, 'Squire Yeates and Moone Abbey' in *Kildare Arch. Soc. Jn*, vol. xii (1935-45), pp. 443-5.

Dunne, Tom, *Wolfe Tone colonial outsider: An analysis of his political philosophy* (Cork, 1982).

—, 'Popular ballads, revolutionary rhetoric and politicisation' in Gough and Dickson (eds), *Ireland and the French Revolution* (Dublin, 1990), pp. 139-55.

Durey, Michael, 'The Dublin Society of United Irishmen and the politics of the Carey – Drennan dispute' in *Historical Journal*, vol. xxvii (1994), pp. 89-112.

Elliot, Marianne, 'The origins and transformation of early Irish republicanism' in *International Review of Social History*, vol. xxii, pt. 3 (1978), pp. 405-28.

—, *Partners in Revolution: The United Irishmen and France* (New Haven, 1982).

—, *Wolfe Tone: Prophet of Irish Independence* (Yale, 1989).

—, 'The Defenders in Ulster' in Dickson, Keogh and Whelan (eds), *The United Irishmen* (Dublin, 1993), pp. 222-33.

Fitzgerald, Frederick, 'An account of the arrest of Lord Edward Fitzgerald' in *Kildare Arch. Soc. Jn*, vol. ii (1898), pp. 350-3.

Fitzgerald, Walter 'The Co. Kildare Cavalry in 1796' in *Kildare Arch. Soc. Jn*, vol. iv (1903-5), pp. 65-6.

Fitzpatrick, W.J. *The life, times and contemporaries of Lord Cloncurry* (Dublin, 1855).

__, *The sham squire and the informers of 1798* (3rd edn, Dublin, 1895).

Furlong, Nicholas, *Father John Murphy of Boolavogue 1753-1798* (Dublin, 1992).

Gahan, Daniel, 'The "Black mob" and the "Babes of the wood": Wexford in the wake of the rebellion, 1798-1806' in *Wexford Historical Society Journal*, no. 13 (1990-1), pp. 92-110.

—, *The people's rising, Wexford 1798* (Dublin, 1995).

Garvin, Tom, *The evolution of Irish nationalist politics* (Dublin, 1981).

—, 'Defenders, Ribbonmen and others: underground political movements in pre famine Ireland' in *Past and Present*, no. 96 (1982), pp. 33-55.

Gough, H., and Dickson, D. (eds), *Ireland and the French Revolution* (Dublin, 1990).

Graham, Thomas, '"An union of power"? The United Irish organisation 1795-8' in Dickson, Keogh and Whelan (eds), *The United Irishmen* (Dublin, 1993), pp. 244-55.

—, 'Dublin in 1798: the key to the planned insurrection' in Keogh and Furlong (eds), *The mighty wave: The 1798 rebellion in Wexford* (Dublin, 1996), pp. 65-78.

Hayden, Tadgh 'Castledermot in 1798' in *Castledermot* (1954), pp. 15-18.

Hayes, R., 'Priests in the independence movement of 1798' in *Irish Ecclesiastical Record*, vol. xxxvi (1945), pp. 258-70.

Hill, J., 'The meaning and significance of "Protestant Ascendancy" 1787-1840' in *Ireland after the union* (Oxford, 1989), pp. 1-22.

Horner, Arnold, 'The pre-famine population of some Kildare towns' in *Kildare Arch. Soc. Jn*, vol. xiv (1969), pp. 89-95.

Hume, Geraldine and Malcolmson, Anthony, *Robert Emmet – the insurrection of 1803* (Belfast, 1976).

Johnson, E.M., *Great Britain and Ireland 1760-1800* (Edinburgh, 1963).

Kavanagh, Patrick, *A popular history of the insurrection of 1798* (4th edn, Cork, 1898).

Ann C. Kavanaugh, *John Fitzgibbon, earl of Clare: A study in personality and politics* (Dublin, 1997).

Kelly, Rev. L., 'Defenderism in Leitrim during the 1790s' in *Breifne*, vol. vi, no. 24 (1986), pp. 341-54.

Kennedy, Denis, 'The Irish Whigs, administrative reform and responsible government 1782-1800' in *Eire-Ireland*, vol. vii, no. 4 (1974), pp. 55-69.

Keogh, Dáire, '"The most dangerous villain in society", Fr John Martin's mission to the United Irishmen in Wicklow in 1798' in *Eighteenth-Century Ireland*, vol. vii (1992), pp. 115-35.

—, *The French disease: The Catholic church and radicalism in Ireland 1790-1800* (Dublin, 1993).

— and Nicholas Furlong (eds), *The mighty wave: The 1798 rebellion in Wexford* (Dublin, 1996).

Landreth, Helen, *The pursuit of Robert Emmet* (Dublin, 1949).

Lindsay, Deirdre, 'The Fitzwilliam episode revisited' in Dickson, Keogh and Whelan (eds), *The United Irishmen* (Dublin, 1993), pp. 197-208.

Longfield, A.K. , 'Prosperous 1776-98' in *Kildare Arch. Soc. Jn*, vol. xiv (1966-67), pp. 212-31.

Lindsay, John, *The shining life and death of Lord Edward Fitzgerald* (London, n.d.).

McAnally, Henry, *The Irish Militia 1793-1816: A social and military study* (Dublin, 1949).

McClelland, Aiken, *The formation of the Orange Order* ([Belfast, 1971]).

MacDermott, Frank, 'Arthur O'Connor' in *I.H.S.*, vol. xvi, no. 57 (1966), pp. 48-69.

McDowell, R.B., *Irish Public Opinion 1750-1800* (London, 1944).

—, 'The Fitzwilliam Episode' in *I.H.S.*, vol. xvi, no. 57 (1966), pp. 115-30.

—, 'The Age of the United Irishmen' in Moody and Vaughan (eds), *A new history of Ireland vol. iv eighteenth century Ireland 1691-1800* (Oxford, 1986), pp. 289-370.

—, *Ireland in the age of imperialism and revolution 1760-1801* (Oxford, 1979).

MacSuibhne, Padraig, 'Notes on 1798 in Kildare' in *Kildare Arch. Soc. Jn*, vol. xiv (1966-7), pp. 163-7.

—, *The priest's grave at French Furze: A victim of the Gibbet Rath massacre* (Naas, 1967).

—, *'98 in Carlow* (Carlow, 1974).

—, *Kildare in '98* (Naas, 1978).

Madden, R.R., *The United Irishmen: Their lives and times* (7 vols, Dublin, 1842-6, 2nd edn, 1858-60).

Malcolmson, A.P.W., *John Foster: The politics of the Anglo-Irish ascendancy* (Oxford, 1978).

Millar, David, 'The Armagh Troubles' in S. Clark and J.S. Donnelly (eds), *Irish peasants: Violence and political unrest 1780-1914* (Manchester, 1983).

Defenders and peep of day boys (Belfast, 1990).

Moody, T.W., 'The political ideas of the United Irishmen' in *Ireland Today*, vol. iii, no. 1 (1938), pp. 15-25.

Murphy, John A. (ed.), *The French are in the bay, The Bantry Bay expedition of 1796* (Cork, 1997).

O'Brien, Gerard, *Anglo-Irish politics in the age of Grattan and Pitt* (Dublin, 1987).

— (ed.), *Parliament, politics and people: Essays in eighteenth Irish history* (Dublin, 1989).

O'Dea, Michael and Whelan, Kevin (eds), *Nations and nationalisms: France, Britain and Ireland and the eighteenth century context* (Oxford, 1995).

O'Donnell, Ruan, 'The rebellion of 1798 in County Wicklow' in Hannigan and Nolan (eds), *Wicklow: History and society* (Dublin, 1994), pp. 341-78.

—, and Reece, Bob, '"A clean beast" Crofton Croker's fairy tale of General Holt' in *Eighteenth Century Ireland*, vol. vii (1992), pp. 7-42.

O'Flaherty, Eamon, 'The Catholic convention and Anglo-Irish politics' in *Studia Hibernica*, vol. xl (1985), pp. 14-34.

—, 'Irish Catholics and the French Revolution' in Gough and Dickson (eds), *Ireland in the French Revolution* (Dublin, 1990), pp. 52-67.

O'Lionsigh, Seamus, 'The rebellion of 1798 in Co. Meath' in *Riocht na Midhe*, vol. iii-v, (1966-71).

O'Murthuile, Seosamh, 'Meascra de thaighdighthe maidir le dinnsheanchas Choill Chluana Gabhann agus na duthaighe ina timcheall' in *Kildare Arch. Soc. Jn*, vol. xii (1935-45), pp. 375-95.

—, 'An t-eiri amach i gCill Dara 1798' in *Feasta*, i, uimh. 2-12 (Bealtine 1948-Marta 1949), ii, uimh 1 (Aibrean 1949).

—, *Kildare 1798 Commemoration* (Kildare, 1948).

O'Snodaigh, Padraig, '*98 and Carlow: A look at the historians* (Carlow, 1979).

—, 'Notes on the politics of Kildare at the end of the 18th century' in *Kildare Arch. Soc. Jn*, vol. xvi (1981-2), pp. 264-71.

O'Tuathaigh, Gearoid, *Ireland before the famine 1798-1848* (Dublin, 1972).

Pakenham, Thomas, *The year of liberty: The history of the great Irish rebellion of 1798* (London, 1969).

Powell, Thomas, 'An economic factor in the Wexford rebellion of 1798' in *Studia Hibernica*, vol. 16 (1976), pp. 140-57.

Ronan, Myles V., *Personal recollections of Wexford and Wicklow insurgents of 1798 as collected by the Revd Br. Luke Cullen 1798-1859* (Enniscorthy, 1958).

Ryan, Eileen, 'Monasterevan in '98' in *Monasterevan Parish* (1958).

Senoir, Hereward, *Orangeism in Ireland and Britain* (London, 1966).

Smyth, Jim, *The men of no property: Irish radicals and popular politics in the late eighteenth century* (London, 1992).

Snoddy, Oliver, 'The Volunteers, Militia and Orangemen of Co. Kildare in the eighteenth century' in *Kildare Arch. Soc. Jn*, vol. xv (1971-6), pp. 38-49.

Stewart, A.T.Q., 'The harp new strung: Nationalism, culture and the United Irishmen' in MacDonagh, Oliver and Mantle, W.F. (eds), *Ireland and Irish Australia: Studies in cultural history* (London, 1986), pp. 258-69.

—, *The summer soliders: The 1798 rebellion in Antrim and Down* (Belfast, 1995).

Synott, P.N.N., '1798 Rising – some records from Co. Kildare' in *Kildare Arch. Soc. Jn*, vol. xv (1971-6), pp. 448-67.

Taylor, Ida A., *The life of Lord Edward Fitzgerald* (London, 1903).

Tenison, Graves, 'The officers of the Kildare Militia 1794-1817' in *Kildare Arch. Soc. Jn*, vol. xii (1935-45), pp. 194-7.

Thuente, Mary Helen, *The harp re-strung: The United Irishmen and the rise of Irish literary nationalism* (Syracuse, 1994).

Tierney, Martin, 'William Aylmer 1772-1820' in *Irish Sword*, vol. vi, no. 23 (1963), pp. 103-7.

Tillyard, Stella, *Citizen Lord: Edward Fitzgerald 1763-1798* (London, 1997).

Wall, Maureen, 'The United Irish Movement' in J.L. McCracken (ed.), *Historical Studies*, vol. v (London, 1965), pp. 122-40.

Wells, Roger, *Insurrection: The British experience 1795-1803* (Gloucester, 1983).

Whelan, Kevin, 'The role of the Catholic priest in the 1798 rebellion in County Wexford' in Whelan, Kevin (ed.), *Wexford: History and society* (Dublin, 1987), pp. 296-315.

—, 'The religious factor in the 1798 rebellion in County Wexford' in P. Flanagan, P. Ferguson and K. Whelan (eds), *Rural Ireland 1600-1900* (Dublin, 1987), pp. 62-85.

—, 'Catholics, politicisation and 1798 rebellion' in R. O'Muiri (ed.), *Irish church history today* (Armagh, 1990), pp. 63-83.

—, 'Politicisation in County Wexford and the origins of the 1798 rebellion' in Gough and Dickson (eds), *Ireland and the French Revolution* (Dublin, 1990), pp. 156-78.

—, 'Catholic mobilisation 1750-1850' in Bergeron and Cullen (eds), *Culture et pratiques* (Paris, 1991), pp. 235-58.

—, 'Reinterpreting the 1798 rebellion in County Wexford' in Keogh and Furlong (eds), *The mighty wave: The 1798 rebellion in Wexford* (Dublin, 1996) pp. 9-36.

—, *The tree of liberty: Radicalism, Catholicism and the construction of Irish identity 1760-1830* (Cork, 1996).

Whitaker, Anne Maree, *Unfinished revolution, the United Irishmen in New South Wales 1800-1810* (Sydney, 1994).

'William Aylmer (1772-1820)' in *Irish Sword*, vol. ix, no. 34 (1969), pp. 72-3.

William Aylmer and the men of Kildare (London, n.d.).

Zimmerman, G.D., *Songs of Irish rebellion: Political street ballads and rebel songs 1780-1900* (Geneve, 1966).

SECONDARY SOURCES: OTHER PUBLISHED WORKS

Andrews, J.H., *Kildare* (Irish historic towns atlas, no. 1, Dublin, 1986).

Aylmer, Sir Fenton, *The Aylmers of Ireland* (Dublin, 1931).

Aylmer, Hans Hendrick, 'The Aylmer family' in *Kildare Arch. Soc. Jn*, vol. i (1891-5), pp. 295-307.

'Ballads and poems of the Co. Kildare: no. 10, The Clane Rangers: a contemporary ballad of the Volunteers' in *Kildare Arch. Soc. Jn*, vol. vi (1909-11), pp. 347-52.

Beckett, J.C., *The making of modern Ireland 1603-1923* (London, 1969).

Bergeron, Louis and Cullen, L.M., *Culture et pratiques politiques en France et en Irlande, xvie-xviiie siecles* (Paris, 1991).

Bowen, Desmond, *Paul Cardinal Cullen and the shaping of modern Irish Catholicism* (Dublin, 1983).

Lena Boylan, 'The Conollys of Castletown, a family history' in *Quarterly Bulletin of the Irish Georgian Society* (Oct.-Dec., 1968), pp. 1-46.

Brenan, Martin, *Schools of Kildare and Leighlin A.D. 1775-1835* (Dublin, 1935).

Cantwell, Brian, 'Notes on Young's tour 1777-1779' in *Kildare Arch. Soc. Jn*, vol. xiii (1946-63), pp. 135-6.

Comerford, M., *Collections relating to the diocese of Kildare and Leighlin* (3 vols, Dublin, n.d.).

Connell, K.H., *The population of Ireland 1750-1845* (Oxford, 1950).

Corish, P.J., *The catholic community in the seventeenth and eighteenth centuries* (Dublin, 1981).

— (ed.), *Rebels, radicals and establishments, Historical Studies* xv (Belfast, 1985).

—, *Maynooth College 1795-1995* (Dublin, 1995).

—, *Looking back: Aspects of Kildare history* (Naas, 1988).

—, *Kildare: Saints, soliders and horses* (Naas, 1991).

—, *Guide to County Kildare and west Wicklow* (Naas, 1991).

Cullen, L.M., *An economic history of Ireland since 1660* (London, 1970).

—, *The emergence of modern Ireland 1600-1900* (London, 1981).

Delany, V.T.H. and D.R., *The canals of the south of Ireland* (Plymouth, 1966).

Devitt, Fr Matthew, 'Rathcoffey' in *Kildare Arch. Soc. Jn*, vol. iii (1899-1902), pp. 79-86.

Donnelly, J.S., 'The Whiteboy movement, 1761-5' in *I.H.S.*, vol. xxi, no. 81 (1978), pp. 20-54.

—, 'Propagating the cause of the United Irishmen' in *Studies*, vol. lxix, no. 273 (1981), pp. 5-23.

—, 'Irish agrarian rebellion: the Whiteboys of 1769-76' in *R.I.A. Proc.*, vol. 83, sect. C, no. 12 (1983), pp. 293-331.

Doyle, Sean, 'Squire Yeates and Moone Abbey' in *Kildare Arch. Soc. Jn*, vol. xii (1935-45), pp. 443-5.

Drennan, John, et al, *Cannonballs and croziers: A history of Maynooth* (Maynooth, 1994).

Dunlop, Robert, *Waters under the bridge, the saga of the La Touches of Harristown, John Ruskin and his Irish rose* (Kildare, 1988).

—, *Plantation of renown: the story of the La Touches of Harristown and the Baptist church at Brannockstown* (2nd edn, Naas, 1985).

Fitzgerald, Brian, *Emily, Duchess of Leinster 1731-1814: A study of her life and times* (Dublin, 1949).

—, *Lady Louisa Conolly 1743-1821: an Anglo-Irish biography* (Dublin, 1950).

Fitzgerald, Charles William, *The earls of Kildare and their ancestors: From 1056 to 1804* (3 vols, Dublin, 1858-72).

Fitzgerald, Walter, 'Belan' in *Kildare Arch. Soc. Jn*, v (1907), pp. 239-52.

Foster, Roy, *Modern Ireland 1600-1972* (London, 1988).

Froude, J.A., *The English in Ireland in the eighteenth century* (3 vols, London, 1874).

Hannigan, Ken, and Nolan, William (eds), *Wicklow: History and society* (Dublin, 1994).

Hobsbawm, Eric, *Primitive rebels: Studies in archaic forms of social movement in the nineteenth and twentieth centuries* (2nd edn, New York, 1959).

—, *Bandits* (2nd edn, London, 1972).

Holmes, John, 'Monasterevan Distillery' in *Kildare Arch. Soc. Jn*, vol. xiv (1964-70), pp. 480-7.

Horner, Arnold, *Maynooth* (Irish historic towns atlas, Dublin, 1995).

Johnson, E.M., *Ireland in the eighteenth century* (Dublin, 1974).

Kelly, James, 'Prosperous and Irish industrialisation in the late eighteenth century' in *Kildare Arch. Soc. Jn*, vol. xvi (1985-6), pp. 441-67.

—, *Prelude to union: Anglo-Irish politics in the 1780s* (Cork, 1992).

Lecky, W.E.H., *A History of Ireland in the eighteenth century* (5 vols, London, 1892).

Leighton, C.D.A., *Catholicism in a Protestant kingdom: The Irish ancien regieme* (Dublin, 1994).

Longfield, A.K., 'Prosperous 1776-98' in *Kildare Arch. Soc. Jn*, vol. xiv (1966-67), pp. 212-31.

MacSuibhne, Padraig, *Rathangan* (Maynooth, 1975).

Mayo, earl of, *History of the Kildare hunt* (Dublin, 1913).

Milne, Kenneth, 'The council book of Naas 1665-1842' in *Kildare Arch. Soc. Jn*, vol. xiv (1964-70), pp. 262-6.

Moody, T.W. and Vaughan, W.E. (eds), *A new history of Ireland vol. iv eighteenth century Ireland 1691-1800* (Oxford, 1986).

Moore, Anne Tower, countess of Drogheda, *The family of Moore* (Dublin, 1906).

Murphy, Denis, 'Kildare, its history and antiquities' in *Kildare Arch. Soc. Jn*, vol. ii (1898), pp. 289-302.

Nelson, Gerald, *A history of Leixlip* (Lucan, 1990).

Newman, Jeremiah, *Maynooth and Georgian Ireland* (Galway, 1979).

O'Casaide, Seamus, 'Patrick O'Kelly, the translator of MacGeoghegan' in *Irish Booklover*, vol. xxxviii (Feb. 1942), pp. 84-6.

O'Connell, Maurice, *Irish politics and social conflict in the age of the American revolution* (Philadelphia, 1965).

O'Grada, Cormac, *A new economic history of Ireland 1789-1939* (Oxford, 1994).

O'Tuathaigh, Gearoid, *Ireland before the famine 1798-1848* (Dublin, 1972).

Oughterany: Journal of the Donadea Local History Group, vol. i, no. 1 (1993), no. 2 (1995).

Power, T.P. and Whelan, K., *Endurance and emergence: Catholics in Ireland in the eighteenth century* (Dublin, 1990).

—, *Land, politics and society in eighteenth century Tipperary* (Oxford, 1993).

Price, Liam (ed.), *An eighteenth century antiquarian, the sketches, notes and diaries of Austin Cooper* (1751-1830) (Dublin, 1942).

Richardson, E.M., *Long forgotten days (leading to Waterloo)* (London, 1928).

Sadlier, Thos. U., 'Kildare members of Parliament 1559-1800' in *Kildare Arch. Soc. Jn*, vol. vi-x (1903-22).

Sherlock, W., 'Donadea and the Aylmer family' in *Kildare Arch. Soc. Jn*, vol. iii (1899-1902), pp. 169-79.

Stewart, A.T.Q., *A deeper silence* (London, 1993).

Tillyard, Stella, *Aristocrats: Caroline, Emily, Louisa and Sarah Lennox 1740-1832* (London, 1994).

Vaughan, W.E. (ed.), *A new history of Ireland vol. v Ireland after the union I: 1801-1870* (Oxford, 1989).

Wall, Maureen, *Catholic Ireland in the eighteenth century*, ed. Gerard O'Brien (Dublin, 1989).

Williams, T. Desmond, *Secret societies in Ireland* (Dublin, 1973).

Wolfe, George, 'The Wolfe family of Co. Kildare' in *Kildare Arch. Soc. Jn*, vol. iii (1899-1902), pp. 361-7.

Wolfe, Major R., *The Wolfes of Forenaughts, Blackhall, Baronrath etc., Co. Kildare, Ireland* (n.p., 1885).

Young, M.F., 'The La Touche family of Harristown, County Kildare' in *Kildare Arch. Soc. Jn*, vol. vii (1912-14), pp. 33-40.

SECONDARY SOURCES: UNPUBLISHED WORKS

Aylmer, Richard J., 'The imperial service of William Aylmer 1800-1814', unpublished paper (1996).

—, 'William Aylmer of Painstown, County Kildare and the battle for the metropolis, May 1798', unpublished paper (1996).

Chambers, Liam, 'Politics and rebellion in county Kildare 1790-1803' (M.A., Maynooth, 1996).

Duggan, Mary L., 'County Carlow 1791-1801: a study in an era of revolution' (M.A., UCD, 1969).

Kerrane, J.G.O., 'The background to the 1798 rebellion in County Meath' (M.A., UCD, 1971).

Kinsella, Anna, '"Who fears to speak of '98" The nineteenth century interpretation of 1798' (M. Litt., TCD, 1992).

O'Donnell, Ruan, 'General Joseph Holt and the 1798 rebellion in County Wicklow' (M.A., UCD, 1991).

Index

Murphy, Michael, 68, 94
Musgrave, Richard, 10, 67, 73, 75, 78-80, 82, 88-9, 96, 101, 103

Naas, 17-18, 24, 26, 31, 34-8, 42-3, 45, 48, 52, 64-5, 69, 71-83, 85, 89, 93-4, 96-7, 109, 111, 113-17
Naas, borough of, 21-2, 51
Naas, North and South, barony of, 58-9, 63
Naas Volunteers, 24
Nagle, James, 104-6, 109-10, 113-14, 117
Nangle, Christopher, 24, 26, 31
Napier, George, 35
Napier, Sarah, 35
Narragh and Rheban, East and West, barony of, 57-9, 78-9, 84, 101
Narraghmore, 21, 7-7, 85
Neale, Captain, 104
Neilson, Samuel, 41
Nelson, Oliver, 109
Nevill, Richard, 18, 34-5, 46, 52, 55, 62, 107
Newbridge, 62, 97
Newbury, 98
Newry, 40
Ní Cinneide, Sile, 18
Nicolson, Patrick, 55
North Cork Militia, 84, 104
Nowlan, Christy, 111
Nurney, 29, 79

O'Brien, John, 54, 113
O'Connor, Arthur, 39-40
O'Connor, Lawrence, 13, 33-8, 43
O'Connor, Patrick, 91
O'Donnell, Ruan, 75, 96
O'Ferrall, Ambrose, 31
Offaly, see King's County
Offaly, East and West, barony of, 29, 58, 63, 78, 92
Ogilvie, William, 67
O'Kelly, Patrick, 10-11, 54-5, 57, 68, 73, 76-7, 79-80, 82-3, 87, 101, 112
O'Muirthuile, An tAth Seosamh, 11-12
Orangeism, 13, 45, 60, 64, 66, 69, 107, 109
O'Reilly, Dominic William, 23-7, 46, 50, 78

Orleans, duc d', 39
Ormsby, Lt.-Col. Arthur, 21, 25
Ormsby, Major, 98
Osberstown, 28, 68
O'Snodaigh, Padraig, 13, 25
Ovidstown, 87, 92, 94-6

Pack, Captain, 93
Packenham, Admiral, 117
Painstown, 28, 62, 87, 90-1, 95, 99
Pakenham, Thomas, 12, 23, 121
Palmer, Charles, 46
Parrott, John, 111, 118
Parrott, William, 111, 118
Patrick Street, Dublin, 110-1, 114
Patrickson, William, 46
Pelham, Thomas, 42, 48, 51-2, 63, 110
Pender, Mr, 61
Pendred, John, 67
Perkins, Joseph, 82
Perry, Anthony, 100
Philipstown, 54-5, 98
Political structures, 21-3
Pollock, Mr, 53-5
Ponsonby, W.B., 46
Population, of county Kildare, 19-20
Portland, earl of, 34, 40, 49, 61, 67
Portland Whigs, 31
Prendegast, Fr Edward, 92, 103
Press, The, 54, 62
Proclamation, 43, 45-7, 63-5, 119
Prosperous, 18-19, 37, 40-2, 67, 73-4, 82, 85, 90, 93-4, 96-7, 101, 110-11, 116

Queen's County, 14, 18, 26, 29, 63, 65, 78-9, 84, 113
Quigly, Michael, 110-14, 116, 118

Rankin, George, 112
Rathangan, 10, 18, 78, 80, 83, 85, 90, 93, 104, 109, 110
Rathcoffey, 28, 87, 90, 112, 116
Rathcoole, 116
Rathmore, 35
Ratoath, 81
Rawson, Thomas James, 11, 15, 18-19, 62-4, 69, 75-7, 85, 103, 105, 113, 117